TRAVELSAFE

PETER CONSTERDINE

PROTECTION PUBLICATIONS

in association with

SUMMERSDALE PUBLISHERS LTD

Peter Consterdine

TRAVELSAFE

Copyright © Peter Consterdine 2000

All rights reserved.

No part of this book may be reproduced by any means, nor transmitted, nor translated into a machine language without the written permission of the publisher.

Protection Publications
51 - 53 Unity Business Centre
26 Roundhay Road
Leeds LS7 1AB
United Kingdom

Published in Association with
Summersdale Publishers Ltd
PO Box 49
Chichester
West Sussex
PO19 2FJ
United Kingdom

A CIP catalogue for this book is available from the British Library.

Printed and Bound in Great Britain by:
Bath Press Group Ltd, Wiltshire, Great Britain
Typesetting, Photographic Scanning and Origination: Protection Publications, Leeds.
Cover Design & Origination: Ian Gordon, ArtStyle, Leeds.

ISBN 0-9537638-2-X

Please Note: The author and publishers cannot accept any responsibility for any proceedings or prosecutions brought or instituted against any person or body as a result of the use or misuse of any information described in this book, or any loss, injury or damage caused thereby.

CONTENTS

caveat viator

............traveller beware

CHAPTER 1

A Journey into Danger

We are told that in 1955 there were approximately 45 million people around the world travelling from one country to another. As we turn the corner of the century, less than 50 years later, there are now over half a billion of us travelling internationally. For the vast majority, their travel will be uneventful, whereas for some it may be both eventful, worrying and traumatic. The current trend, in tourist terms, is to refer to those journeys where 'interesting' events may happen, as 'adventure holidays'. The truth is that many could be more aptly, although uncommercially, described as 'danger holidays' and for an unacceptable number of tourists this is what their journeys have turned into. The ancient Chinese curse *"may you live in interesting times"* could be the motto for many of today's international travellers, be they tourists or those on business.

The figures relating to the volume of world travel have become truly staggering and over the past 30 years the tourist industry has grown 1-2% faster than the global economy and it is slated to become one of the three key industries in the 21st century. Currently one job in ten in the global economy is linked to travel or tourism, with over 80 million people employed directly by the industry worldwide and another 150 million indirectly, accounting for some 11.12% of global gross domestic product - worth about $4.5 trillion in 1998.

In 1997, 612 million tourists spending $448 billion visited a foreign country, which was up 75% on 1987. It is estimated by 2010, the number of vacationing travellers could top 1 billion.

It would be comforting to think that since the demise of the Soviet Bloc and it's confrontation with the West that world peace had taken a few steps forward. In the sense that global, nuclear *"mutual assured destruction" (MAD),* no longer hangs over us, then I suppose it has, but in terms of world peace taken as meaning 'a safer world to live in', then we are heading backwards at a great rate of knots. There cannot have been a time when global conflict rages to the extent it currently does and social disorder affects the lives of so many people worldwide.

The end of the 'superpower' conflict is only one contributor to the overall demise of the safety and security we would hope to enjoy as we travel around the world. It is easy and convenient to simply believe that the more backward a country, the worse security will be and to ignore the risks on our own doorstep. The Oklahoma bombing in the States was the wake-up call to it's citizens about home grown terrorism. The World Trade Centre bombing could be sidelined as a one off incident perpetrated by foreigners, but Oklahoma, Atlanta Olympics, the Unibomber and numerous incidents of domestic terror have now alerted people to the potential for social disorder in their own backyard of the United States. In the U.K. we have had a bombing campaign waged by a curiously titled 'Mardi Gras bomber' who has targeted not only a major bank, but also a well known U.K supermarket chain. Now caught and sentenced, we can see that he looks like everyone's grandfather who, by the way, carried a stun gun disguised as a mobile phone.

In Northern Ireland since the cease-fire, we have had the horrific bombing at Omagh. Following the 'Mardi Gras bomber' in the U.K., we had a further series of home made explosive devices targeting 'gay' bars and multi-racial areas of London. Originally thought to be the work of a right wing gang turned out to be one individual with a warped thinking about the world and how he would like it to be.

There are views being propounded, which argue that governments will have to increasingly fight to keep the loyalty of it's populace and to ensure that a growing sentiment against the centralised control of the state does not increasingly turn to violence. The Marxist sponsored terrorism of the 60's and 70's in Europe is now a distant memory, only to be replaced by committed individuals who embark on reigns of terror, in the name of even more obscure dogma. Europe has, in the nineties, been the hunting ground of Islamic terrorists from Algeria and their bombing campaigns in France left many dead and reminded us all how vulnerable we are if we happen to be in the wrong place at the wrong time. The demonstrations and violence in Seattle and Washington against the World Bank and IMF, are seen as a backlash against globalisation, at least of the commercial kind.

The demise of the superpower conflict has lifted the lid off the pressure cooker in which has stewed, for over 50 years, national, regional, ethnic and tribal conflict. Suppressed and controlled under the totalitarian regimes of the soviet bloc there are now no former soviet republics without ethnic violence, nor few former communist countries free of the troubles created by islands of ethnic minorities abandoned in countries who no longer want them, yet whose presence gives reasonable excuse for their country of origin to enter into major conflict on their behalf. Albanians in Kosovo, Montenegro or Ngorno Karabak are a small example. Most are what could be called 'low level' conflicts, although in Tajikistan this is anything but the case and the country should be avoided at all costs.

From former Yugoslavia to Rwanda and the Middle East, old scores have still to be settled. The past 5 to 10 years has seen tribal violence erupt with a ferocity that continues to shock, both in the West and in the Third World. The violence and ethnic cleansing in Bosnia, Croatia and now Kosovo has been no less inhuman than that of Rwanda and elsewhere. The Khmer Rouge still clings onto some semblance of regional power and the murder, following his kidnap, of the British bomb disposal expert, who was working for a charity operating in the region, has been laid at the door of Pol Pot's successor.

The results of civil war - Beirut. Probably the most dramatic example of how a modern society can slaughter its way almost back to the stone age.

The International Arms Trade

It is a chilling fact that 4 million civilians have been killed in wars since 1990. According to the United Nations, of the 80 something armed conflicts fought around the world in the mid 1990's, only 3 were between nations. The rest were civil wars and insurgencies.

At the centre of all this slaughter is the international arms trade. Oxfam has estimated the global small arms trade between 1990 and only 1995 at some $22 billion. Arms controls only ever work against costly and hard to hide tanks, missiles and aircraft. It does not work against man-portable weapons.

"Small arms proliferation is a major political and security issue at local, national and regional levels in Africa" says Peter Batchelor of the Centre for

Conflict Resolution at the University of Capetown. There are some 1.5 million assault rifles missing in Mozambique and since El Salvador's civil war ended in 1992, murder rates have soared by 36% and as we report elsewhere gunshot wounds in South Africa are on the increase. The CIA has spent $millions to recover the 'Stinger' shoulder-mounted missiles it gave to Afghan rebels fighting the Russians. Interestingly British Airways flights from Islamabad to London take a long westerly detour to avoid the possibility of Stinger anti-aircraft missiles. The collapse of the Soviet Union has thrown millions of weapons into the hands of criminals and terrorists.

As I write this introduction, the British papers have carried the horrific stories about the atrocities carried out by the Sudanese military against the Christian tribes in the south of the country, clearly following a policy of genocide. The Sudanese, not happy with slaughtering their own, finance and give aid to one of the world's most despicable murderers of the 20th century - Joseph Kony and his Lords Resistance Army, operating in Uganda. As the requirement has diminished for the superpowers to slice up the world for political influence, little has

The Russian White House about 18 months after the seige and still being repaired. Bullets fired in the conflict went through offices nearby, rented by Western businesses.

changed as they continue to support totalitarian regimes for their economic value. France and Russia's reluctance to apply force to Saddam Hussein at the time the U.N Inspection teams were evicted, rested on purely economic imperatives. Someone eventually will get the country's oil and again Russia's reluctance to intervene with force in the prevention of Slobodan Milosevic's Serbian police! Slaughtering Albanian civilians in Kosovo only typifies how alliances are still ordered along ethnic and potentially commercial lines.

I have heard the current situation described as the *"new world disorder".* What this means is that no longer will committed and murderous tribal or ethnic terrorist factions be guided by, nor listen to a superpower. Writing this book straggled the atrocities against tourists in Yemen by Muslim fundamentalists and in Uganda by the Interahamwe Hutu rebels. Both these situations have been studied in more detail in Chapter 2, but both clearly indicate the unstructured nature of central government control in many countries of the world. Less structure means countries are open and opportune for capital, tourists, business and exploitation, but also for criminals and extreme terror inclined factions.

Unfortunately such countries have become the destination of the 'adventure tourist' where the adventure is of a degree not portrayed in the tour brochures. I hold many tour operators guilty of negligence in the promotion of such geographies as suitable for vulnerable, unprepared and unprotected tourists. The same applies to companies who are prepared to send their employees to such parts of the world where anarchy reigns. Chechnya is a good example where, in 1988, four British telecommunications engineers were kidnapped and subsequently beheaded by Chechen rebels.

Chechnya can not even be compared to Lebanon in the height of it's troubles. The gangs operating in Lebanon and Beirut had lines of communication and, usually, a state sponsor, i.e Iran, Syria, Israel etc, through whom negotiations could happen, should a kidnapping occur. Often through pressure from one of these sponsors a victim would be released. No such structure or understanding exists in Chechnya. If you are kidnapped, there is no higher authority who can be called upon to intercede on your behalf. Whether another factor had a bearing on the attack on the camp or not we will never know, but the company that employed the men has admitted it agreed with the British Foreign office to supply intelligence from Chechnya - spy! To put it's employees at risk in this way is unconscionable. To also believe that you can protect a company's compound against attack from a people who held up the Russian war machine is equally naive or negligent.

At the Inquest in November 1999 the verdict of unlawfully killed was given and the solicitor for the men's families said that in the light of evidence given, the families may sue their employer. For some time following the kidnapping it seemed as if negotiations would prove positive and it is still not known whether the kidnappers suspected an armed assault to free the men, or whether their deaths were as a result of some internal feud between the captors.

Prior to the attack they were housed in a walled compound, with steel gates, around the clock surveillance and four to six armed guards. Despite these precautions, the guards were overwhelmed. An accurate risk assessment in October 1998 should have concluded that despite precautions, the risk to Western workers, without massive Chechen military support, was too extreme to send people out there. A parallel with Algeria could have been made and a study of security practices in place there for foreign workers would have given some idea as to the monumental size of the task - one poorly protected compound would not do it.

This whole region remains a powder keg just ready to explode. In March 1999 a bomb in the market place of the capital of North Ossetia, Vladikavkaz, which is some 30 miles from Chechnya killed in excess of 60 people. The country is in dispute with it's neighbour Ingushetia and clashes in the early nineties killed hundreds.

But what does all this have to do with travel security. It is all part of the bigger picture that is contributing to instability in many parts of the world into which we venture to do business, or see the sights. It is a fact of international business that those countries which have the natural resources, cheap assets and cheap labour are by definition unstable regimes. Much of what the West wants is still in the Third World. By Third World I also include the Former Soviet Union now known as the Confederation Of Independent States (C.I.S), as it was succinctly said to me that ***"Russia is a third world country with a first world intelligence".*** Which makes it even more difficult and potentially dangerous to do business with.

Just as there is no corner of the former communist bloc which is free of ethnic tensions there is certainly no corner which is free of the heavy and all controlling hand of organised crime. My own business, over many years, has been to provide the personal protection for senior business people as they travel around the world. This is an extension of the broader work I do for their corporations in the field of Risk and Crisis Management. Over the years I have organised and run executive protection operations (bodyguarding) for some of the worlds wealthiest, corporate individuals. The reason they require such protection is obvious, particularly when you put their individual profile against the environment they are travelling in.

It is now a fact of corporate life that the opportunities in the world exist in those countries which are described as third world or those which have escaped from under repressive and protectionist regimes, such as the former Soviet Bloc, Vietnam, China and elsewhere. It seems to be a natural corollary that where the opportunities lie there also lies the very evident dangers.

Emerging Markets

Over the past ten years the world, as a market place in which international businesses have an interest, has doubled in size as previous restrictions to travel and trade have been removed. The prime example must be Russia and it's former Republics, with their huge natural resources. It is a market place where labour is cheap and rarely organised along union lines and it is a market place with little business acumen. As such, what one might be fooled into thinking, is that it is a recipe for exploitation by the West - wrong. The reverse is true and one only has to look into the hollow eyed stare of business executives coming home from Moscow to know they have added themselves to the ever growing list of those who have been comprehensively shafted by their Russian partners, distributors or associates.

Corruption At The Top

In September 1999, allegations were made about the laundering of $15 Billion by Russian organised crime and that much of it was via Western banks, in particular the Bank Of New York. Some of this money, it is alleged, may include portions of loans from the International Monetary Fund (IMF). At least five members of the Kremlin inner circle, including President Yeltsin's daughter and ex-Prime Minister Chubais, are alleged to be involved. There was a separate allegation that the Swiss company Mabatex had provided Yeltsin and his daughters with a £1 million kickback for lucrative contracts in Russia

Murder Inc.!

The Federal Security Services (FSB) formerly the Russian KGB was accused by some of it's senior officers as being run like a private militia and a 'murder incorporated'.

Orders to murder and kidnap personal enemies were commonplace as were attempts to silence officers who protested. Officers were accused of setting up their own private criminal groups. These accusations were at a press conference by officers who said they had received orders to murder the controversial, Boris Berezovsky, one of the country's richest businessmen and bankers - known commonly in Russia as Oligarchs.

A Col. Alexander Litvinenko said the service had almost been privatised by senior officers who behaved little better than Mafia godfathers. Supposedly, activities they had ordered included terrorist acts, murders, kidnappings and extortion of large sums of money from commercial firms. One officer claimed he had been ordered to kidnap the brother of a prominent Moscow businessman.

A KGB training facility in Kazakhstan - now redundant. The authorities were keen to lease it out to a Western security company for training purposes.

The British newspaper the Daily Telegraph, in 1996 reported that according to the Russian Interior Ministry's National Research Centre - ***"1 in 4 Russian citizens has a tendency to display criminal behaviour".*** Experts at the Centre warned that the country's criminal potential was growing. Some 3 million crimes are recorded in Russia every year, but the number of unrecorded crime is, however, estimated at between 6.5 million and 7 million. Most of the 'new' markets have endemic corruption, organised crime and lawlessness on the streets. One week's news from around the world should convince even the most sceptical observer of the inherent risks of doing business in emerging markets.

Not Important Enough To Kidnap?

But don't think that you need to be prominent and wealthy to be kidnapped. It can happen by accident as much as it can by design. Kidnapping may be for profit or political gain and if it is the latter often any European or American body will fit the bill. There is still no word from Kashmir as to the fate of four kidnapped backpackers, although it would now seem likely that they are sadly no longer alive.

Only this week I was reading in a British newspaper of another backpacker who has disappeared whilst trekking in the Australian outback. Don't always think of kidnappers being terrorist organisations. Serial killers kill following abduction - kidnapping takes place prior to the murder. In Russia it is common practice and no longer a remarkable event for a rival businessman to be kidnapped off the street and held until he complies with the perpetrators wishes and the same happens to prospective partners when something is required of them.

I am led to believe that in the first half of 2000, Kroll Associates, had worked on half a dozen kidnappings. Kroll reported that this was a doubling of their work in this area and that, unfortunately, victims were being held for longer. A trend has been for kidnappers to hold their hostages even after the ransom has been paid in the hope of more money.

Ronald Sander, an American oil executive was found dead in a remote jungle near the Colombian border, having been shot in the back five times. This followed his kidnapping three months earlier along with seven others from an oil farm in the El Coca region outside Quito.

A note with the body attributed his killing to the non payment of the ransom.

Lack Of State Control

Unfortunately all those aspects which make these new markets attractive and opportune also contribute to its risk and danger. We know from simple experience that when labour is cheap often life itself is cheap. We should know that when business experience or acumen is low in a foreign business partner then business ethics are usually a complete mystery. We are also now finding out that when the heavy hand of state control is lifted in a country that criminal elements who previously operated unseen, crawl out of the woodwork as if there had been a house fire, to take a grip of society and adequately fill the vacuum left by the withdrawal of the state machinery. The reason the state control was lifted in Russia is the same reason communism collapsed - the state was bankrupt and it could no longer afford to maintain its internal security organisations, whilst satisfying the IMF (from whom it requires a few $billion in aid) as to it's seriousness about economic and fiscal management.

There was a joke going around some few years back that officers of the anti-mafia unit of the St Petersburg police had to queue to use the one phone in the department. The meteoric rise of Russian **Organised Crime Groups (OCG's)**, could never have been predicted, but so it will be with China, albeit in a more controlled way.

The China Syndrome

Don't believe that China has no crime. Some towns in the country are criminal controlled 'no-go' areas. Prior to China taking over Hong Kong, armed gangs of robbers were coming over the border and raiding jewellers shops. Highly organised crime exists in China, it's just that as yet we hear little about it, but rest assured when the western businessman turns up in force with his pockets bulging with dollars we will.

The following gives a view of how even a totalitarian regime such as China is unable to suppress criminal activity. It may be that, as with Russia, the influence of corruption and organised crime go all the way to the top.

Macau

In the last days of this Portuguese colony, a vicious Triad war has broken out for control of the territory's lucrative gambling industry before it is handed back to China in December 1999.

After a 442 year rule from Portugal, the last few years have seen an upsurge of violence. Despite the arrest of ruthless gangland bosses such as Wan Kuokai-koi, better known as 'Broken Tooth Koi', a campaign of terror has continued. The local gangs are jockeying for position before the arrival of the Chinese mainland's Triad gangs headed by and this is the interesting fact, former Peoples Liberation Army (PLA) officers, who run substantial 'business' organisations ably assisted by their former colleagues still in the military.

Racketeering schemes based on the casinos makes $millions per month. Despite being behind bars, gang leaders still manage their empires and hire contract killers, mainly from the mainland. Whilst some of the remaining Portuguese have become victims of the violence, it is not directed toward visitors, but it would not be difficult to be in the wrong place at the wrong time and care must be taken. For the businessman travelling to China, events in Macau should serve to highlight that though we sometimes don't hear of the real state of lawlessness in some of the cities and regions of China, it is there and it will get worse. As with any emerging market, the Western business proves an attractive and 'soft' target for organised crime.

Business and Russian Organised Crime

In Russia and the former Republics the 'mafia' has a stranglehold not only on indigenous businesses, but on nearly every Western business brave enough, or foolish enough, to have attempted to establish a legitimate toehold there - whether they care to admit to it or not. Hand in hand with the business 'sea change' that many former communist countries have gone through, is the collapse of society. Where once upon a time a family had to think, or certainly worry little about the future, given the 'state engineered' ethos of full employment, it now has to think forward if only to determine where the next meal is coming from. Some workers are six months in arrears in pay and as I write, in an effort to save the Rouble, the Russian Government has raised interest rates by 150%. Panic is close to setting in and there is no telling how matters will turn out. The Rouble will have to be devalued despite the brave words of the President and by that time foreign reserves will be more than half in a futile attempt to support the currency.

The exponential growth of organised crime in Russia and the former Soviet Republics is not only an issue of personal security and economics it is becoming an issue of national and international security. Former Soviet military, fully automatic weapons now appear on the streets of most western major cities, having been acquired in the escalating cycle of drugs, money laundering and weapons exchange.

In Russia itself no one is safe from the attentions of the Organised Crime Groups (OCG's) or Russian Mafia as they have become known. The Moscow Times in August 1995 reported the death, by poisoning of a prominent banker Ivan Kivelidi, a departure from the 26 other bankers killed previously, where all but 4 were killed by gunfire.

Kivelidi was the founder of the Russian Roundtable and president of Rosbizbank and one of Russia's most visible businessmen. The Russian Association of Bankers released a highly unusual survey giving details of the 85 contract attacks on bankers in the previous three years leading up to August 95, which resulted in 47 deaths. Bodyguards, relatives and employees made up the total. Nearly all the shootings occurred near the home either on the way to or back from work, at or near their vehicles

A Bodyguard team in practise prior to deployment in the former Soviet Union.

Of the 85 attacks 23 of them left bankers or their bodyguards permanently maimed. Most of these 'injury' attacks were the result of explosions.

The attraction to the Mafia of controlling the Russian banking system is obvious. The huge cash 'mountains' being generated through their activities need laundering and what better way than to own or control the banks and even the banking system. Despite Russian Central Bank initiatives, both in improved systems and computer controls, billions of Rubles of mafia money circulates through not only the Russian, but also the International banking systems.

It is a known fact that the London property market is in no small way buoyed up by the 'weight' of Russian 'new' money finding it's way into the market. Whilst most of it is from legitimate businessmen from the emerging stable of Russian, billionaire businessmen, many a cloud of suggestion of the wrong connections hangs over many of these people. Often they have political careers as well as the wide ranging business interests.

Russia, especially in it's larger metropolitan areas always had 'big city' problems. However, in Soviet times crime was hidden and often repressed. The period of stress and uncertainty of perestroika in the mid 80's allowed criminal activity to become more visible. The change was possible by the realisation that many of the state structures, not least the criminal justice system and the police were bankrupt. Penal taxation has turned even the most law abiding person criminal as they operate within the 'black economy', declaring little if anything of their earnings. It is a 'gold rush' mentality and lack of state control over 'privatisation' issues has allowed criminal elements to exercise control over many major industrial concerns.

Those banks that the mafia were unable to coerce into their sphere of influence by violence have possibly been bought by Mafia front companies.

Igor Timofeyev, a Moscow investigative journalist, believes the pivotal point for the explosion of violent, criminal activity came some eight years ago when groups of thugs in the region of Kazan suddenly became more violent. They briefly terrorised Moscow before being rounded up and imprisoned, but the mould was formed and those criminal groups already in existence for many years began to seize control of business, both legitimate and illegal. They have their people in the police, justice system, former KGB and in every state and political faction that matters when it comes to exerting influence and ensuring that their activities go unnoticed. Today there are some 24 Russian organised crime groups operating and identified in the USA and they have forged international links with most of the important, organised criminal groups around the world. Even the holiday beaches of southern Spain are now the preserve of Russian Mafia who have shot and bombed their way to criminal supremacy in this region.

It is difficult to walk anywhere in Cyprus without hearing the guttural tones of a Moscow accent and it would be hard to estimate the volume of new bank accounts being opened on the island by the 'new rich' of Russia, but it is very high.

For any Western business to operate in this environment certain things need to happen. Keeping a 'low profile' is one way, but even this is no guarantee that your enterprise goes unnoticed. Often a Mafia approach follows a visit from the 'Tax Police' and shortly after the official visit there occurs the second visit by people who seem to know a great deal more about your company's finances than they should. The reason they do is because the tax police in some instances are selling your information. Most Russian businesses are, as a consequence, keeping two sets of books.

Russia serves as an example as to how a well ordered society can disintegrate in a few short years. But, what has all this to do with executive travel security? Everything is the answer. When a society breaks down the first victim is law and order. Crime both highly organised and highly disorganised will very much affect a foreigner in a foreign land. It wasn't always the case that poor equalled lawless, but these days it is hard to find a community that is prepared to suffer poverty in silence and without turning to less than honest ways to earn a living. Some societies have lawlessness bred into them over millennia. Without being unkind, Chechnya, prior to it's first invasion by Russia, was a mafia country. It's head of the state Dudieff was no more and no less than a mafia godfather and banditry by the chechens had been a way of life for centuries.

After the invasion the world conveniently forgot the two bus loads of Russian schoolchildren kidnapped by Chechens for ransom and other acts of criminal violence that preceded Russia's intervention in their affairs. Yet despite this and in the hope of doing business, the international businessman will continue to travel to such regions and, in most cases, survive. However, he or she survives probably in ignorance of the true picture. I am uncertain whether there is true ignorance of the dangerous reality of where they are, or they simply choose to ignore the evidence they have read, seen and been told. This certainly happens with business ventures in Russia. I have found the average businessman deaf to the reality of what is likely to befall him in doing business in that geography. Their belief is that they have found the 'honest broker' in town, that their deal is sound and they are covered. I know it's trite to say it but if I had a pound for all the times I have heard this and then seen the result, I wouldn't be writing books for a living.

One could be forgiven for uncharitably labelling the root cause of the problem as greed, rather than a more benign title of 'seizing emerging market opportunities', but however we perceive the cause of the blindness to reality, the end result can be the same. The British Department of Trade and Industry cautions anyone who is thinking about doing business in Russia to first formulate a 'Security Plan' and this should include extortion response. All foreign businesses will be targeted. The United States still links the killing of Paul Tatum, an American citizen with his former business partners and one, 39 year old Chechen, Umar Dzhabroilov, is still denied a U.S.visa.

A British TV producer was found stabbed to death in his flat in Moscow in September 1999. Christopher Rees 34, worked for STS Television. Over the past few years there has been a spate of 'contract killings' of TV personalities in the city, although STS was outside the mainstream of the companies engaged in the 'media wars'. As there was no forced entry it is likely he knew the killer.

World Tourist Risks

In a recent article in the security magazine **Intersec**, Henryk Handszuh, Chief of the Quality of Tourist Development Programme at the World Tourist Organisation (WTO), reiterated that ranking tourist destinations according to their perceived security and safety status has become a common media feature. This is particularly so when public attention is focussed on spectacular events such as terrorist attacks, kidnapping, aircraft crashes, sea accidents or natural disasters. Handszuh remarked, however, that in reality, such events claim relatively few victims among travellers, albeit that their potential to discourage tourism from the destinations is proportionately much higher than common crime, car accidents, health problems or drowning. His reference to the media is probably the key to the problem.

In the U.K., surveys show that the public's perception and fear of domestic crime is out of proportion to the way it would, statistically and in reality, affect their lives. Their perceptions are gained from alarmist media articles narrowly focussing on one or two, untypical outrages. So it is with tourism. Clearly the more media focus, the greater the impact on a destination. Handszuh succinctly summarises the three types of tourism destination, affected by safety and security image problems.

Country destinations usually associated with such problems: These, typically, will be parts of Africa, Asia, Eastern or Southern Europe, Latin America and the Middle East. He makes the point that the dangers of these destinations, for which a strong bias has developed, will only happen with major campaigns and very efficient emergency management should incidents occur.

Destinations believed to be safe: This we perceive to be Western and Northern Europe, America and East Asia. This is the case, even if the frequency and volume of their tourist victims may actually exceed the figures from the "bad reputation destinations". The point was made in the article that the misconception was based on the fact that people are deceived by the similarity in the culture of the destinations to their own and are often well known to the traveller, particularly the businessman.

Local areas known for crime within safe destinations: The article quotes such places in the U.S. as New York, Miami, Washington, D.C., New Orleans etc. Interestingly though and despite some very bad reports from particular quarters in such cities affected by notorious crime problems, visitor reputation is not shaken. Again this may be a cultural response or it may be simply 'out of sight out of mind'.

It can be as dangerous in some parts of Washington as it could in any Third World city.

This book is equally aimed at the businessman who is now asked to travel to many of the unstable and potentially dangerous regions of the world we have mentioned previously, often with little corporate support, resources, training, education, or information.

This should not, however, be the extent of the target audience. Travel is now on the agenda for everyone. The tourist industry is experiencing a growth of immense proportions and the projections are equally staggering. Even the remotest corners of the world are feeling the tread of the trekker or eco-tourist, from the Antarctic to the jungles of Papua New Guinea. It is no more safe though to be travelling as a tourist than it is to be travelling on business, in fact, for many reasons we will look at it is less safe. For many dissident anti-government rebel forces in countries around the world the tourist has become to be seen as a very opportunistic, soft target.

For many Third World countries tourism now comprises the principle source of foreign revenues, or any revenues for that matter. This has been recognised by the Fundamental Islamic movement in Egypt and after years of attacks on tourists they perpetrated their worst atrocity on the visitors to Luxor with the massacre of 58, outside the Tombs of the Kings. The person who finds him or herself in such a predicament as the victims at Luxor there is little in the way of individual opportunity to help oneself, but there are still things which one could do at that late stage and no one should simply become a victim through ignorance.

High Profile?

The vast majority of us are what we can term 'low profile' travellers. We are not famous, wealthy beyond imagination, nor work in government service and when travelling can safely use our own name. For the high profile world traveller, however, certain precautions need to be rigorously adhered to.

First you need to ensure that your hotel bookings are not in your name or the name of your company, as criminals and others require information about the victim to allow them to plan. This may be achieved through surveillance or by gathering information, or by a combination of the two. Information has a value and people are ready and willing to sell information about you and your company.

Some Basics

So two things - ensure that details of your travel arrangements are known to as few people as possible and avoid falling into patterns of movement and behaviour. Routine is the key to a kidnappers plans and at this point it is important to differentiate between the problems of being an expatriate, who is domiciled in a country for months or years and a visitor who may be there for a period measured in days or a week at the most. Herein lies one of the biggest safety factors for the occasional traveller in that they are not on the ground long enough for people, who would have a nefarious interest in them, to be able to establish a pattern of movement and plan the kidnap or robbery or attack. Also the more difficult it is for the offenders to get information on a victim, the less attractive that person becomes. When you know the process of kidnapping you realise it is seldom, if ever, a spontaneous affair.

There is the initial victim selection, followed by the acquisition of information to fill out the plan of attack. This will include careful enquiries about the intended victim, analysis of information, observation to establish patterns and habits, choice of the attack site, rehearsal, further reconnaissance, study of timings, routes, mapping, simulation of action, withdrawal, destruction of evidence. In essence no action is taken without careful preparation.

This is however, in contrast to the almost opportunist, abduction of people who are in areas of severe instability or rebel activities. Aid workers are still missing in Chechnya and people have been seized off the street in many parts of the world. In the Philippines it is estimated that half of the kidnappings are carried out by or with the collusion of police officers. In these environments, you can be taken off the street at a whim, simply by being in the wrong place at the wrong time.

Offenders normally rely on catching the victim off guard and by the use of surprise and shock. A vulnerable victim therefore, is one who offers the offenders a quick and easy attack and a safe getaway. This very basic requirement applies in a kidnapping, an assassination or a street mugging. Often the majority of people who are kidnapped are not in any way alert to the pending danger until it is too late. All the techniques of anti-surveillance and avoidance of patterns must be an active and continuous process and we will study this later.

All executives must be aware of the possibility of being singled out and attacked at any moment for no other reason than the fact they may be employed by a particular company, agency or are representative of a disliked or even hated nation state. Western tourists are equally at risk for the same reason as illustrated in two separate incidents, the first in Yemen in the Middle East and the other in Uganda, Central Africa We will look at these in more detail later.

A Quick 'Once Around The World'

All the following countries made the news in 1999. This is by no means an exclusive list of trouble spots, but it is a cross section of internal strife and external incursions. All have a potential impact for the business traveller and tourist, although becoming a victim is primarily a matter of being in the wrong place at the wrong time. That having been said, increasingly, the foreigner is a 'soft option' with high publicity potential. It is academic, if you are caught in the middle of a violent conflict, to be able to determine whether it is a border clash, internal insurgency, political hostage taking or out and out war. Prior knowledge can however, make you reappraise your decision to go and if you do, what to expect and where.

Even in Europe

The most dangerous places for tourists stretch from the inner cities of North America, most cities and tourist areas in Mexico, most of sub-Saharan Africa, South East Asia in places such as Cambodia, Northern Sri-Lanka, the Philippines (188 abductions in 1998), Latin America (Brazil for example has critical levels of criminal activity), to even Paris with it's gangs of predatory Gypsy thieves. To be fair we can find problem areas in most regions of the world, especially Europe. We often ignore the problems of society on our own doorstep.

For example late in 1999, four leading Stockholm newspapers took the unprecedented step of publishing the names and photographs of 62 of Sweden's neo-Nazis and biker gang members. These people were described as a threat to the nation's democracy. The articles revealed the methods of these fascist and criminal groups who targeted attacks on police, politicians and journalists. Recent murder victims included a well known trade unionist and 2 policemen. Astonishingly the articles stated that 90% of Sweden's policemen and 59% of it's state prosecutors had received threats, with 37% of the prosecutors admitting that they had dropped charges because they or witnesses were threatened. Some years back international co-operation between European nations in the fight against terrorism was non-existent. Now matters have much improved. A recent example was in 1998 with a choreographed sweep in May just before football's World Cup in France. Hundreds of arrests were made on the same day in France, Belgium, Switzerland and Italy of people suspected of planning attacks in France to coincide with the event. The intelligence for the arrests came from an earlier arrest in Belgium of suspected members of Algeria's Armed Islamic Group, the G.I.A.

The change came about around 1995 after a number of bombings by Islamic terrorists in France which left 9 people dead and more than 170 injured. All European nations realised it could have been them just as easily. Since the demise of the Soviet Bloc, the traditional hiding places for Europe's home grown terrorists, such places as Hungary, East Germany and Bulgaria have also ceased to exist. Terrorists such as Ilich Ramirez Sanchez, better known as Carlos The Jackal, have had nowhere to hide and he now languishes in a French jail, having reportedly spent months at a top hotel in Bulgaria's capital, Sofia.

However, the statistical reality is that half the world's violent conflicts are in Africa - this is according to **Fabienne Hara**, a Nairobi analyst for the Brussels-based **International Crisis Group**. A short tour around may give you a better picture as to how potentially dangerous the world really is and represents a very small window onto the wider landscape of the world's trouble spots. Remember though that it is not simply a question of being aware of the problems a country may have, it is important to know when and where you may be at risk. According to Philip Perry a terrorism underwriter for Hiscox, a LLoyds of London syndicate, which specialises in insuring against special risks, says, the danger lies not in particular countries, but, in 'soft targets'. He said ***"I would be extremely vigilant anywhere there are American interests"***. What this means is avoiding such places as McDonalds, Hard Rock Cafes and Planet Hollywood. U.S airlines could be targeted too, but the difference is they already have risk control systems in place, whereas restaurants won't have, which makes them very vulnerable. The following 'quick tour' is in no order, certainly not comprehensive and simply an overview of some extremely complex situations.

Greece

An intelligence report by the U.S State Department, released in May 2000, says Greece led Europe in the number of anti-American attacks in 1999, second only to Colombia. In fact there were 20 terrorist attacks against American targets in a 12 month period, a combined 40 strikes on U.S., French and British interests, 7 rocket attacks and 52 anti-American protest marches.

In the latest attack by the shadowy Revolutionary Organisation 17 November, the British defence attache, Brigadier Stephen Saunders, was tragically assassinated as he drove to work. This group has claimed the lives of 22 Greek and foreign citizens and despite supposed efforts by the Greek authorities, no members have ever been arrested never mind brought to trial. There are very strong suspicions that November 17 and the some 80 other terrorist groups who operate in Greece have more or less a free hand. The situation was very succinctly summed up by Wayne Merry a former U.S. embassy official when he said, "It's not that Greece has the world's worst terrorist problem, it's that Greece has the world's worst counter-terrorist problem". November 17 was also responsible for gunning down Richard Welch, the CIA's station chief in Athens in 1975.

Any U.S or European company operating in Greece should ensure that it's threat assessment and procedures that flow from it reflect the true sentiment which exists in the country towards the U.S and other Western interests. Greek people have, clearly, more sympathy with the Eastern view of the world than that of the West and this was evidenced by the increased terrorist activity following the bombings of Kosovo.

Angola

There is no tourist market in the country, which is currently to the good. A country with over a quarter of a century of internal warfare, it has been listed by the U.N as the worst place in the world for a child to be born. The victims of this conflict run into millions. From a guerilla insurgency against the Soviet backed government which took over from the Portuguese in 1975, the opposing sides, which are now Jonas Savimbi's UNITA against the Luanda government have continued the fight. In 1999 13 aid workers were killed and 2 U.N. aircraft were shot down with the loss of 23 lives. The number of land mines which litter the country run into millions. Three out of every 10 Angolan children die before the age of 5. Forget the politics of democratic revolution here, the war is being waged for control of the countries vast natural resources, particularly the diamond mines.

Sri Lanka

By contrast, the Island of Sri Lanka is a popular tourist destination, yet it has one of the most vicious of wars raging in it's northern provinces. Whilst there is no tourism in these areas, the conflict spills out to the capital with regularity, usually in the form of bombings. Only in December 1999, a bomb exploded outside Colombo's City Hall, killing

Galle Face Road leading south from Columbo and seemingly peaceful, but at any time a Tamil separatist bomb could shatter the peace.

15 and the President Chandrika Kumaratunga received medical attention for injuries she received from a suicide bomb during an election rally. At one time the Tamil Tigers targeted the tourist market directly with a massive truck bomb which destroyed some of Colombo's largest Western hotels. As I write, in May 2000, the Tamil rebels are making a massive push to retake the City of Jaffna and many elements of the Sri Lankan army are cut off.

Algeria

Still to be considered the most deadly place in the world for foreigners. With 50,000 dead over the past few years there is little sign of matters improving. In late 1999, the slaughter of the innocents continued with over 100 villagers being killed by the Armed Islamic Group (GIA) in an attempt to de-stabilise the cease-fire announced between the Government and the Islamic Salvation Army.

Yemen

Tourists must be armed with knowledge. On the 29th December 1998, 3 Britons and one Australian were killed when Yemeni security forces stormed a mountain hideout where 16 Western hostages were being held by Islamic militants who had kidnapped them. Since 1992 more than 100 foreign visitors have been kidnapped, but it was the first time any hostages had been killed.

The leader of the kidnap gang Abu Hassan 28, described in court how he used the hostages as a 'human shield' when the security forces attacked. He called the tourists *"the grandchildren of pigs and monkeys. God sent them to us, so we took them. I hope those who are still at large will continue the 'Jihad' "*. As with this group many of the world's Islamic terror groups owe their allegiance and possibly their training to the millionaire dissident Saudi Osama Bin Laden.

The Islamic Jihad group or more accurately the Aden-Abyan Islamic Army, made up in the main of Arab volunteers who had fought in the Afghan war, had been responsible and the name has been used countless times before by dissident Islamic groups from Lebanese hostage takers in the 80's to an Egyptian group responsible for attacks on tourists.

Many of the kidnappings in Yemen in the past have been by tribal groups who in exchange for the release of hostages, had wrung concessions from the Yemeni government for such basic needs as new roads, water supplies and health clinics. Whilst Yemen is not on the British Foreign Office's 'banned' list of 26 countries it remains one of the most heavily armed of the world's countries with some 50 million automatic rifles in a population of 16 million - an explosive backdrop for any tourist. The emergence of this group is a turning point in hostage taking in Yemen, but the risk existed already and such information must be made available to 'adventure' tourists before they decide on such a visit.

The tour group responsible for the visit of the group who were kidnapped advised they handed out the Foreign Offices warnings, but this is simply not enough. There should be a detailed 'risk assessment' available for any country or region where the potential for problems may arise. A very simple analysis of the upward trend of kidnappings, should have been enough to set the warning bells ringing. The first kidnapping of a foreigner took place in 1991. Since then the numbers have grown to 15 in 1996 and more than 20 in 1997, with the 1998 figures around 100. When not kidnapping tourists, armed tribal groups turn their attentions to government troops, killing 250 in June and July 1998 and also attacking oil pipelines operated by Hunt Oil in the north and Canadian Occidental in the south. Widespread disaffection with a repressive and tribal partisan government, unable nor inclined to feed it's people and provide even basic conditions, are the recipe for serious internal problems.

A Stuart Poole-Robb, from the U.K's Merchant International Group, a firm that advises companies and individuals travelling to inhospitable parts of the world, believes the dangers of Yemen had always been underplayed. *"Tourists will always want to go to slightly dangerous places, but I don't believe there has been enough caution exercised over Yemen"*. I concur, but would level the same accusation at many other parts of the world. For entirely different political reasons the following example further illustrates the dangers of being a tourist from the West.

Uganda

The brochure of Acacia Expeditions, given to 15 tourists, who travelled with them to see mountain gorillas, described the trip as *"the opportunity of a lifetime"*. It turned into a jungle massacre when about 80 Hutu, Interahamwe rebels burst into 3 safari camps armed with assault rifles and machetes, killing 4 Biwindi Park staff and taking 31 Western tourists hostage.

Later in the morning the rebels selected English speaking tourists and force marched them through the jungle. Subsequently and horrifically 8 were killed - 4 Britons, 2 Americans and 2 New Zealanders. The rebels had trekked from their camps in the Congo where they had been rearming and reorganising since having fled from Rwanda. These were the same Hutu militia who had perpetrated genocide on nearly 1 million Tutsi neighbours in 1994. This was clearly an attack aimed at destroying Uganda's struggling tourist trade and revenge on the West's support of the Tutsi led Rwandan government. Uganda has also been on the side of the rebels attempting to wrest power from the Democratic Republic Congo leader Laurent Kabila. The Interahamwe (*those who kill together)* rank as probably the most murderous of all rebel groups operating around the world and have been hiding the 1 million Hutu refugees in camps in the eastern Congo and have found themselves fighting on the side of Kabila who has now turned against his own Congolese Tutsi minority.

Uganda is assailed on all sides by rebel activity either from the Alliance of Democratic Forces (ADF) a Muslim based group,

Interahamwe rebels, to the Lords Resistance Army or LRA. Joseph Kony it's leader has to date kidnapped some 8,000 children of all ages since he began his campaign in 1990. Most remain unaccounted for.

The Great lakes region of Central Africa remains a dangerous place to visit, with tourists at risk from armed groups that roam the region. Also the continuing involvement by neighbourning countries in the Congolese struggle makes it even easier for these disparate and murderous groups to ply their trade.

Eastern Europe

The effect of organised crime from the former communist countries is inexorably moving west. We will look in detail at the problems of the new Russia, it's spiral into lawlessness is not an isolated event. Gangs from the East - Russia, Ukraine, the Caucasus and Turkey all now operate from Central Europe e.g Poland, Hungary, Czech Republic and Slovenia. With most of these countries knocking on the door for Europen Union membership, they are a perfect 'jumping off' point for organised crime groups (OCG's).

It is now estimated that 80% of heroin in Europe comes via the Balkan route from Afghanistan, Pakistan and Turkey. Two groups - one controlled by ethnic Turks and the other by ethnic Albanians dominate the trade and have divided almost all of Central and Western Europe between them. The East-West drugs trade fuels both violence and gun-running across the continent.

Former military hardware floods across Europe, with Serb gangs tapping into the arms surplus from such places as war-torn former Yugoslavia. The weapons and ex-military explosives from the Eastern Bloc have led to a large increase in incidents of violence. Bombings in Slovakia rose from 15 in 1995 to 98 in 1997, whilst violent crime rose from 6,260 in 1989 to 11,564 in 1997. Whilst violent crimes peaked in Poland in the mid 90's, in the Czech Republic, Hungary and others it continues to rise. The Russians and Ukrainians are also into prostitution, extortion, debt collection, car theft and money laundering, with massive profits from smuggling cigarettes and 'black market' oil.

Piracy

The effect of Balkan criminals is not restricted to the land. Recently the Greek government sent out gunboats to discourage Albanian pirates from crossing the 3km Corfu channel and preying on yachts around the island.

Whilst most international acts of piracy or armed robbery (whilst in port) are against unarmed merchant ships, there is an increasing trend of attacks against pleasure craft. According to the London based International Maritime Bureau, incidents of piracy in general were up from 90 in 1994, 187 in 1995 and 224 in 1997. By far the majority of incidents go unreported due to the high cost of delays to a ship whilst investigations take place. The most dangerous waters are the seas off Indonesia and the Philippines, but the South China Sea, the waters off West Africa and the eastern seaboard of South America as well as the eastern Mediterranean, have all been areas where attacks have occurred.

South Africa

"A serious crime is committed every 17 seconds".

"There are 4 million illegal weapons in circulation and most robbers are armed."

" A rape every 28 seconds".

"A murder rate running at some 27,000 per year".

" 7,000 qualified lawyers, businessmen, and doctors are leaving every year".

South Africa now has a crime rate 80 times higher than that in the U.K. In addition to a soaring crime rate, South Africa's mixed race townships have long been notorious for fringe, fanatical Islamic groups. Every evening at sunset, thousands of Muslim militants gather in mosques in the lee of Table Mountain, many wearing Palestinian-style keffiyeh head scarves. Some carry guns and all offer their commitment to Islam and their loathing of America and Israel. Whilst such radicals are in a minority in the Cape's sophisticated Muslim communities, they are in the vanguard of a tide of Islamic militancy which, analysts say, is growing all over Africa.

From being at the forefront of the fight against apartheid they have now turned their anger from Pretoria to Washington. Muslims Against Global Oppression (MAGO) is one group linked to the bombing of Planet Hollywood. Whilst Cape Town has traditionally been a safer bet for tourists than Johannesburg, which is named in some surveys as the world's unofficial murder capital, this may change. Over the past 4 years there have been hundreds of pipe bomb attacks. In a recent police raid near the Mozambique border, some 5,600 assault rifles and 3 million rounds of ammunition were discovered. In fact there has been a flood of weapons into South Africa following the end of the civil war in Mozambique.

The nature of criminal gangs in South Africa is changing. There is a trend for experienced and well organised gangs to be taking over. The Nigerians are a good example of this where, from a base of supplying local gangs with crack cocaine, they have now established themselves in the mostly white, Sea Point suburb of Capetown. The Russians are now also in town, with both lots heavily involved in commercial crime, money laundering and fraud, some 59,000 cases in 1997. They recruit both State and corporate employees to help with the frauds.

The local 'taxi wars' have taken on an international gang flavour and a strong cocaine route has been established with Brazil, Colombia, Bolivia and Peru. Even if the South African economy soared to 8.5% growth, it would take 10 years to provide a job for every person who needed one. Even with 15,000 new houses being completed a month, some 10 million people (a quarter of South Africans) still live in shacks and as squatters. In 1999 some 42% of black adults are still unemployed (only 4% of whites). Despite huge achievements of the government, the changes are too slow for many who see the 'new rich' in the BMW's and Mercedes (both black and white).

The result is that violent crime like murder, assault, rape and robbery have almost doubled since 1994. A serious crime is committed every 17 seconds, a murder every half hour, a burglary every 2 minutes and an assault and rape every few seconds. From 'car-jackings', perpetrated in people's own driveways, to knifings during home burglaries, whites protest, yet it is the South African black population that is most at risk.

The police have had 1,000 of their own killed whilst on duty in the last 5 years. Morale is low and staff are poorly paid. Violence in Johannesburg has so far closed down a MacDonalds and a Holiday Inn and the Carlton Hotel.

When in Africa remember - don't get close to the real wildlife either!

Former township crime barons have turned their attention from local crime to the rich pickings of the white and affluent black communities. Bank hold-ups, hijackings, burglaries, kidnappings and heists are becoming commonplace. In car hijackings there is less than a 50% chance of survival. After the driver has disabled the alarm he or she is likely to be killed to prevent identification. Most crime in South Africa is becoming more brutal according to the Crime Information Management Centre - murder, attempted murder, and violent robbery are all on the increase.

In Johannesburg, the country's financial heart is slowing down. It is losing it's most prestigious companies as office workers can no longer put up with lawlessness on the streets. The centre of financial services is now Sandtown, a few kilometres north and even the Stock Exchange and Price Waterhouse Coopers and Ernst & Young have moved from the old centre. The crime wave is probably the single largest contributor to the 'brain drain'. 1998 was the fourth successive year the country experienced a net loss of people. A Business Time survey found that 74% of 11,000 skilled and highly qualified respondents were considering emigration because of crime and violence. Much of the recent crime has been attributed to Mandella's early release of 9,000 prisoners, as part of his 80th birthday celebrations! Anglo-American Corporation will shift it's corporate HQ and primary stock listing to London.

To provide some Western assistance to the crime problem, a British police chief has taken up the challenge to help lead the fight against crime in the city of Durban. Chief Superintendent John Sanderson will be on a year's secondment from November 1999.

The contrast couldn't be more stark. Sanderson comes from the U.K's Humberside police authority, where out of a population of 900,000, the annual murder rate varies between 10 and 12. In greater Durban, with a population of 3 million, there were 2,435 killings in 1998, 4,000 plus rapes, (compared with 150 in Humberside), 15,884 robberies, 18,222 burglaries and 21,370 assaults. Car-jackings were some 1,931. The contrast in the relation of police resources to crimes is also very dramatic, where in the U.K. 40 officers may be assigned to one murder, in Durban one officer may have to handle 40 murders.

Despite AIDS being a latecomer to South Africa, the numbers are now desperate. It is reported there are 1,500 new infections each day and the Department of Health estimates that at least 20% of the work force will be infected by the virus by the year 2000. Over the next three years the annual death toll will be 250,000. Insurance company actuaries estimate the epidemic will peak between 2005 and 2010 with some 6 million infected.

Indonesia

Jakarta has always been a violent city, but since the economic upheavals and political problems throughout 1999, street riots by students and others can erupt at any time. The instability has led to a rise in street crime and one should not venture out after dark.

Philippines

Crime is on the increase. Always a dangerous and often lawless country, criminals are now getting bolder. Many now don't even wear masks or blindfold kidnap victims. They know the judicial system has collapsed, mainly as a result of the country's economic ills. The police are starved of resources and earn barely enough to survive. Corruption in the government, police and judicial system all contribute to an out of control crime wave. Most kidnappings in the Philippines, are directed at the Chinese business community, with little directed to Westerners. This does not apply though with general crime, which is completely multi-racial. This last statement would have held good up to the kidnapping of 21 Western and Asian tourists from the Malay island of Sipidan by the Islamic terrorist organisation Abu Sayyaf who moved them to the island of Jolo and subsequently made demands on the Philippines government for both money and release of terrorists in jail

Almaty - Kazakhstan

Once the capital and also once a reasonably safe place for a foreigner to wander, violent crimes against foreigners is on the increase. On my one visit some years ago I felt much safer than in many other

Republics, but this has now changed. There is car theft and crime against motorists.

Pakistan

At times, this country can seem to be one of the most dangerous places in the world, from taxi drivers who steal luggage to police who have a record of sexually assaulting female victims of crime. Foreigners should be aware at all times.

Many parts of Pakistan, in particular the North West, are essentially ungovernable from Islamabad. The warlike tribes which have controlled these regions are simply a law unto themselves. It is a country which still works actively at isolation and is, as a consequence, one of the poorest in the world. It is also, despite its poverty, a highly militarised country and its on-going conflict with India - even to the extent of nuclear sabre rattling - is one of the most worrying aspects for the safety of the world, not just the region.

Be very careful if you visit Karachi. It is violent and whilst most of the violence which erupts suddenly is of a political nature and directed at each other, you could get caught up. Robbery, kidnapping and even bombings of government buildings is now almost commonplace.

The country is corrupt from top to bottom and crime is rampant. Most Pakistanis when they travel, have luggage locked, strapped and secured more tightly than 'Fort Knox', which should tell you something. Don't let anyone know your schedule, avoid lone travel and keep all your money and valuables in a money belt. Carry the customary 'give away' wallet and out of date credit cards, as well as some small denomination notes. Be very wary at all times and avoid leaving anything of value in your hotel room. Travel to Pakistan should be 'light'.

India

There are few of the regions of this populace country that do not suffer from separatist violence or rebel activity. Sectarian violence between Hindus and Muslims can flare up at any time and as a traveller you could find yourself embroiled. Riots can occur at a moment's notice in India, but are more likely around election, holy days, or after significant political events. Therefore, monitor political developments carefully if you are resident in the country. Visitors should not visit urban areas without first checking the security situation.

Sectarian and caste violence, manifested in regionally based insurgencies have accounted for most of the country's bombings, assassinations and kidnappings. There is not much violence against Western businesses, but as a nation it's politics are corrupt and often linked with organised crime. Certain states, such as Jammu-Kassmir and Bihar have ongoing insurgency problems and should be avoided. Trains and buses are still the favourite targets for attacks by terrorists and are also frequented by criminals. Pickpocketing and muggings are a continuing problem, so maintain a high level of awareness at all times and don't overburden yourself with too many packages when out and about. If a curfew is imposed by the military then obey it - often the army enforces such curfews with a 'shoot to kill' policy.

Foreign women should dress and behave conservatively when in public, but still risk being singled out for sexual harassment by Indian men. Foreigners of either sex should avoid public transport, as buses, trains and crowded terminals are frequent venues for criminal and terrorist attacks. Always research thoroughly the particular places you will visit, prior to travel.

Kashmir

This remains one of the riskiest destinations. The kidnapping in 1995 of 5 tourists by another Islamic group was followed by the beheading of one of the five, Norwegian, Hans Christian Otto. The other four, including two Britons are still in captivity. Bombs placed on trains and buses and in other public places are a common hazard. It has been reported that there are some 500 people kidnapped in Kashmir each year and many don't survive the experience.

Islamic mercenaries are penetrating Kashmir and carrying out attacks on Indian security posts. The Indian security forces estimate that 70% of the rebels operating in the Kashmir valley are from Pakistani fundamentalist groups, supported by a smaller number of local militants, some Afghans, Sudanese, Arabs and Chechens all linked to the Saudi millionaire terrorist, Osama bin Laden. Some terrorists who were killed in July 1999 were identified as belonging to the Harkat al-Mujahideen ul-Ansar, formally known as the Harkat ul-Ansar, the group responsible for killing 6 Western tourists, including 2 Britons some 4 years ago. Reports indicate some 1200-2000 guerrillas now operating in the region. Clearly the rebels operate with the blessing of Pakistan and since the military takeover in October 1999 in the country, it is unlikely that they will be made to cease their activities.

Many other parts of India have increasing problems with separatist rebels and general lawlessness. Make stringent enquiries before you embark to far flung regions, particularly in the North.

Colombia

The majority of kidnappings in Columbia go unnoticed and even when someone from the West is taken it makes only a few lines. The UK's Financial Times gave only a few lines to the kidnapping of a Mr Alistair Taylor feared kidnapped by left wing rebels in August 1999. Mr Taylor had been working for a US oil company, under contract to BP Amoco. In 1995 the reported kidnappings in Latin America were some 6,500 although the real figure will be much higher, but Colombia was at the top of the league with 1,500. It is estimated that Colombian kidnapping is a $200 million a year industry, carried out by guerrillas, ex-guerrillas, drug gangs, criminal gangs and the police.

At one time, the economy of Colombia was regarded as the most successful in Latin America, but it is now in it's worst recession for 50 years, but this hardly makes a dent on the revenues from drugs and kidnappings earned by the left wing guerrillas and paramilitary fighters. It is a country considered by some to be the most dangerous in the Western hemispher and rebels control over half of the country and are effective in the running of 60 percent of local municipalities. The murder, robberies, druggings, kidnappings and general mayhem practiced against tourists should be enough to frighten even the most foolhardy from a visit.

The Revolutionary Armed Forces of Colombia (FARC) is Latin America's oldest guerrilla group and has become, in many areas, the surrogate police force, judicial system and government, all in one. Stronger now than at any time in it's 34 year history, it's 15,000 strong army control some 60 active fronts, but a stalemate with the Colombian military has now been reached. FARC raises some 60% of it's multi-million dollar income from abduction. Neither side is capable of defeating the other and high level talks are currently taking place to reach an accord on a number of issues, mostly going in favour of the guerrillas. Their finances come from extortion, (the wealthiest families paying what is known as a 'vaccine' to stay alive), from kidnappings and increasingly from the country's multi-billion dollar a year drugs trade.

In July 1999 the biggest battle ever between the Government forces and FARC guerrillas took place following FARC's attack on 15 towns in southern Colombia as it broke out of it's de-militarised zone. Crime has reached a point where the authorities no longer exercise any control. With some 4000 or more police officers killed since 1990, they are rightly more concerned with their own survival than with the plight of Western tourists.

Expatriates working for international organisations rarely operate without a Western specialist security presence, but as with the case of

Mr Taylor, it is not possible to look after everyone all the time. A new twist in the standard FARC kidnapping routine occurred in April 1999, with it's first hijacking of a commercial flight. A 52 seat Fokker, bound for Bogota with 41 passengers and 5 crew was forced to land at a clandestine airfield some minutes after take-off.

Mexico City

There are some 6 million visitors each year to Mexico City and local tourist officials admit that some 23 tourists are attacked each day in the city - more than half are foreigners. Crime in Mexico has spiralled since the Peso crashed in 1994. Since then crime has doubled and the government has singularly failed to halt the rise. We report elsewhere about the problems of taxi's in the city and tourists are warned about flagging down cabs in the street.

It is reported that hundreds have been beaten, robbed and raped by rogue taxi drivers who are closely linked with street gangs. Package tourists to the more popular beach destinations are fairly safe, but there is an increasing level of crime in rural areas. An American woman was dragged off a beach in Oaxaca, raped and drowned. Two German tourists were robbed and shot in the middle of a busy city centre restaurant.

Mexico Police

To quote the newly appointed Chief of Police, Alejandro Gertz, *"they control the thieves who steal cars, the thieves who steal people and the thieves who steal from stores"*. He is not talking about some organised crime group, he is talking about his own police force.

The 94,000 strong city police force is riddled with corruption and successive governments have been able to do little to improve matters. In November 1998, 200 street-level policemen were arrested on charges ranging from robbery to murder. There are what is known as "brother-hoods" controlled by powerful police commanders who head up kidnapping and car theft rings. A 1995 survey revealed that 80 per cent of the capital's residents had no faith in the police.

Rogue police are widely considered to be the backbone of Mexico's billion-dollar kidnapping industry, as well as serving as strong-arm men for drug cartels. In January 1998 Armando Martinez, head of the anti-kidnapping police unit in Mexico's central Morelos state, was charged with running his own multi-million dollar abduction ring, after he was caught dumping the body of a murder victim. He is also accused of being part of the network of Mexico's recently captured 'most-wanted' kidnapper and ex-Moreles cop Daniel Arizmendi Lopez.

The problems of a violent, criminal and corrupt police force are not confined to only Mexico. In **Guatemala**, Gabriel Celada a diligent police detective reported regularly to a family about the progress in the investigation of their 19 year old daughter who had been abducted in December 1996. He comforted them and urged them to pay the $19,000 ransom demand only to be subsequently charged with the kidnap himself. He and four colleagues had kidnapped the girl and was also charged with the kidnap of two others.

In **Brazil** in January 1998, federal agents arrested Manoel Cavalcante, a military-police lieutenant, an alleged boss of a murder-for-hire mob made up of state police, called the Uniformed Gang. The group is under investigation for bank robberies and political assassinations. His underlings have revealed the gang's rates - including a $44,000 fee to kill top state politicians.

In **Rio de Janeiro** the Institute of Religious Studies, an independent think tank, says military police kill as many people each year (almost 400) in that city of 5.5 million as all U.S cops do in the line of duty in a country of 260 million.

In **Sao Paulo** cops commit an estimated 10% of all homicides - the city had 4,778 in 1997.

Officials in Argentina's **Buenos Aires** province conceded that in 1997, their 48,000 strong police force had become a major source of car theft, house burglary and murder-for-hire. In the 90's criminal cops in Latin America have become so blatant and prolific they are the prime movers in the violent-crime explosion that is the continent's reality today. Latin America suffers the worst robbery and assault rates and also tops the homicides charts, with some 30 murders per 100,000 people, some six times the global average.

Whilst the main victims of 'cop crime' in Latin America are native residents, foreign visitors are not exempt from their attentions. Close to 100 foreigners were murdered in Mexico City in 1997. The U. S. Embassy was blunt in it's warning some time back that U.S citizens who are victims of crime "report that uniformed police are the perpetrators". The rise of crime against foreigners began in 1996. The kidnap for ransom of Mamoru Konno the Japanese president of Sony in **Tijuana** was a turning point. He was released after the payment of $2 million. Officials believe the kidnappers were Baja policemen.

Precautions:

- 'Greet and Meet' at the airports.
- No Taxis.
- Restrict travel.
- Do business in your hotel.
- Dress down.
- No cameras.
- No watch (buy a cheap plastic watch, cut the straps off and carry it in a pocket).
- Take a 'Palmtop' instead of a notebook computer.

Bogota

The main airport is a hunting ground for kidnappers.

Laptops/Bags will be stolen. One scam is for someone to

sprinkle dust on your jacket, point out the mess and help you dust it off, whilst at the same time an accomplice steals your belongings.

◆ Don't let drivers write the company name on the greeting board.

◆ Don't label luggage.

Osama Bin Laden

It is probably appropriate, at this point to give some of the background of this financier and mastermind of world terrorist activity. In his early forties and with an estimated wealth of between $100-$300 million inherited from his father, who made a billion in the construction industry. He allegedly channels millions of dollars through Islamic banks and charities to terrorist groups in Egypt, Algeria, Yemen, Sudan, Philippines as well as financing Islamic movements in Bosnia, Kenya, Tajikistan, Chechnya, Somalia, Albania and Afghanistan.

The mastermind behind the U.S. Embassy bombings in Africa in 1998. In January 1999 the London Evening Standard reported U.S intelligence sources as saying that he had plans to kidnap a high-profile American. He is reported to have operations in over 50 countries and training camps in 20. His operation is called Al Qeada. Following the U.S attacks on Afghanistan, which country harbours the Saudi terrorist, and also on Sudan in an attempt to destroy his operations, incidents of terrorism around the world increased.

The Bin Laden Influence

The prime, potential areas where Bin Laden has associates operating are Pakistan, Egypt, Yemen, South Africa and Central Africa. Secondary targets include such places as Turkey, Israel, Saudi Arabia, Jordan and Lebanon. The bomb in Planet Hollywood in Cape Town and the U.S Embassy bombings in Central Africa are all part of an orchestrated campaign against the West and the U.S.A. in particular by Bin Laden and his followers.

South East Turkey

This area is on the U.K's Foreign Office list of 'no-go' areas. Westerners have been kidnapped and one Briton killed in 1994 in the resort of Marmaris. There have been kidnappings near Mount Arat in the east of Turkey and attacks against tourists in Istanbul with bombs in cafes. The capture, trial and death sentence on the Kurdish rebel leader, Abdullah Ocalan only raises the stakes and subsequently 17 people have been injured in a grenade attack on a coffee shop in Istanbul and 3 people killed in the south east town of Genc in another attack on a cafe.

Should Turkey execute the Kurdish leader the whole of Europe could go up in flames. His arrest led to violent protest in many European capitals with some demonstrators setting themselves alight. The main Kurdish separatist organisation the PKK was founded in 1978 and began the guerrilla fight against Turkey in 1984 from bases mainly in Syria and took the fight to Iraq after the Gulf war. There are some 10,000 soldiers under arms in the PKK and although outlawed in Germany and France, it is well organised in Europe as a whole. There is a strong political Kurdish base in Brussels - the National Liberation Front of Kurdistan.

Spain

Whilst the Basque separatist terror group ETA may have declared a cease-fire, political terrorism was exchanged for economic terrorism in the form of an extortionist bomber. A Spanish pensioner was killed and a civil guard injured in two separate incidents on a beach in the resort of Salou, 60 miles south of Barcelona. The local tourist office, it emerged, had received threatening letters demanding almost £500,000 in cash in return for a promise not to plant bombs on the beach.

It was common practice for ETA to target the tourist trade, setting off bombs in summer 1996 in the resort of Almunecar, beside the Alhambra in Granada, in the centre of Malaga and at Reus airport near Barcelona - 35 tourists, mostly Britons were injured. The campaign of violence by ETA has lasted some 30 years and claimed over 750 lives. The short-lived cease fire looks to be at an end, when in January 2000, 2 car bombs exploded in Madrid, the first killing a Lieut. Colonel Pedro Antonio Blanco age 47, who regularly waited for an official car to take him to work. Several people were injured in both blasts. Police are now on full alert again and just before Christmas 1999 they intercepted two vans en route to the capital packed with explosives, almost two tons and a third car bomb was discovered near Bilbao.

A new generation of fascists now plagues Spain. Believed to be responsible for 21 murders in the past 8 years, far-right gangs now recruit members on the internet as well as in the school playground and football terraces. Most attacks have been against immigrants, tramps and prostitutes. Spain's far right is a mixture of youth, skinhead gangs (some based on football clubs such as Real Madrid and Atletico Madrid), the old Falangists and the followers of the most vocal of the right wing activists, Ricardo S. de Ynestrillas, 33 and head of the Alliance for National Unity. He is the son of a former Franco army officer and is about to begin a 7 year sentence for murder. The number of youths in such xenophobic groups has grown fourfold in four years.

China

As with the Republics of the former Soviet Union, crime in China is flourishing in the vacuum left behind as the authoritarian rule of the Communist party and as the power and economic ability to continue the fight against Triad gangs and secret societies declines. In late 1998 it took the British consulate in Guangzhou to put on record what everyone already knew who travelled to the booming southern Chinese coastal provinces, that organised crime is booming and that robberies, muggings, kidnappings and murder are no longer rare events.

The consulate formally advised Britons to take care because armed gangs were targeting expatriates in parts of the city where foreigners frequented, such as cheap restaurants and late-night bars.

It is understood that following a stabbing of a member of staff of the consulate and an attack on a businessman, British diplomats took the unusual step of holding a meeting with senior officers of the city's public security bureau.

If further proof were needed, one needs to look no further than the capture by the police of South China's most notorious gangster Cheung Tze-keung, known to friend and foe as 'Big Spender'. Guilty of a host of crimes as well as the kidnapping for ransom of two of the richest men in Hong Kong. The victims were Victor I, son of Hong Kong's most famous tycoon, Li Ka-shing, and Walter Kwok, the property billionaire. Neither family reported the crimes to the Hong Kong police and vast ransoms were paid.

It was only when the business community leaders complained to Beijing that a crackdown began and Cheung was caught. Matters will not get better and once the true worth of Western business is realised by the crime groups, it is likely to become a free for all. Only restrictive Chinese reporting prevents us knowing in the West the true nature and dangers of crime in the country. What was reported in January 1999 was the murder of 23 sailors by pirates who, armed with machine pistols, boarded a China bound ship, dumped the bodies into the sea and escaped with a cargo of mineral ore. The ship, registered in Panama and bound for Guangzhou, was not the first in a long list of acts of piracy in these waters. Again, the Chinese authorities seem powerless to prevent the incidents. The attacks on the U.S Embassy in Beijing by mobs following the accidental rocketing of the Chinese Embassy in Kosovo, shows how quickly anti-Western sentiment can be whipped up.

Egypt

Nowhere has suffered more in tourist trade from terrorist activities than Egypt. When it was just recovering from the effects of 18 Greek tourists who were gunned down in Cairo in 1996, it was rocked again a year later when three men in business suits opened fire with automatic weapons and hurled gasoline filled bottles at a group of German tourists boarding their bus outside the Egyptian Museum in the city centre. The Egyptian driver and 9 Germans were killed immediately and 12 other Germans and 15 Egyptians were injured during a 10 minute gun battle between the attackers and security forces. Two assailants were captured and one escaped. One of the captured men had been responsible for a previous attack in 1993 on a Cairo hotel in which two Americans and a Frenchman were killed. The man had escaped from a mental institution.

The massacre of 58 tourists at the Temple of Queen Hatshepsut in Luxor, by Islamic extremists, became too much even for the worst elements in the country and, following a massive crackdown by Egyptian authorities, the terrorists have now declared an end to their armed struggle and attacks on tourists - it remains to be seen. Egypt's tourist trade had still not recovered in 1999. It was reported in 'Time' magazine that Egyptian Officials suspect that the attack was financed by Osama bin Laden. This was according to the head of Switzerland's Federal Police. The Swiss still have an 'open investigation' on the atrocity in which 35 Swiss lives were lost. Although supposedly financed by bin Laden, Urs Von Daeniken, the police official, said the attack had been ordered by Mustafa Hamza, a fugitive leader of al-Gamaa al-Islamiya (Islamic Group).

Argentina

In the same issue of Time magazine (May 1999), Argentine's Supreme Court blamed the radical Islamic Jihad organisation for the 1992 bombing of the Israeli Embassy in Buenos Aires in which 9 people died. The court also ordered the arrest of 6 policemen suspected of being indirectly involved in a subsequent bombing of a Jewish community centre 2 years later, which killed 86.

Jamaica

Once a place where violent crime against foreigners was a serious problem, Jamaica is now much more benign. Both regular and 'tourist police' now patrol downtown Montego Bay, but one should still be cautious and travellers should still be wary of robbery attempts, particularly after dark.

In a country with a population of only 2.6 million there were 953 murders in 1998 - most in the capital Kingston (population 707,000). There were also 145 suspected criminals shot dead by the police.

In the Caribbean, many of the island states have had their share of problems arising from small, vulnerable economies, corruption, money laundering and drug trafficking, but most have managed some progress, unlike Jamaica. It's economy is declining and the government is struggling to maintain law and order. In many parts of Kingston such as Mathews Lane and Tivoli Gardens it is the local gang leaders who keep the lid on petty crime and who kill suspected informers. They control the drugs and protection rackets. Gang disputes can flare at short notice and after a gang member's mother was punched in June 1999, nine neighbours were shot dead in three weeks.

Social discontent due to the crumbling economy and living conditions of the poor has twice in 1998 led to riots. One impact of all this has been a declining tourist trade, further affecting the economy. Since July 1999, the army has been patrolling the streets and beaches jointly with the police. Supposedly as a result, the murder rate has fallen, but tourists need to be careful as to where they visit on the island and when. The north is still considered a 'safe tourist destination'.

Israel and the Middle East

The election victory of Ehud Barak, the Israeli Labour leader, in August 1999 is likely to further de-stabilise the region. Not that as Prime Minister he holds any extreme right wing policies, just the opposite, but his desire for peace with both the Palestinians and Syria, has posed a new threat to Iran. Tehran's total opposition to any Arab peace agreement with Israel has caused it to give an estimated £3,000,000 to the militant Palestinian group Hamas, to fund terrorist attacks on Israel.

It is believed Palestinian terrorists have already drawn up a list of targets. Previous attempts by the Israelis and Palestinians to reach agreement and understanding over issues was undermined by a series of devastating suicide attacks by Hamas activists against Israeli targets in Tel Aviv and Jerusalem.

Tehran is anxious to forge strong links with what are known as the 'external' Hamas groups in Lebanon and Syria. A meeting between all parties held in Khartoum, the Sudanese capital, agreed that any attempt at a treaty between Israel and the Arabs was "contrary to the laws of humanity". They planned a series of terrorist attacks which will have a 'spin off' effect of diverting attention from Israeli's domestic troubles - student riots and a crumbling economy. In late 1999 a new twist to the normal tale occurred when a series of bombings turned out to have been perpetrated by Arabs domiciled inside Israel.

This is unprecedented and has caused major concern as it is the first occasion that Israeli's have felt the enemy is actually in their midst. Israeli's now believe that the country's 1 million Arabs may be harbouring a fifth column of potential terrorists who are tied to Hamas. Israeli Arabs make up 20 % of the population and are a natural target for a group such as Hamas, although they have lived peacefully for the most part with their Jewish neighbours. Whilst Palestinians from the West Bank and Gaza must pass through army checkpoints to enter Israel, Israeli Arabs have always been able to travel freely in and out of the country. There will be little chance of peace if there is a backlash by Israeli authorities and hard liners against these atrocities. Tourists may find themselves once more in the thick of things. Just prior to my completion of this book, Israeli police were fighting violent demonstrations by stone-throwing youth in the West Bank, which Palestinian police seemed unable to control.

Somalia

The descent into anarchy is probably now complete in what could now hardly even be described as a country. There is no infrastructure and the control of the Warlords and their murderers is absolute, despite the growing influence of Islamic courts. There is anarchy, murder and chaos.

International Security

As early as 1980 the World Tourism Organisation (WTO) in a conference proclaimed that "tourists have the right to travel in safety". Following numerous requests by governments and the tourist industry (usually voiced at times of crisis) the current WTO programme provides for the establishment of an International Facility on Tourist Safety and Security. It has been conceived as a comprehensive service, based on a network of focal points representing governments, other international bodies, tourism industry organisations, experts in the field and the media. Accordingly, partners to the project will be surveyed as to their needs and co-operation requirements, so as to benefit the public and to establish a comprehensive facility to cover:

- tourist safety and security information
- expert advice
- safe destination criteria and clearance
- early warnings (crime, health, natural disasters)
- research

A very praiseworthy and hopefully achievable list of aims. We will watch that space with interest.

CHAPTER 2

Preparing To Go

I want to approach this chapter from the perspective of addressing the novice business and tourist traveller. This way I can dot the I's, so to speak, and the seasoned, street smart, 'seen it all', professional traveller can tell everyone that he knows all this and always prepares according to the book. The point should be made though that, strangely, as many seasoned and supposedly experienced travellers are attacked, mugged, kidnapped and fall seriously ill as do the novices. With experience comes complacency and denial.

In business we are only ever as good as our preparation and nowhere is this more apt than when preparing to travel. In my profession I can be called abroad at the literal drop of a hat and it may be to somewhere which is -20 degrees or somewhere where even thinking in the heat of the country is an exhausting, physical activity. I stepped off a plane onto the airport tarmac at a place called Hassi Massoud in the Algerian interior with a wind blowing across the airfield and it felt as if I'd put my face into a fan assisted oven on it's highest setting.

Clothing

As a consequence, over the years, I've equipped myself with clothing suitable for most environments and most situations within those environments. In Russia for example even when it gets to one hundred in the shade, a very rare occasion I might add, businessmen will still be wearing a suit and tie. This is with the exception of the more obvious mafia types who still insist on wearing the ubiquitous, black roll neck sweater with a suit and leather overcoat. There is still a formality about doing business in the former Soviet Union and you need to conform. By contrast, in Central Africa, the climatic conditions have created a more relaxed approach to the attire of business. Dress conservatively, suitably and in keeping with the country you are in. Avoid garish clothing which may be designer wear and attracts attention to you.

The Statistical Crutch

There is a certain nonchalance about the seasoned traveller, but often this is simply the result of that individual's 'statistical crutch', as I call it. This is, that so far it has simply not been their turn for something very horrible to happen to them. The longer this happy state of affairs continues the more that person believes either, that the environment is benign, or they are so adept at managing the situation and have become so 'street smart' that they are actually in control of their own destiny. Whilst many people travel on a wing and a prayer and live to tell the tale, some do not. We are not simply talking about personal security, but health risks and also avoiding the often very high risk of accidents.

Preparation is not simply limited to suitable and appropriate clothing, but it is a comprehensive checklist of actions, education, training and procedures and suitable kit. What we will look at first are the final checks we all should make if we are to ensure a safe and smooth trip.

We are talking about mental preparation. If your destination is the Third World then you will need a good dose of'frustration adjustment'. You will only increase, to a very high level, your travel stress if you do not spend some time in adjusting your expectations to the reality of how it will actually be on the ground.

Some tourists should get the praying done before they leave home - Machu Pichu - Peru.

You will not out-argue authorities abroad, you will not be able to bring your own, home-grown self-importance to bear on people and you will not beat a country's ingrained bureaucracy, inefficiency and laissez faire attitudes. You are also puny in the face of third world corruption and, sadly, institutionalised dishonesty. You are seen as fair game and the moral codes which they may apply to their dealings with one another, often does not extend to overbearing and over-wealthy foreigners.

Prepare mentally and learn as many useful phrases as you can. There will be delays, frustrations, inefficiency, prejudice and sometimes active efforts made to defeat your best endeavours. Equally though, you will meet people who cannot do enough for you and who genuinely want to help, you just won't be able to identify them from the others. Therefore treat everyone with respect and be friendly, courteous and, above all else, keep a smile on your face. Do not expect to learn cultural differences overnight, but make a start. Be someone who says very little when first abroad, rather listen, observe and 'see' what is going on around you, don't simply look.

The House You Leave Behind

◆ Make sure your property and contents insurance is up to date and will cover you for the time you expect to be away.

◆ Consider putting all valuables in a safe deposit box.

◆ You should have good locks on all doors and windows.

◆ If you have a trusted neighbour leave a key with them as well as a contact number abroad.

◆ Never leave a key hidden anywhere.

◆ Don't change the message on your answering machine to say you are away and for how long.

◆ Turn down the ringing volume on your phone. If there is a burglar near your house he won't hear the phone keep ringing.

◆ Leave your curtains in the normal position.

◆ Cancel newspaper and milk deliveries and arrange for post to be held or redirected.

◆ Leave a car in the drive. If you would normally have two cars in the drive then leave them both as normal. If you have a trusted neighbour he can move them around.

◆ Also have a neighbour put out your garbage can and also put some rubbish in it.

◆ Arrange a system of timer switches to turn lights on and off. A timer can also turn the television and radio on and off.

◆ Ensure you arrange regular gardening or snow removal.

Important Papers

If you travel regularly or even infrequently, it still behoves on you to leave at home a well ordered system of personal documentation:

- Will.
- Birth and Marriage certificates.
- Power of attorney for spouse or relative.
- Any deeds, stocks and shares, investments.
- Insurance policies both personal and property.
- Tax and accounting papers.
- Deeds, mortgages, stocks , shares etc.

Information List

You might also want to make a detailed information list. This would be particularly important if you are planning to be abroad for some time.

- Bank account numbers and addresses.
- Passport number.
- Driving license numbers, both home and abroad.
- Social Security number.
- Credit card numbers.
- Travellers cheques numbers and issuing bank.
- Medical and dental information and any distinguishing marks.
- Medical and spectacle prescriptions.
- Assets and debts listed.
- Names and addresses of important business and professional contacts.

◆ Also, depending on where you plan to travel to - fingerprints, current photo/video and handwriting samples of you and your family.

Leave behind a comprehensive telephone list for emergency contacts by your family. This may be the local embassy/consulate, local company office, insurance broker, or emergency evacuation company.

To Travel Light Or Not? - This Is The Question

As a professional observer of my fellow man, I am for ever appraising the amount of luggage people travel with, never ceasing to be amazed at how some people are able to circumvent the world with nothing more than one 'carry on' bag. Minimalist, doesn't do justice to how some travellers are able to equip themselves for a journey abroad. Often though, I am not party to knowing the length of their stay, which is probably to the good as I would be a broken man if I was to discover that the man with only the suit carrier, taken on board the flight, was going away for a fortnight.

My standard fayre is a medium sized suitcase, suit carrier and a soft, computer style briefcase. Both the case and suit carrier go in the hold as a consequence of not wanting to get to the departure gate and then find that the carrier is 'bounced' into the hold.

Recently whilst travelling to Uganda on Alliance Air, part of South African Airways many passengers fell foul to a particularly pedantic and somewhat unpleasant ground hostess at the departure gate who weighed everyone's hand baggage. It was a strict rule of one item and only a certain weight. There was some leeway for business class ticket holders, but she was even making people with camera equipment consign it to the hold. This, when you're travelling to a country promoting the photographic qualities of it's wildlife seemed a bit O.T.T. In practise there never seems to be any hard and fast rules about the amount of carry on luggage, although there has always been some broad guidelines which we will look at later.

Luggage

◆ It is a personal choice, but I would recommend older model luggage and buy cheap, but sturdy. The hard shell variety are the best, but massively increase the weight.

◆ Don't buy expensive, designer labelled luggage - it looks as if there will be expensive items inside.

◆ Also avoid any stickers which proclaim nationality.

◆ No home telephone numbers on your ID stickers and use a business address. Keep safe your baggage claim stubs, if it's lost you will have problems without them.

◆ Do not try and conceal weapons, particularly firearms. Stowed luggage is X-rayed so don't put electrical goods such as tape recorders in stowed luggage

◆ Put nothing of value in your checked baggage. No money, cameras, computers, business documents. Obviously you won't put your travel documents in your checked luggage, but I have known people split their tickets if they have multiple destinations and put the other tickets in the stowed luggage. If the luggage is lost so are your return tickets.

◆ Additional safety straps are a good idea and make the prospect of someone breaking into it whilst being handled more unlikely, but by no means impossible.

◆ Fix a name tag on the outside of the case which is difficult to remove, but use your initials not your full name. On the inside lid glue another name and address tag.

◆ Use a colourful strap to help identify your luggage.

◆ If you are in a malaria area, then keep your repellent in your hand luggage for when you are at the airport, particularly if you are arriving or departing at dawn or dusk.

Luggage Security Equipment

There are a number of products on the market which can help both deter and prevent theft of or from your luggage. Broadly, they divide themselves into three types - **straps, locks** and **alarms**. Some are combinations of all three.

An example of the alarm comes from **ASF International** who produce the ***'Bodyguard Personal Security Alarm'.*** At only £9.99 and weighing 96g, this battery operated alarm has a 130 dbs siren, audible up to half a mile. It is compact and lightweight and has a belt clip/wrist cord for attaching it to the person, or luggage and comes with a mounting bracket for a room. (Tel: 0116 2490434). There are also alarms which work on motion detection and not just the 'pull type'. One such device comes from **Catch 22** (01257 473118) and is the ***'Micro Alert Multipurpose Alarm'.*** It operates with different sounds depending on either motion or mechanical detection. It is designed for door entry as well as luggage and is operated by entering a code, with the sensitivity to movement being adjustable. It has a 130 dbs alarm weighs 150g and costs £19.99. On a more basic front the ***'Lock A Way',*** from **BCB** (01222 464463), has a 1.5m wire cable emerging from a 3 digit combination lock and can be used for attaching luggage to any fixed item like a table leg. It weighs only 70g and costs £9.99.

Always remember that however good the lock you may use to secure straps around your suitcase, the strap can always be cut if it is of canvas material. The answer to this is steel cable and the **Eagle Creek**, ***'Super lock and Cable'*** has a 2-in-1 padlock and cable set and comprises a very sturdy 3-dial combination padlock and an optional 1.20m steel cable, with PVC covering, at £10 or less without the cable. Another **Eagle Creek** product is the ***'Alarm Lock'***, weighing in at 183g and is a motion-activated device with a retractable 1.07m steel cable, housed in a black plastic casing, with a 3-in- lock. The cable will go around luggage, or a doorknob and the battery cover even locks automatically when the alarm sounds so as to prevent its removal. Not the cheapest device at £35, but it is also weather resistant.

If you have any doubts about the efficacy of the baggage handling of the airport you are transiting through, then only have your luggage checked through to that airport, then collect it and recheck it into the system. This is my standard operating procedure at Heathrow, after two losses. They seem unable to handle the volume of traffic.

Carry-on Luggage

To avoid both delays and the potential for lost luggage we are increasingly pressured, particularly on a short trip, to take all our luggage as a 'carry-on'. Over the years luggage manufacturers have responded to this need with the manufacture of the **MLC** or 'maximum legal carry-on'.

Whilst this type of bag conforms to the airline size and weight restrictions, it can be big enough for some spare clothes a notebook computer and papers. The most popular are the wheeled variety with the pull-out handle, but on numerous occasions I've seen such bags refused entry to the cabin, only to be consigned to the hold. It may have passed muster at the check-in desk only to come up against the cabin staff at the flight departure gate.

There are many variables as to why your carry-on luggage will meet with a positive nod through or a flat refusal and aircraft type have a lot to do with it, as the overhead bin size varies considerably. How full the flight is and the class of seat you have booked are all factors and most long-haul operators allow club and first class passengers more generous carry-on allowance, usually a bag (MLC), suit carrier or second bag and a briefcase.

The other factors are weight and dimensions. KLM, for example, allow a single 50cm by 40cm by 24cm bag, but with a measly weight limit of 5kg. The bag itself is likely to weigh close to 4kg before you put anything in it. IATA, recommends a total size of 115cm, but no airline conforms to this. Sometimes you will see a tubular metal frame in use at gates, through which your MLC must pass, although this is usually restricted to economy passengers. I can only recommend being sensible, because trying to take advantage of the system may backfire and you can find valuable papers and equipment confined to the hold and the attentions of baggage handlers.

From the point of view of personal security, it is far preferable, as a businessman, to travel light. If you can manage with one suit, a jacket one pair of extra shoes and work on the basis that you can keep your shirts and the rest of your laundry circulating through the Hotel's laundry system, then go ahead and keep things to a minimum. The least you have to worry about the better and if you can get the suit carrier on board all to the good. If you are being met at the airport it becomes problematic if you don't emerge for over an hour due to you having had to report the loss of your luggage.

Resource Data

If you are travelling to anywhere outside western countries you need information about the places you are planning to visit. This is, in broad terms, the socio-political background of the country. This is the starting point to assess the factors which will specifically impact on the conditions that you will experience on the ground. Chapter 3 will deal with the mechanics of this, but at the moment I want to deal with who is responsible for it's production and dissemination.

For me, if we are talking about the business traveller, there is no argument as to who is responsible for ensuring that a person is correctly briefed as to the potential dangers of geographies employees will visit and that is the corporate employer. Companies owe a duty of care to their employees to ensure that all reasonable steps have been taken to provide a 'safe working environment'. This extends to wherever an employee works, not restricted to the corporate HQ in the rolling hills of upstate New York or Oxfordshire, but also if that person has occasion to be wandering in the outback of Indonesia or the back streets of Manila.

It is not possible for the company to alter the conditions of those environments, but it is possible and also the company's responsibility to prepare that person, in advance, through the provision of knowledge and training, as to how to conduct him or herself both proactively and reactively to possibly dangerous environments. If this is not being done then scream. There is a dereliction of the duty of care if people are sent abroad unbriefed and unprepared.

If, as an individual, you feel powerless to say anything, then the ultimate responsibility is your own and you must put together your 'Regional Threat Assessment' and 'resource pack' yourself, but keep the pressure on. For the tourist and the self employed then it is down to you and, hopefully, Chapter 3 will help.

Preparation

◆ As a general rule safety begins when you pack. Aim to travel light and dress conservatively. Avoid the look of affluence and looking flashy. If you travel light you can move fast, not become tired and not have to stop to put bags down and may be able to keep a hand free.

Cash, valuables and paperwork need consideration as to storage whilst with you and when you are separated, i.e. in the hotel. As a general rule avoid 'bum bags' ('fanny bags' if you are American), back pockets, hand bags. A sturdy shoulder bag worn across the chest with concealed money pouches is the transport of choice. If you wear glasses, bring an extra pair.

◆ Prior to any trip, I prepare a 'packing list'. By this I mean everything from the colour of the ties to the type of film. I break the list into clothing, documentation, kit and financial. Under documentation I will have my resource sheet and shortened threat Assessment.

Packing List

I pack in accordance with the list and tick off as things go into the case or bags. My own way of doing this is to lay everything out prior to packing. This means everything, cash, cards, visas, vaccination certs, clothing, kit, etc etc etc etc etc and check them off. My rule is "take nothing with you you cannot afford to lose". e.g.

- Valuable or expensive looking jewellery.
- Irreplaceable family items.
- All unnecessary credit cards.

◆ Leave a copy of passport, visas, traveller cheque numbers, Itinerary, drivers license, birth certificate at home. Take the other copy with you.

◆ Obtain an international driving license.

◆ If you are travelling to a particularly difficult region you may want to consider leaving another set of copies with your local embassy or consulate.

◆ Try to memorise you passport number and date and city of issue.

◆ For extended trips you should register with your embassy or consulate.

◆ On the travellers cheque numbers cross them off as you use them.

◆ If you are on business ensure you have the address and a map of your local office or offices you intend to visit together with the phone numbers.

◆ Plan also for emergency notification to you. Your family should have all necessary phone numbers - the embassy or consulate, local company office, hotel, etc. They should have a detailed itinerary of your visit.

◆ Your home office should have a complete itinerary as well as the local office manager.

◆ Prepare a card giving details of your blood type, health problems and known allergies, required medications, travel insurance company details and emergency person contact number - give more than one.

You may wish to take the gold Rolex so as to impress the people you are meeting, but if you value anything over and above it's replaceable insurance value then leave it at home. Remember it is not simply the value of the item stolen it is the significance of the long term damage. Computer notebooks are a good example of this. The physical loss can be insured, but not the loss of vital information, nor the loss of that information to others who will profit from it's acquisition. If you have a back-up disc then don't carry it in the convenient floppy holder in your notebook case. Keep it elsewhere.

Preparedness also means mental readiness.

Insurance

If you wouldn't dream of sky diving without a parachute, then you shouldn't think of travelling internationally without insurance as the consequences could be equally disastrous. The corporate traveller often makes the assumption that he travels with adequate cover, but I would suggest that nothing be taken at face value. Check as to whether the sums insured are adequate. A travel policy acquired when journeys were limited to European destinations will be inadequate for the array of potential problems in a Third World environment.

I started my working career in the insurance industry and spent some time in the Personal Accident section, which at that time issued travel insurance policies, both the 'packaged' holiday ones and the more flexible, group travel policies. Over the intervening years, the holiday packages have become more flexible, comprehensive and moved away from the restrictive levels of sums insured they used to contain. Broadly, though, they still contain all the elements the typical tourist should require - cancellation and curtailment, medical expenses, personal accident, personal effects and money.

Interestingly, claims against such policies are usually in the following ratios: 40% are concerned with medical expenses, 30% relate to loss of luggage and 20%-25% are for cancellation.

So what about sums to be insured. Don't be conditioned if you come from the U.K, as we have been accustomed to paying little for our medical treatment. In the Third World or even in the States as a visitor, emergency treatment and the cost of repatriation could be staggering. If you have to be repatriated by air-ambulance from a remote location, together with an emergency medical team, the cost can run into hundreds of thousands of pounds.

Over the years, the variety of sources where one can buy travel insurance in the U.K has widened immensely such as the Post Office, chemists, banks, travel agents and a host of others. Bear in mind, however, that on a pure cost basis, you should look to buy from an accredited 'broker' as the insurance premium tax is only 4% as distinct from 17% that has to be charged by a travel agent. In most 'secondary' outlets you will get little professional advice and you should be guided to an insurance broker. Most other outlets have brochures, which are comprehensive and self-explanatory.

In the UK, Boots the Chemist have a very comprehensive 'single trip' package underwritten by the insurers Royal Sun Alliance. With medical expenses at £10 million and the same amount for emergency repatriation (by air ambulance and with a doctor if necessary) you have the basis of a very effective package. It also covers on the medical side, hospital stay benefit, fly a relative out, emergency despatch of prescription glasses, cosmetic surgery (following an accident overseas), emergency dental treatment, hospital stay benefit and more, all with appropriate sums assured. On the 'Personal' side there is cover for holiday cancellation, loss of baggage, loss of money/travellers cheques, missed departure, travel delay, baggage delay, travel abandonment, passport replacement, personal liability, legal protection, personal accident and more.

There is another section to the policy i.e 'Assistance Benefits' which provide an advice section, emergency home return if the police require you to return in the event of a burglary, flood or fire, other ancillary benefits together with a 'Helpline' card giving a 24 hour emergency number. The premiums are reasonable and this package represents how comprehensive cover has become. Seldom though will the policy cover on the personal side 'high value' items such as the gold watch or video equipment.

The policy above, whilst it provides £1,500 for loss of personal effects the single article limit is only £250. If you are taking items of value these are no doubt specified on your Household policy and you may need to widen the geographic limit as an extension of this policy. You will need up to date valuations, but once in place it will be a more permanent solution, particularly if you make several trips a year.

Check your policy with regard to your notebook computer. Ensure that the cover provided is worldwide, not just U.K or Europe, or worse only covered if stolen from your office. There will also be 'restrictive' clauses in your travel policy as to how high value personal effects and cash must be secured whilst abroad, e.g. locked and occupied bedroom, hotel safe or safe deposit or on your person. They won't be covered if you simply leave the items in your room when you are out.

Reciprocal Arrangements

If you are travelling from the U.K you are fortunate to benefit from a host of reciprocal arrangements with other countries over medical treatment and the attendant expense. These are technically referred to as Reciprocal Health Care Arrangements.

This is for urgent treatment only and the agreement provides for substantially reduced and in some cases free treatment. Get the booklet **Health Advice for Travellers** available from the **Post Office** or **Department of Health, P.O. Box 410, Wetherby, LS23 7LN.**

This very useful booklet not only concerns itself with the inter-country arrangements, but is an invaluable source of advice on health for travellers. It also contains **form E111**. This is for travellers to countries within the European Economic Area i.e. 15 member states plus Iceland, Norway and Liechtenstein and it's production, at the time you may require urgent medical treatment, will ensure free or reduced cost treatment. There is no time limit on the form

This does not let you off the hook, however, from ensuring you have adequate private cover. Not all countries provide free cover and in some you will have to pay the full cost of the treatment and reclaim it at a later date, this from the DSS Benefits Agency. The booklet gives you a run down on each country and what you can expect. It guides you through the process of dealing with Doctors and hospital services, obtaining receipts, contacting local sickness funds and what amount you will be expected to pay at the time.

The E111 must be completed and taken to a Post Office to be accepted and stamped. It is free and should be kept with your passport - staple it to one of the pages. The E111 will only cover you for temporary stays and will not cover you for long periods of working abroad. It will apply for temporary work postings abroad, but not if you work for a foreign employer. Broadly, it covers for stays of less than one year, during which you must have maintained your U.K National Insurance contributions. Apply for your form up to 2 months prior to departure.

We have not dealt with the subject of insurance cover for participating in hazardous pursuits whilst abroad. If you are going mountain climbing, white water rafting, or the like you need to speak to people like **Club Direct on 0500 787838.**

If you are planning to be away for some time, or you are a frequent business traveller, then the simple 'over the counter' package insurance is not going to be for you. Seek advice from a Broker.

Documentation

Passport

We speak the blindingly obvious, but well before you travel ensure your passport is 'in date' and has a good 6 months unexpired. Many countries won't let you in with a short time of unexpired portion left. Also remember to take it with you (use the 'checklist'). You may believe it's in the same place it always is, but if it has been away for a visa it may still be on your desk or in a file somewhere.

Under the section to do with visas, I have mentioned the benefits of a second passport, a matter for consideration, if in the old days you travelled to the former South Africa or Israel. Now South Africa is no longer the pariah state it was, this only leaves, unfortunately, Israel, where having an entry stamp in your passport will prevent you from entering most Middle Eastern countries.

When you travel to Israel you will fill out the obligatory immigration form on the plane before landing and on arrival ask Immigration to stamp this form not your passport. They are used to this and do not take offence. However, all those who have travelled to Israel know how 'interrogative' the procedure is on leaving and the stamp on the form will be one of the questions. Simply say that you did not ask, but it was offered.

They give the impression they have taken offence, but it is all part of the process. If you are with a business colleague make sure you tell the same story about your purpose there. They will cross examine both stories to ensure they are correct in detail.

Tickets

Remember it is problematic these days to travel without a return ticket. In many parts of the world you could be refused entry despite being able to demonstrate that you have the financial wherewithal to be able to leave the country. Even a gap in a journey can cause problems. My partner was on a trip to Australia and the South Pacific to meet a client and had tickets for every aspect of the journey with the exception of Australia to Tahiti. The reason for this was that she would be flying on that leg in the client's private jet, but the lack of a ticket for this leg caused major problems when she was trying to leave Heathrow and only sheer force of will won the day.

Visas

If you are travelling on business, we assume your company will have an established system of obtaining visas. For the European holiday traveller no visa is required and for many parts of the Middle East, including Lebanon, you obtain your visa on arrival for a nominal fee. Very broadly, visas divide themselves into four types - tourist, business and then single entry or multi-entry. Be prepared for business visas to cost more and take longer. If you plan on travelling to a country often, say for example Russia, then weigh the cost/convenience benefits of a multi-entry visa. These usually run for twelve months and allow unlimited entries. The advantage is that you can go at very short notice and your passport is only away the once.

Don't take people's 'advice' as to the visas required for certain countries. Because someone has heard that you can 'buy it at the border', doesn't mean the border guards have heard the same story. If you simply had no time before you left then you may throw yourself on the mercy of the court, so to speak, but if in any real doubt check with the Embassy or Consular office of the country to be visited. Even in parts of the Soviet Union you may be able to buy a visa at the border or once in country, but these concessions are fluid and not guaranteed. I've arrived in Ukraine from Russia by train and been allowed in without a visa, on the understanding one will be bought when there, otherwise one won't get out. I've turned up at the frontier of Kazakhstan without a visa, but been allowed entry on the basis I had a Russian multi-entry visa. Again the directive was that I was to have purchased one within the first few days. This wasn't clearly outlined to me and after three days of non-compliance due to pressure of work they charged me $100 when I finally got around to it.

Visa Agents

The majority of the countries you intend to visit will have an Embassy or Consulate in London and you have the choice to turn up with your passport, photos and the fee and queue, which process may take an hour or so, or post it and possibly wait weeks. The third choice is to use a visa agent. For many years I and colleagues of mine have utilised the services of **Portman Travel** in London. Run by a friend of mine **George Coombes**, they have on many occasions pulled the proverbial chestnut out of the fire. They are specialists in visa acquisition for the former Soviet Bloc, (they can obtain the necessary invitation letter from former communist countries), but are very effective across the board. They are by the way one of the most helpful and effective travel agents I have dealt with. **Telephone: (44) 0207 2556555.** They are also great for travel, hotel and transportation bookings.

Having applied and received the visa as a stamp or separate document - check it! Check the date, type of visa e.g. business, tourist, single entry or multi-entry. Impossible, by the way, in the case of the Australian visa as it is invisible to the naked eye. If your trip involves leaving a country, even if only for a few hours, a single entry visa may not allow you back in. You will need a multi-entry if they are issued or ensure it mentions the two visits. On occasions you may be better served by applying for a 'tourist' visa, particularly in respect of speed of issue and simplicity. But, keep to the story line when you get to passport control. Sometimes I will travel on a tourist visa, if it has been the convenient course of action.

Be aware that in some countries your visa will not allow you total access to all it's regions. There may be a requirement for additional 'special passes' and the more remote you get the more you will be at the whim and mercy of local government officials. Be prepared to pay! Also be prepared not to hand over original visas or special passes. Arm yourself with a number of photocopies. Have 2 copies of your passport and the visas and plenty of passport size photos.

The visa itself may be a stamp in your passport or a separate document. If your visa is a loose, separate document, then use a paper clip or staple to secure it to a page of your passport. It's no good getting to the airport with your passport and no visa. For some countries the 'check-in' staff will ask to see your visa, but even if you discover the omission here it may still be too late to go back for it - you only get one chance to get out of your own country and into another!.

One problem you may face as a frequent traveller is the problem of having to travel abroad whilst your passport is away for a visa for another upcoming trip. The answer is to obtain a second passport and it is quite legitimate for this purpose.

Cash/Cards/Travellers Cheques

If this book was 500 pages long we could still not exhaust the arguments about what 'fiscal' support to take with us abroad and how we carry it and safeguard it. There is no right or wrong answer, but there are certain guidelines which should be borne in mind.

If you carry a credit card or travellers cheques, be sure to check you are still in possession of them every day. In the case of travellers cheques, thieves have been known to rip out the bills from the back of the book so you won't notice the loss immediately. This could have happened in your hotel room. Keep any unused cheques on you or in a hotel safe deposit box.

Cash

It is possible to travel with no or very little cash, particularly in the West. The further afield one goes the cash required rises in direct proportion to the distance travelled, particularly if the destination is a Third World environment. That having been said I will travel with a minimum of £500 in cash approx $750 even in Europe and if only for a few days. Cash is still the 'emergency' fuel. The most careful plans which may depend on the use of credit or charge cards can often go awry.

The taxi you have booked which takes credit cards fails to turn up and you are forced to flag one down which doesn't. I can think of numerous occasions where a gratuity has worked wonders and one still needs cash for this. As an Englishman I hate to have to admit it, but the 'lingua Franca' of the cash world is the U.S Dollar. Wherever I travel I will have dollars and local currency. The situation was exemplified some years ago in Russia, when after the fall of the old regime prices in shops were in U.S Dollars. Initially one could pay in dollars, but over the past few years this changed to goods being priced in dollars, but paid for in Roubles.

Change your hard currency into local currency in small amounts. Don't carry large amounts of local as you will inevitably find yourself with buckets of it left over at the end of the trip and problems converting it back. Remember in many countries it is illegal to take local currency out of the country - god alone knows why. If you are away for anywhere between 5-7 days in a third world geography then I would submit a minimum of $1,000 be the amount you should take with you. It is both a working fund, but more importantly an 'emergency' fund.

This amount will not be sufficient to meet hotel bills. Even in the most underdeveloped countries the hotels in major cities will take credit or charge cards. The biggest are usually operated if not owned by the international groups. Travel only 50 kilometres, however and the picture changes and your cards are next to worthless. Your pre-trip planning and enquiries should have warned you about the situation, so your cash fund should be capable of meeting these demands. Local, rural hotels are usually very cheap and are seldom a drain on the cash resources.

Travellers Cheques

Travellers Cheques (TC's) are useful in the case of theft, but still do not have universal acceptance. You should not rely exclusively on TC's when you are likely to be in a remote or Third World environment. As we have reported elsewhere American Express, Thomas Cook and Visa are going to be the most widely accepted and if you are in any doubt, make enquiries prior to leaving. Have some of the cheques in small denominations.

I seldom travel with travellers cheques. Don't ask me why? I know the benefits over carrying cash, but it is another piece of documentation which requires safe keeping and I know from experience that seldom have I got time to queue to affect an exchange. Every time you change money someone is likely to be watching you.

The benefit though is that if lost or stolen they can be replaced. However, if you also lose the issuing receipt you lose everything. Travellers Cheques are expensive and depending on where you are going, you should probably go for $ denominated ones.

After you have signed each cheque on receipt then DO NOT countersign until you come to cash the individual cheques. Keep your passport, TC's and the issuing receipt all separate. Put the issuing receipts into the bottom of your suitcase and don't take them out.

Personally I would go for Amex cheques as they usually have the best all round fees/commission and having their cheques often entitles you to have mail held in their Poste Restante facility for up to 30 days. Employees, however are encouraged travel with travellers Cheques.

Money & Carriage

◆ Leave all unnecessary valuables at home.

On occasions it may not be possible to land in a country with local currency in your possession and I have learned to my cost that it is not always possible nor practical to get it at the airport when you land. Often you need to exit the airport as swiftly as possible. In Russia and some countries you cannot declare that you are taking local currency into the country, primarily because you should not have taken any out, so one is constrained to carrying small denomination dollars. Even US$1 bills are good for tipping.

You have a number of options as to how to carry cash and cards. There are the waist money belts, leg belts or you could have sewn into a jacket a zip-top money pocket.

◆ The rule is keep your money next to your skin.

◆ Do not carry cash, cards and cheques in the same place and remember to keep handy small 'giveaway' amounts.

◆ Never change money on the street or black market. The risk of getting a bad rate, receiving counterfeit money, robbed, or arrested is very high.

◆ Carry a small calculator for quick conversion of your money into local currency.

◆ Always know the exchange rate you should expect, although you will seldom get it.

◆ Carry cash in small denominations.

◆ In most parts of the world U S dollars are best.

If you are concerned about the cash you have being required for emergencies, then you need to have two separate amounts. We will look at how best to travel with cash later, but for the moment don't let the security aspect hinder or restrict you taking the amount you may need. If you are going to have a financial emergency abroad it certainly pays to be a U.S citizen. Their Department Of State, in particular the Overseas Citizens Services can come to their aid. The State Department for a small charge approx $20 will open a trust account to facilitate the transfer of money abroad which can be done in conjunction with Western Union and the use of a credit card or money order. The alternative is Bankwire or to post money order or cashiers cheque to Washington. The service is efficient and as speedy as any system in getting money into the hands of those who need it abroad.

Credit & Charge Cards.

◆ Don't take every card you possess. One charge card and one major credit card should be sufficient. I go everywhere with an Amex and have few, if any, problems.

Hotels, taxis, restaurants, car hire, train services, internal flights all work.

◆ Limit the use of your cards as fraud is common, particularly in such places as Hong Kong.

◆ Because of fraud only use your card in what appear reputable outlets.

◆ Always ensure you have a 'card protection plan'. For a few pounds a year it is stupidity not to have the cover provided.

◆ Never throw away sales vouchers. An innocuous purchase of a few Rupees can end up on your statement with a few noughts on the end.

◆ Don't write your PIN number down - memorise it.

Credit card security whilst abroad is essential. It's too late when you get back to find additional items on your bill that you never spent.

◆ It is easier said than done, but in regions with high incidence of kidnapping and extortion, travellers should avoid the use of 'corporate' credit cards.

◆ Prior to leaving ensure your limits will be sufficient.

◆ Be aware that if your average purchase is small, your card company may react to a very large foreign hotel account being requested. They may ask you, whilst at the hotel to supply further ID such as your code word, usually your mothers Christian name - don't forget it.

◆ Write the number of your credit cards, licenses etc on a piece of paper and keep it in a separate location such as a piece of luggage.

◆ Get all copies and the carbon back after a purchase.

◆ In many countries 'tax' is added to the bill. Ensure that if tax is applicable that it is added at the time you settle your account and cross out all the empty boxes, otherwise you may find it has been added later plus some other spurious charges. Insist if anyone tells you crossing out the boxes is not permitted.

◆ Make a note of your credit limit on each credit card you take. Make certain not to charge over that amount on your trip. In some countries Americans have been arrested for innocently exceeding their credit limit.

◆ Find out from your credit card company how to report the loss of a card from where you are going.

Purchase Tips

You always stand the chance of being 'ripped off' when making foreign purchases, for example when the gold chain and diamond ring is anything but. Apart from the most obvious fraud, you should be aware of the following:-

◆ Your change - always count it and know how much change you should expect. Always ensure you ascertain the price of an item before you buy itand not after, otherwise it could be astronomic.

◆ If a purchase is wrapped up make sure you see it happen. If someone's back is turned or it happens out of sight you may not get what you bought when it comes to unwrap it.

◆ When you change money, even at a bank, do not move away from the counter until you have counted the notes. Know how much local money you should receive, both before you make the purchase and after you receive it. Don't do it away from the counter as it will be too late.

◆ Take all the money and any documents and put them away in your safe places before you leave the bank. Ensure that you are not being watched.

◆ Be extremely vigilant when you leave the bank. Any foreigner leaving a bank must be assured to have received cash and not made a deposit. You are a target.

◆ Purchasing antiques in some foreign countries like Turkey, Egypt and Mexico, could lead to arrest. If genuine, you may need an export permit. If the item is 'reproduction' get documents to state this is the case. Westerners have been arrested for trying to take out reproductions which were be believed to be national treasures.

Kit

The travel kit should include a detailed folder of your important information, together with some useful kit - door wedge, torch, electrical plugs, smoke mask and possibly a utility tool such as a Leatherman or multi-purpose penknife. If security is an issue take a door alarm and portable smoke alarm. Your torch should be a Mag-Lite or similar. At night keep it on the nightstand together with the room key and smoke mask.

Technical Equipment

Notebook computers, cellular phones, satellite phones and Global Positioning Systems can all be problematic depending on where in the world you plan to take them. In many totalitarian regimes, such equipment is seriously frowned upon and may be banned from entry.

Such restrictions are a fast moving target and change from one year to the next. If you plan on taking any equipment which is of a radio communication service or similar, then contact that country's embassy or consulate or your own consular affairs department. Russia was a good example of this. In December 1997 a U.S citizen was imprisoned in Rostov-na Donu for 10 days on charges of espionage for using a GPS device to check the efficacy of some newly installed communications equipment. Unfortunately he was near some government installations.

No traveller to Russia or the CIS should seek to import or travel with any such equipment unless it has been properly and thoroughly documented by the traveller in accordance with instructions of Glavgossvyaznadzor (Main Inspectorate in Communication) and is declared in full on customs declarations at the point of entry to Russia. Notebook computers and AM/FM radios are okay these days into Russia and you may try your cellular phone, but in the case of the latter you still need to check with your consular office. You may still have to register it.

Planning

Do your research and get your countries official 'country briefing' prior to your trip. Start a file to include newspaper cuttings.

◆ Know any expected extremes of weather or geological activity. Is it a seasonal period of extremes, eg monsoons etc.

◆ In the Middle East, parts of Africa, still in some parts of the former Soviet Union, there may be strict regulations against photographing military bases, military officials, or airports. Check before you do and also check what, if any, restrictions apply to having a camera with you. Don't photograph civil disturbances - shooting journalists (e.g someone with a camera) has become a sport in many parts of the world.

◆ Some countries restrict or prohibit the importation or consumption of alcohol. This will be common in most Muslim countries.

◆ Many Middle Eastern and North African countries have strict laws and severe penalties regarding pornographic material.

Personal

◆ Avoid carrying any objects or written material which identifies your religion.

◆ Learn a few words of the language of the countries you travel to. Don't decry the typical tourist habit of carrying a small phrase book, it may be a life saver. Learn all greetings and thanks.

◆ Don't take alcohol into fundamental Muslim countries, even in such benign concoctions as cough medicine or mouth wash.

◆ The same goes for what may be considered (by them) pornographic material. Even a TV guide could fall foul of this one.

◆ If travelling with friends, family or business colleagues establish code words for danger. See Colour codes in Chapter 5.

A private hotel beach in Fiji - and an idyllic scene, but taken only weeks before an armed coup and hostage seige nearly toppled the government and brought riots to the streets.

Abroad in Jail

In 1997 an average of 2,350 Britons were in prison abroad every day - an increase of 17.5%on the figure for 1996. Also in 1997 overseas posts of the Consular division of the FCO were notified of 5,822 arrests and the number grows each year. As a matter of interest in 1997 Britons took 47 million trips abroad.

You should know that the current FCO policy is to site posts in commercial areas not tourist areas, so as a tourist to a remote area you need to be particularly careful.

According to the 1969 Vienna Convention, consular rights include visiting prisoners, making representations about their conditions in prison, any unfair treatment and attending trials to see fair hearing which conforms to recognised codes of justice. It does not extend to being able to get people out of jail.

The Convention places responsibility for an arresting nation to inform, within 48 hours, a Consulate of an arrest. The longest was Venezuela which took 8 years. If you are arrested abroad:

◆ Do not argue with the police as it will only aggravate matters.

◆ Always try to keep possession of your passport.

◆ Offering bribes could make matters worse.

◆ Demand the police inform your Consulate if it appears you will not be released.

◆ Tell the Consulate how you are being treated. They should get you some essentials such as soap, toothpaste, writing paper.

◆ They can only provide names of suitable lawyers - they cannot provide legal representation.

Remember that in the very poorest and remote countries even being fed as a prisoner will be a problem. In some parts of the world (Morocco is an example) prisoners rely on their families bringing food on a daily basis. There are two organisations in the U.K. which have an excellent reputation for helping Britons in prison abroad:

The National Council for the Welfare of Prisoners Abroad, 72-82, Rosebery Avenue, London EC1R 4RR (0171 833 3467) and **Fair Trials Abroad Trust, Bench House, Ham Street, Richmond, London TW10 7HR (0181 332 2800).**

CHAPTER 3

Risk Assessment

Business First

If your company was to embark on any business venture, it would carry out a commercial risk analysis of the merits of the proposed action. These would be fiscal in nature and lead to the conclusion that profit, at some time, acceptable to the potential risk of the venture, should flow from a particular course of action. Judging by the volume of business ventures which fail, there would seem to be less of a science at work in this process than business schools and business gurus would have us believe.

At least there is some semblance of analysis carried out when a commercial business venture is proposed, whereas often, when the decision is made to send an employee abroad, little if any thought is put into the assessment of the potential dangers. This, despite the fact that each day there are some 4 million business travellers flying around the planet. From my experience, few companies will embark on a detailed risk assessment until the stable door has banged shut very firmly into someone's face.

The American Society For Industrial Security (ASIS), conducted a survey in which over half of the 520 respondents indicated that domestic terrorism in the States had altered their thinking, as corporate bodies, on how to handle travel in the U.S They also indicated that more companies now enquire of their travel arrangers about trouble spots around the world and information about the safety record of airlines.

The survey was mailed to 7,633 ASIS members and returned by 520. The results prove interesting reading and somewhat restores one's faith in the body corporate, as 65% said they had a longstanding practise of the company's security department disseminating travel security information to employees upon request before they travel. The figure fell to 53% who had a longstanding practise of 'proactively' providing such data to employees before they travelled.

A good number of companies had in place a system whereby the State Department's Overseas Advisory Council (OSAC) data was supplemented by 'open intelligence' from such sources as newspapers, as well as sharing information between themselves and other companies. Many of the respondents gave both hostage survival training, how to behave at airports, and how to maintain a low profile whilst travelling.

My concern is however, about what the other 7,113 non-respondent companies are doing. It is probably the case that the respondents are likely to be the one's who are taking a positive approach to the problems. There are tens of thousands of companies who are not ASIS members who may do nothing at all to protect their staff who travel. Some do have systems in place which are designed to protect the upper eschelons of the company's management whose untimely death, injury or kidnap would have a very negative effect on the fortunes of the company.

For these people, this is the point at which I may be called in either to carry out a detailed 'in-country' analysis or provide Executive Protection for the executive should his status so demand. Strangely or possibly not so, the higher up the corporate the ladder we move the more proactive the company is about underpinning the security for a foreign visit, particularly to a non-compliant geography.

Often the decision to provide a personal protective detail (bodyguards) is at the behest of the company's legal counsel, who has an eye firmly fixed on the potential legal liability. It may also be a prerequisite of the individuals Kidnap & Ransom insurers that on visits to certain locations, protection must accompany. So much for the CEO, but what about the poor middle ranking exec who finds him or herself in some god forsaken Third World airport surrounded by large men in leather jackets, with unknown intent. They may be lucky to get to their intended location, (which is marked out on the wall map in their bosses office by the ubiquitous pin), in one piece

I do a great injustice to those reasonably altruistic corporations which do have procedures in place to ensure as best as possible the safe journeys of their people. Motorola would be a good example of this where the company's Global Security has set up an internal web site for employees to access the latest real time regional risk assessments and security advisories. By contrast to those companies that do make some effort, I find that those companies which fare badly in difficult geographies are often those which have no formal security procedures laid down for their operations in the West. Those companies which have an experienced security manager, a liability conscious legal counsel and a mandated corporate security policy will have the best chance of operating abroad.

I should make the point that the issue of responsibility is a two-way street and any employee in a substantial multi-national must exercise some personal responsibility in not simply jetting off to some war zone without having the trip approved by corporate security. One way of preventing this is to ensure the travel agencies which employees use, must secure approval from corporate security prior to proceeding with a booking.

It is far easier to append travel security briefings and regional threat analysis to an existing security policy. Such a policy usually means employees already have an awareness of security issues and their importance not only to their companies well being, but also to their own. Also the presence of a **Crisis & Contingency** policy enables a company to add on to it's normal corporate business disaster recovery continuity plans such extensions as **Kidnap & Ransom (K & R), Extortion** and **Evacuation Procedures**. If such procedures are in place an employee can operate as an expatriate, confident in the knowledge that the company is prepared and has the assets in place to deal with an emergency abroad. Crisis planning should be at both corporate and regional level with regular local planning meetings being held to play out contingencies well before they may be required. Intelligence should be regularly fed into local alert states, with contingency evacuation based on the result and options available for partial or full evacuation - by public or charter carrier, overland and with what level of logistics required. A company should have two practises in place for it's people who are either working abroad or are going to work abroad.

The snow-clad mountains contrast with the mediteranean holiday image - but this is Beirut and only yards from where the old U.S. Embassy stood before being blown up.

1. Travel Warnings

These serve as a way of keeping people who are working abroad up to date on matters which may effect them. Companies should not believe that 'people on the ground' are always aux fait with what is happening. Often and particularly in more repressive countries, internal news is severely repressed. Warnings are also a way of enhancing travel briefings for people about to travel.

2. Pre-Travel Briefings

These should be structured around a 'generic', core theme which deals with such factors as awareness, avoidance of routine, maintaining a low profile, crime prevention, aspects of anti-surveillance, how to protect proprietary information etc.

It will specifically contain country or regional specific intelligence embracing the topical, travel warnings. On occasions the briefings can extend to intensive practical courses on such matters as 'Defensive' Driving, First Aid and Survival Skills in hostile environments.

Business people are at risk either as casual travellers to a region, regular travellers to that region or, eventually, expatriates operating in a region for a year or more. The risks increase progressively and in all cases the company should have carried out it's own analysis of the potential risks to it's people or it should have paid a company who specialise in such matters to carry one out. Often this comes with the acquisition of K & R insurance, providing not only pre-travel briefings, but a response facility and even hostage negotiation services. For most companies and individuals who could not secure such costly outside services, it will be necessary to identify the risks and the resultant precautionary measures for themselves in a more DIY manner.

Before we look at some specific risks we need to see in a simple way where we fit into a Threat Scale. If we rate our attractiveness, so to speak, to a kidnapper or terrorist we may fit in one of the categories below:

5. Royalty, Head of State, Very High Profile Corporate Leader.
4. Foreign Minister, High Profile Corporate Leader.

3. CEO's, Senior Military, In-Country Manager (International Corporation).

2. VIP's, Security Personnel, Government Personnel.

1. Mr and Mrs Tourist and Business Traveller.

Such a defined scale would go out of the window if you were to put them all together in a bus and drove around Algiers town. Everyone, ignoring rank, noble birth and position would be at the same risk - death. So never ignore the threat your geographic situation imposes and don't think that because you are poor, or at the bottom of the corporate ladder that you are not at risk.

The Range of Risks

It may be useful to look at the range of untoward things that could befall us whilst abroad.

Criminal

Whenever I put together a Threat Assessment I always refer to ***'Organised Crime'*** and by contrast and somewhat sarcastically, ***'Disorganised Crime'.*** By the first I mean where the crime is the product of an organisation operating against both the business entity and the individuals within it and the latter I am really referring to 'street' crime, which is random, opportunistic and rarely the product of a long term operation. This is not to say that street crime is not operated by large criminal organisations, who control street thugs, but simply that as victim you are probably in the wrong place at the wrong time as distinct from being the target of a detailed and long term operation. In by far the majority of cases, street crime around the world is non-violent - some small comfort I suppose.

A long term operation, on the other hand, could be a kidnap and ransom scenario for either criminal or terrorist gain. The latter may be for fiscal gain or it may be to exact some concession out of the local government ie release of prisoners (the kidnap of tourists for hostage in the Yemen). Terrorist organisations are often less concerned with the fiscal background of the person they kidnap, simply that they are foreign, Western and, as such, a person whose kidnap will elicit exposure on an international stage.

Almaty - the former capital of Kazakhstan. A deteriorating social fabric and an increase in street crimes. Still a focal point for oil negotiations however.

Don't discount, however, the requirement of terrorist organisations for money and as well as outright theft and robbery they will kidnap for financial gain. It is estimated that ETA the Basque terrorist group in Spain has made some $12,000,000 from kidnap ransoms in the past ten years. In late 1998 they declared a cease fire, but it's longevity remains to be seen, as 2 years later they have embarked on another bombing campaign

Organised crime, particularly in Eastern Europe has corporate extortion high on their list of money making schemes. Threats, to the business, owners, workers and partners are all practised as a way of extorting money. Product contamination, product theft, product diversion, the theft of proprietary information all serve to make very healthy returns for the Russian Mafia as an example.

Complex and very sophisticated fraud against both individuals and companies have been developed to the level of a national pastime by such countries as Nigeria.

Acts of crime against the individual range from a street assault, to car jacking, to kidnap, fraud, a snatch theft, assault and robbery whilst in transit on either trains or buses, to being drugged by a prostitute and/or accomplices and robbed, blackmailed and possibly murdered. The list is by no means comprehensive and to make matters worse, in some parts of the world such acts are actually being carried out by the very people employed to prevent them - the police.

Are you throwing away paper data which could prejudice your company's business or your people's safety - Shred it!

Terrorist Threats

1. There has been an emergence throughout the eighties and into the nineties of targeting the tourist as a means of anti-government factions bringing attention to the world of it's on-going course, whilst at the same time seriously effecting the economic well being of that country.

The murder of the tourists at Luxour in Egypt.

The kidnapping and subsequent murder of tourists in Yemen.

The kidnapping and subsequent murder of British and American tourists in Uganda.

The murder of any foreigner in Algeria by Muslim fundamentalists.

The kidnapping of tourists in Kashmir.

The attacks on tourist centres in Turkey.

The assassination of the British military attache in Athens.

In economic terms terrorism constitutes the greatest threat to tourism, particularly in those places where attacks have been against civil aviation, tourism property and the international visitor. According to IPCO-Interpol statistics, 22 tourism related cases of terrorist attacks have been reported since 1990. They claimed 92 deaths and 96 injuries. Their effect on the destinations concerned was powerful and cost $billions in lost business and job opportunities.

2. Increasingly there are retaliatory attacks being carried out around the world against Western targets, particularly U.S. ones. Attacks can come from organisations previously unknown, but who feel some solidarity between themselves and, say, the state of Iraq, Kosovo or elsewhere.

Whereas airports and planes were the targets for the terrorist of the seventies, there is now a shift to 'soft' targets, as was the case of the bombing of the Planet Hollywood restaurant in South Africa. The bombing attacks against the American Embassies in East Africa in August 1998 were part of the orchestrated campaign by the Islamic Fundamentalist movement under the control of the Saudi terrorist Osama bin Laden -more later.

3. There is then the threat to tourists from internal strife where the potential for death or injury is as a consequence of simply being in the wrong place at the wrong time, as acts of violence against the state are perpetrated by dissident groups.

In March 1999, following the capture by the Turkish authorities of the Kurdish terrorist leader Ocallan, a wave of violent demonstrations occurred around the world directed at the Embassies of countries the **PPK (Kurdish Peoples Workers Party)** felt had some involvement in the capture. Subsequent to that the PPK has now begun a campaign of grenade attacks in Istanbul.

Some Statistics

Safety and Security

In 1997, the World Tourism Organisation, held a seminar in Warsaw on tourist safety and security in Europe. At the conference, the European Travel Monitor revealed that in a major survey (380,000 interviews), that more than 8,000,000 Europeans on trips abroad, or over 3% of all travellers, fell victim to serious criminal offences. The most common events were car break-in/theft, handbag theft, money exchange fraud, theft of cash, credit cards and cheques.

Interestingly, but not surprisingly, the incidence of crime increases with the independent traveller and decreases in package holiday travel. The risk also depends on the type of holiday, with winter holidaymakers in the mountains facing the highest likelihood of problems - strange as this may seem. The report went on to say that hotel accommodation is safer. Young travellers, especially women, are more susceptible to crime than the over 50's, or parents with small children. Parents with small children are more likely to be hotel bound in the evenings as distinct from wandering the streets of a city.

Health

The report went on to say that health problems affected some 4% of the survey, or 11,000,000 European travellers, the principle problems being food-associated diseases, allergies and infections. Travelling further afield carries a health risk four times higher than travelling within Northern Europe. Hotel accommodation and visits to friends and relatives are three times safer than staying in other accommodation and the all-inclusive trips are safer than independent travel. Interestingly, common health risks decrease as the traveller's age increases, which can probably be attributed to greater caution, although the findings do not include health problems which may arise upon returning home as in the case of the strain of air travel on senior citizens. The statistics would probably be little different in percentage terms for travellers from the States. A useful source of advice on regional health matters is the web site of the **U.S Centres for Disease Control and Prevention.**

What will the basic conditions be like where you are travelling to? How safe is the water? Here, a well is dug in the North African desert and finds water - it doesn't get any purer.

Health and Safety - General

Anyone who visits Third World countries must be adequately briefed not only on the security issues, but also on the whole range of issues which effect health and safety. The safety aspect is really one of avoiding accidents. I carried out a Risk Analysis, some years ago in Russia for a company which was building a factory some way out of Moscow, really in the middle of nowhere. The assessment highlighted a whole range of corporate security issues, but at the top of the list in terms of 'probability' of a serious incident occurring was the likelihood of a traffic accident to a senior executive whilst travelling between Moscow and the south on what are remote and dangerous roads.

The condition of the roads, poor condition of most vehicles, speed at which vehicles are driven and a complete lack of adherence by most road users to any rules of the road, make any long distance, rural journey in Russia extremely hazardous. Link this to a complete lack of communication in rural areas to summon help and the parlous state of that help, if and when it does arrive all conspire to make a journey dangerous.

The finished factory deep in the backwoods of Russia. The road from the site to Moscow, some 160km was a potential death trap for ex-pats.

The Dangers of Rail

From the backwoods of Russia to the dangers of travel by rail and in this case in India. In August 1999 near Gaisal in West Bengal, India suffered it's worst rail accident, when 2 trains collided head on killing 285 and injuring hundreds more. The trains were, as is often the case in this part of the world, seriously overcrowded with some 2,500 people.

The Business Traveller & The Tourist

The nature of and degree of risk is different for the two broad categories of person abroad. For the average tourist on a package holiday they will not be specifically targeted due to their renowned wealth, political position or business ownership. They are broadly anonymous, but potential victims by dint of the fact that tourists, as a group, are attractive to criminals. They are often in possession, foolishly, of large amounts of cash, cameras - both still and video and are relaxed and careless with their possessions and themselves. Villains also know that their victims are probably never going to return simply to give evidence in a theft prosecution, possibly a year after the event.

For other, less obvious reasons the tourist is seen as fair game and the business traveller needs to maintain some visual distance from being perceived as a casual tourist devoid of 'street smarts'. The businessman abroad is, though, more likely to be the target of a more considered assault, following a longer period of surveillance and this may involve an element of fraud, sexual entrapment, bribery or organised assault.

Business Specific

One specific factor which separates the tourist from the business traveller is that the latter carries with him or her what we know as Proprietary Information - broadly, information owned by a company, or government which, if lost, would cause damage to the corporation or government. In Travelsafe we are only interested in how this may be a problem to the business traveller, but the problem is of such concern to government agencies that we can draw some first class advice about the problem from such sources.

Information Loss

When we go abroad on business we take with us proprietary information in a number of ways - we carry it in our heads, commit it to paper data and these days commit it to digital means and transport it on our notebook computers. We can lose it from all three sources. Substantial and vital information is lost not just from theft, but via disclosure. Businessmen abroad can become victims of organised intelligence gathering carried out by competitors, foreign government agencies and criminal factions who have an interest in business, particularly yours. The former Soviet Union is a good example of this.

Don't believe for one minute that you will be able to detect an approach made to you on a friendly basis which leads to a conversation being struck up and a relationship being established. Self aggrandisement and wanting to appear more important than one is within the corporate structure, leads many people to disclose information that no one else should be party to. This can happen in the bar around the corner from the office at home but it is even harder to resist when one is on one's own and starting to feel lonely in some foreign country.

It is interesting to look at how a U.S. government department deals with the potential problem as it may effect their staff who travel abroad. The department in question is the **U.S. Department of Commerce.** There is actually a directive - **Presidential Decision/NSC-12** ***"Security Awareness and Reporting Foreign Contacts"*** which requires the Office Of Security of the Department to establish and maintain security awareness programmes which include formal briefings of the threat posed by foreign intelligence services. The awareness programmes focus not just on the intelligence gathering of classified, but all sensitive information.

The Department's ***'Defensive Travel Briefing'*** highlights the wealth of information employees have, which is of value to foreign countries and their businesses. These are listed as *trade issues, ongoing negotiations, economic indicators, industrial resources, production capabilities, manufacturing and other critical technologies, satellite data, telecommunications and computer sciences information as well as export data.* It should be mentioned at this point that the Department entreat their employees to be aware of their surroundings and alert to their actions, even when in an 'allied' country. If you study the above list it would it would be equally applicable to a private business and not just government.

The Office of Security mandates some actions to be taken and it is worth repeating them here, albeit that many of the advisory points will be repeated elsewhere in the book, but it is useful to see how adherence to a cohesive programme offers the best protection not only for one's personal safety, but also for the protection of private corporate information. Whilst the following advice, on occasions, requests the individual to make contact with a Commerce Department or State Department office, the reader will on most occasions, be able to identify someone within his or her own corporate organisation i.e. personnel, legal, financial, I.T., or security department to whom they can report.

The guidelines are as follows and comments in brackets are my own :-

PRIOR TO DEPARTURE

1. Contact your Security Officer at the Office of Security to obtain the latest travel advisory information. You may also want to contact the Department of State recorded message. (a business traveller should secure a travel update from either his company's security department or from the Foreign Office).

2. Carefully complete your Visa application, as it will be scrutinised.

3. Ensure that items you carry with you are not controversial or prohibited. Political material or anything that could be considered pornographic should not be carried. If you are carrying prescription drugs with you , be certain they are clearly marked and bring only necessary quantities.

◆ *Carrying letters, packages, or gifts to individuals in other countries should be avoided. You may be viewed as a courier attempting to bring the material for subversive or illegal purposes.*

◆ *DO NOT TAKE CLASSIFIED MATERIAL with you as you travel. Arrange to have the material transmitted by other approved means prior to your departure. Consult with your security officer for guidance.* (For the business traveller this advice could not be more appropriate. Often classified material is taken abroad accidentally, because it travels on the notebook computer you use for everything, even if that information has no pertinence to the deal you are going abroad to conduct).

◆ *Limit the amount of identification you take - particularly office ID's and building entry passes.*

◆ *The carrying of laptop/notebook computers is discouraged, but not prohibited. Consult your security officer and your information technology security officer if you plan to take a laptop.* (This point follows on from the one above and equally applies to anyone travelling on business. Do you take your notebook computer abroad unnecessarily? On the occasions I have, I feel encumbered and only have the additional worry of where I leave the computer when I am not in my hotel room and can't take it with me).

Upon Arrival

1. An accurate declaration of all money and valuables should be made at entry. Some countries give the traveller a copy of the declaration which must be surrendered upon leaving. (Russia is a good example of this). *It is important to keep all receipts of money exchanges, as they are frequently required upon departure.*

2. Declare such items as cameras, radios, etc., to preclude possible explanations, customs charges, or confiscation when you leave.

3. Use of public transportation is recommended, rather than driving yourself, because involvement in traffic accidents can be problematic. Taxis are the preferred mode of transportation. State department travel advisories provide updated information regarding public transport concerns in the country you are visiting. (Good advice for all of us and remember the travel advisory service referred to is available to all of us via the Internet).

Your Activities and Behaviour

1. In all of your activities, show discretion and common sense. MAINTAIN A LOW PROFILE. Refrain from any behaviour that may make you conspicuous or a potential target. NEVER engage in any illegal activity, excessive drinking or gambling. Use your best judgement to carefully avoid any situation which may allow a foreign intelligence agency the opportunity to coerce or blackmail you.

2. ***Do not discuss classified or sensitive information in any vehicle, restaurant, hotel room, hotel lobby, or other public place.*** *In any public place your conversation may be overheard, or you may be monitored..* (In my travels it never ceases to amaze me the way in which businessmen from the West seem to revel in disclosing to everyone in a hotel bar their business. It is often the norm to talk in a loud and clear manner than to be circumspect, talk quietly and select the most tactically sound position from which to prevent being overheard or monitored. They are also totally oblivious of people around them. Often the hotel lounges are the only place where business may be conducted by people who are in business and not government service and there is nothing wrong with this providing you are cautious and LOW PROFILE).

3. If you locate any possible surveillance equipment such as microphones, telephone taps, miniature recording devices, or cameras, do not try to neutralise or dismantle it. Assume the device is operable and that active monitoring is ongoing. Report what you have found to the U.S. Embassy or Consulate. (Don't think electronic surveillance goes on against just foreign government employees. In Russia the former KGB intelligence gathering apparatus is very firmly directed at the theft and acquisition of corporate intelligence).

4. Never leave luggage or briefcases that contain sensitive information unattended. This includes your briefcase in your hotel room. We encourage you to keep your briefcase containing sensitive information immediately in your possession. Departmental personnel frequently report occurrences of their luggage or briefcase being searched or rummaged through.

5. Foreign intelligence services may try to put you under physical surveillance or you may suspect that you are being watched.. It is better to ignore the surveillance than to attempt to lose or evade it. In any event your actions should be prudent and not likely to generate suspicion. Good precautions are to use well travelled highways and avoid establishing routine patterns and schedules.

6. Never try to photograph military personnel, installations, or other 'restricted areas'. It is best to also refrain from photographing police installations, industrial structures, transportation facilities and border areas.

7. Beware of overly friendly or solicitous people that you meet. Do not establish personal or intimate relationships with these people as they may be employed by the intelligence services. ***Do not share any work related information with any person who does not have a need to know.***

8. Do not accept packages and agree to transport them back to the U.S. Even if your friends, relatives and professional contacts make the request do not accept the package.

9. If you are on an extended visit and expect to be writing or receiving mail, remember that it may be subject to censorship. Never make references to any classified or sensitive information.

10. Avoid any areas where there is political or ethnic unrest, demonstrations, or protests.

11. Should you be detained for any reason by the police, be co-operative and contact the Embassy or Consulate immediately. Do not make any statements or sign any document you do not fully understand until you have conferred with an Embassy representative.

12. Do not leave documents in hotel safes.

So there you have it - good advice for everyone not just U.S.Government personnel. The risk of being targeted for intelligence gathering is real for anyone in business and the more your business is at the leading edge of technology, the more of a target you will be.

The Prominent & Wealthy

Often these people, particularly if in business in a major way will not be allowed by the company's legal counsel to travel without the attendant personal protection in the form of security personnel. The potential for loss to the business is high as is the potential for losses by the underwriters of the Kidnap & Ransom insurance and it may well be that they have conditionally insisted on such protective cover during journeys to certain places in the world.

Don't believe for one minute that prominent and wealthy means prominent, wealthy and blessed with common sense. I've known the richest be taken in by fraudsters, robbed of hundreds of thousands of dollars or have jewellery stolen from around their wives neck in highway robbery. By jewellery I mean jewellery which, if sold on the open market, would finance the national debt of many small nations. There seems to be an abdication of personal responsibility by people who travel to foreign parts and some obscure belief that everyone there will be only to pleased to see him arrive, welcome him with open arms and have no thought in mind other than to ensure he has a pleasant visit.

Nothing could be further from the truth and in many parts of the world being from the US or Europe will guarantee you don't survive until the sun sets. If you don't believe me take a trip to Algiers town and go shopping for an hour or two. You probably won't make into the second hour.

The travel press seem to have a blind spot when it comes to the dangers of travel. In 1998 in two separate magazines I have read articles about trekking into the **Rowenzori Mountains** in **Uganda.** In March 98 I carried out a risk assessment in the region, specifically looking at the **Rowenzori (Queen Elizabeth) National Park**, which due to the activities of a rebel terrorist group, infiltrating from eastern Congo, the park had been shut since 1997 and closed to tourists. The articles were ones that were obviously written some years ago, revamped and sold to the magazines who printed them, without checking the accuracy of the information.

In July 1998, the Ugandan army was carrying out a major operation to root the rebels out of the Rowenzoris following the slaughter of 100 school children in a school close by. No one is permitted to enter the park nor have they for two years or more. In the colour plate section there is a photo of an armed army guard I was given just to have a look in the foothills.

The Assessment Procedure

In simplistic terms, the object is to assess the stability of a country or region of that country or city or town in that region. You can even reduce that to the security in a particular part of that town and in particular the security of a specific hotel in that part of town. The exercise doesn't stop there as it is necessary to assess the most appropriate part of the hotel which serves our security best. But lets first backtrack to the wider picture. We need to know the 'socio-political' health of a country that we intend to visit.

It should be an absolute minimum requirement for anyone who travels abroad to keep themselves up to date with world current affairs. It is no good when you are tasked with a trip to some far flung corner of the world to spend the first hour trying to find it on the map.

As a professional security consultant everything that happens in the world is bread and butter to me as I have no way of knowing where I will be going next. One obviously cannot keep an eye on the very fine detail of a region or country, but there is no excuse for not knowing the very broad outlines of what is happening around the world.

As we saw with the former Soviet empire, there has been a breakdown of order and a breakdown in the morality of it's people. Little in the way of taxes are now collected in Russia. This is due the penal taxation levels in force, resulting in its populace hiding most of it's earnings under the floorboards. In doing so they become criminals and are a target for the real criminals who now have a hold over them and who will threaten reporting them to the Tax Police if they do not comply with some favour or action demanded.

Where To Start

In the U.S., the **Department of State's Consular Information Sheets** are available for every country of the world. You do not have to be a U.S. citizen to access this detailed information as it is available via the Internet. The sheets describe such matters as unusual entry, currency regulations or unusual health conditions, the crime and security situation, political disturbances, areas of instability, special information about driving and road conditions and drug penalties.

They also provide addresses and emergency telephone numbers for U.S. embassies and consulates, which will only be available as a resource to U.S. citizens, but the general information is invaluable to anyone. The Information Sheets don't give recommendations, simply facts upon which people can make their own informed decisions. What they may do on occasions is warn people about dangerous situations and this is done by a **Department Of State Travel Warning**. This would recommend that U.S citizens defer travel to that location.

The third way of disseminating information is via the **Public Announcement.** This would highlight terrorist threats and other short-term problem which may have a significant security risk to U.S travellers and would be headed, 'Worldwide Caution'. Generally, Public

Announcements have been issued to deal with short-term coups, pre-election disturbances, violence by terrorists and anniversary dates of specific terrorist events. This latter resource is very valuable as it is indexed by country and month, so that if, forexample, you were travelling to Algeria in June, you could look up any incident of previous terrorist activity which gave rise each year to a celebration, so to speak. The web address is **http://www.travel.state.gov.** It links to the State Departments main Internet site.

Remember that the thin air of high altitudes and helicopters are not a good mix. Don't have all your board members on one flight.

The Variety of Risks

Risk comes in a number of ways from **airline safety, road safety, hotel safety, health risks, street crime, kidnapping, extortion, hijacking, hostage taking, commercial fraud, complete social breakdown, internal violence (coup etc).** In some countries of the world business fraud or 'scams' have become a national pastime. The Russians are developing commercial theft based on direct extortion, leveraged with threats of violence against property or people, through to engaging in joint-venture deals, only to emerge as less than honest at some future point in the relationship. One U.S. multi-national I have had dealings with over a few years, has racked up, over 6 years of operating in the CIS, bad debts of between $8,000,000 and $10,000,000. These are unrecoverable and have arisen as a consequence of fraud by their distributors. The company believed the best at outset about their proposed partners, refused to instigate vetting procedures for either the distributors or their own staff and through staff collusion in the frauds, the products went out of the door and no money walked back in. Some staff and distributors, at outset were not crooked, but were coerced into criminal acts by the mafia, either through direct threats or bribes. Fraud in Russia and the newly independent states is simplistic compared with some countries where the level of sophistication is unparalleled. One such country is Nigeria, which over the years has developed a reputation for acts of state sponsored fraud.

The Nigerian Scams

All the scams are based on one premise - **GREED**! Only the sheer avariciousness of their victims allows them to be so successful and it never ceases to amaze me the seemingly intelligent and successful people who are suckered into giving away thousands or even millions of pounds or dollars. It is reported that the U.S. and other Embassies in Lagos handle several cases each week of business people who have been defrauded.

Scams can start 'in country', but can also be perpetrated at long distance and many companies in the U.K. and the States receive faxes or letters from Nigeria with some 'business proposal'. Scams range from fictitious money transfer schemes, through to supply of goods for nonexistent government contracts. The latter is often supported by meetings in government buildings where offices have been 'borrowed' to enhance the credibility. Deals are often supported by what appear to be genuine government department documentation, appropriately signed sealed and stamped.

Attempted enforcement or escape from these spurious deals can and has lead to violence and even murder. You will receive no help or sympathy from the Nigerian police nor government agencies, many of whom are involved in the scams. The problem reached such epidemic proportions a few years back that the British government refused further dealings unless the Nigerian government addressed the millions of pounds which was owed to British businessmen through fraud. Needless to say little has changed.

Any unsolicited proposal from Nigeria must be treated with suspicion. If you are a U.S company then the **Department of Commerce** and the **Foreign Commercial Service (FCS)** at the U.S. embassy in Lagos can provide information. In fact you can fax the FCS with details of any approach so as to verify the 'bona fides'. In the U.K. the first approach should be made to the '**Nigerian Desk**' at the **Foreign & Commonwealth Office (FCO).** The following may help as indicators of a potential fraud, but remember even the best have been taken in by these 'scams' and they are very difficult to spot. On the basis that there is never 'something for nothing' in this life then believe that when a deal seems too good to be true - it probably is!.

A genuine start!

Many scams start out with small, genuine orders, paid in advance, which are the 'confidence builders'. Then the large order comes in which is required urgently only this time you will probably have a forged cashiers cheque. Ship no product unless you have either full payment or an irrevocable letter of credit confirmed by a U.S or U.K bank.

The '**money transfer scheme**' entraps you through the sheer greed of assisting some Nigerian in evading his countries penal exchange controls and the offer is to transfer substantial monies to your account to escape controls with you getting a percentage. They will request blank letterheads, signed invoices and bank account information. Unfortunately people who have fallen for this have found their bank accounts looted.

Don't get involved in charitable donations, nor 'crude oil' deals. The first will at some point involve you giving your bank details and the second will involve a nonexistent state oil company.

Beware This List

Look out for the following, which may be proposals out of the blue or some request which occurs in the middle of what started out as a genuine deal The following list is not exclusive and there are literally hundreds of variations of what is essentially a 'confidence trick'.

◆ Any deal which sounds too good to be true.

◆ Any request for blank company letterheads, or signed and sealed letters and invoices, or bank account information. You may think that nobody in their right mind would supply these, but the story that usually accompanies the request is often commercially compelling.

◆ Any offer of a percentage of an amount which they wish to transfer to your company's account in exchange for your 'discretion' and 'confidentiality'. They give you to believe that this is some way of helping someone avoid Nigerian exchange controls.

◆ Any letters soliciting money in exchange for high level contacts.

◆ Any cash requests supposedly required in advance to facilitate transfer taxes or incorporation fees.

◆ Requests for urgent air shipment, against an instrument whose validity it is impossible to ascertain quickly.

◆ Any resistance by your proposed Nigerian partner to you vetting him through your Embassy.

◆ Any offer of a charitable donation.

◆ Any offer of crude oil.

◆ Any contract based on the statement that your name was provided by a 'reliable contact' you do not know.

◆ Any proposal that you visit the country for some, 'once in a lifetime', opportunistic business deal, but that you do not require a Nigerian visa and should enter the country overland from a neighbouring country.

This latter 'caution' should be heeded as it has resulted in violence. The object of the scam is to get you into Nigeria, isolate you from friends, associates, family and your Embassy and with the threat of violence or violence itself extort money from you. You are particularly vulnerable if you do not have a valid visa prior to arrival in the country and beware of anyone who tells you one is not required.

In addition to corporate 'scams', Nigeria is a difficult and potentially dangerous environment. Before you travel there carry out the usual checks with either the State Department in the U.S. via the Consular Information Sheets and Travel Warnings and with the U.K.'s Foreign and Commonwealth Office. Travel advice on a regional basis is available on the Internet, in addition to the usual means of access. A friend of mine who works as a security advisor to an oil company operating in the delta region of Nigeria reports that consistently the Americans who are sent to the country by their companies seldom, if at all, receive any travel briefings. His own company experiences one kidnap a month on average, albeit a figure which predominantly includes local employees who have been taken hostage, but also includes westerners. In the majority it has been to secure some concessions for a local village as much as for direct financial gain.

South African Corruption

In Chapter 10 we mention the murder of the Korean head of Daewoo South Africa in a car hijacking in February 1999. South Africa is a classic example of a country of immense opportunity slipping inexorably into social and economic chaos. President Mandela's replacement, Thabo Mbeki is likely to assume power as South Africa's President and leader of the ruling party the African National Congress. Whilst he is likely to institute firmer government than his predecessor, who persistently demonstrated a reluctance to deal with cronyism, corruption and nepotism any real change in the status quo is unlikely.

South Africa is likely to fall prey to the African disease of endemic corruption wedded to a weak currency and high interest rates. Already there is 38% unemployment and a growth rate of less than 1%. Improvements in basic living conditions for many millions over the last 5 years has had little impact on the plight of millions more. The likelihood of democracy surviving the election of the ANC with a two thirds majority is looking remote, particularly as opposition groups are splitting down into ever smaller units, offering a fractured, vote splitting opposition.

A demoralised police force, weakened political will to fight crime and corruption are all contributing to South Africa being one of the most dangerous places in the world for the occasional tourist, businessman or the expatriate worker. Most Europeans who find themselves on long term postings seldom, if ever, leave their place of residence, unless the journey is of necessity.

Information Sources

In very simplistic terms we can look at two broad sources of information: **OSCINT** 'Open Source Intelligence' i.e data which is publicly and legally available and

HUMINT Information obtained from a human source.

The above are terms taken from official intelligence gathering practises, but they serve as a good reference for our risk assessment. We need to not only research, but we need to talk to people.

Internet Info

The Internet and the world wide web have become one of the best sources of world intelligence. There is even a growth in companies who rely solely on the data they can source from the Web to put together detailed intelligence and then sell it back via the Web.

One such company is **Stratfor** at **www.stratfor.com.** The company 'vacuums up' data from all over the world to produce both economic forecasts as well as military-style intelligence. Many of the company's staff come from this latter background. The company accurately predicted the economic crisis in Asia as well as the socio/political troubles in Indonesia and the 1998 India-Pakistan nuclear standoff. It sells it's intelligence analysis to international corporations.

My own sources of information are more traditional, although I make increasing use of the Internet to construct country threat assessments. The methodology I use is simply to cut out and file on a regional or country basis all socio, political, economic, criminal or terrorist information on countries that at some time I may visit professionally for the first time or revisit. My sources have for many years remained unchanged and are traditionally newspapers i.e in the U.K **The Daily Telegraph** and the **Financial Times** (the latter, on occasions, having excellent pull out, country specific supplements). To this I extract articles and reports from the **Economist** and **Time** magazine. The latter has in its 'Notebook' section 'World Watch' reporting in small news items events from around the world. To this I add conversations with my own personal contacts around the world.

When 'in country' I will take the opportunity to bring myself up to date with visits to the British Embassy and, if possible, the U.S.Embassy as well as a meeting with available senior police officers. Local English language newspapers are an excellent source and are often more critical of government, more honest about reporting crime and corruption often suppressed in the national papers. In Russia the

Moscow Times, Moscow Tribune and the St. Petersburg equivalent are excellent sources of intelligence.

Some of the risk consultants are as follows:-

Kroll Associates (Kroll Travel Watch - web site)

Pinkerton Global Int Services (web site)

Control Risks

Merchant International Group

This latter London-based risk consultancy has developed and trademarked a system to rate what is known as 'Grey Area Dynamics' (GAD), by mathematically quantifying the risks facing companies trading abroad. Claiming a worldwide network of some 2,800 contacts, regular intelligence is fed into the system and will rate a country across such areas as bureaucracy, corruption, counterfeiting, cultural issues, legal safeguards, organised crime, unfair trade, unfair competition, asset security, extremism. The GAD 'score' range would be fom 0 to 10 on each area.

0-3 A small likelihood of the factor affecting an investment

3-6 Needs to be taken into consideration

6-8 Highly likely to affect any investment

9-10 Certain to affect any investment

Needless to say such countries as Russia, Pakistan, Indonesia and Colombia all came out with scores across the range of subjects which would make any investing company think twice - at least. The company has, in fact, won awards for this product, which has been endorsed by three FTSE-100 companies

Airline Safety - 'Beating the Odds"

I remember a few years back, in the early to mid 80's, when the former Soviet Union Airline Aeroflot was consistently in the news over it's safety record - or, to be precise, it's lack of one. A safe journey was a lottery, particularly internally and many Western organisations operating in Russia and the Republics banned their people from using the airline. The most tragic crash was where an Aeroflot pilot let his young son pilot the plane who fell onto the controls, bringing the aircraft down. Some sources still put the odds of dying in a Russian crash at seven times the global average

The Airline Pilots Association even went as far as to advise against even flying over Russian airspace, safety aspects were so poor. There is a wealth of anecdotal stories from business people who have flown Aeroflot which, if I did not know from personal experience to be accurate, one would dismiss out of hand. Internationally as an airline standards have improved, but any journey on a Russian plane or into a Russian airport is still an experience which can hold surprises for even the most case hardened traveller.

British Pilots threatened to boycott Greek airspace in summer 1999 unless there were improvements in the country's air traffic control. Greek traffic controllers still rely on voice contact rather than radar systems, a situation which can lead to long delays. Athens is the worst capital in Europe for flight punctuality. **The International Federation of Airline Pilots Associations (Ifalpa)** may, if it so finds from it's investigations, designate Greek airspace as 'critically deficient'.

A Curate's Egg

There's good and bad when it comes to airline safety, just as there's good and bad when it comes to general standards, such as service and reliability.

National socio-economic problems that a country experiences will show through in their national airline and it goes without saying that the more 'Third World' a country is the more 'make do' it's airline gets. Accidents do, however, happen to the best and the crash of Swissair flight 111 in September 98 was a shock to everyone, particularly given the airlines attitude to safety and it's safety track record. We are told that 75% of air accidents happen in countries which account for only 12% of air traffic. Fatal accidents per hundred thousand flights - Africa 21, Asia 13, South America 8, Central America 8, Europe 5, North America 2.

The Black Box

For once in the U.K. when it comes to aircraft safety, we have the lead over the U.S. This is in the area of the volume of information available to air crash investigators following an incident and also to flight engineers who may, as a consequence, be able to avoid one. We, the public, have come to believe in the total efficacy and amount of comprehensive data that is provided by the 'black box' following a crash. We would, however, be very wrong indeed and our faith is sorely misplaced.

The problem is that many users (airlines) see black boxes as little more than a nuisance, causing extra weight and cost. For example, black boxes on 737's were approved in 1969 when the requirement for the number of parameters they were required to record were much less and the information that one of these would provide following a crash is actually negligible. If you crashed in a 737, it would likely be impossible to determine the cause from a black box.

This does not help, particularly when airline safety in the U.S. has been based around the "Autopsy Approach". This means that future safety is based on reaction to what happened and not by using data in flight to prevent what may happen. "The chances of dying in an air crash are the same as they were 20 years ago". It's not that the technology isn't around. The telemetry used by the U.S. navy in testing and that for space travel has been around now close on 20 years and could be used on commercial aircraft.

Some black boxes record 10 or so parameters, not the hundreds they could and there are also big gaps of up to 2 seconds in the data sampling. Flight 427 (a 737) crashed at 300mph when the rudder stuck, killing 120 people. Boeing tried to obfuscate the cause, but eventually had to concede the rudder problem on this and other incidents. Due to the gaps in sampling, they had been able to add data so as to 'self fulfill' their argument.

In the U.K., by contrast, British Airways carry 'in flight' data recorders or as they are known '**Quick Access Recorders**' **(QARs).** In a 777, where a massive total of 20,000 parameters are available, the QAR does some 2,000. What started in the 1960s as a research tool, when BEA wanted to install a system called 'Autoland' in a Trident, the QAR has become an invaluable interrogative and proactive tool whilst the plane is in flight. Airlines in the U.S. are only just starting to use QAR. The U.S. Government is still trying to get its country's airlines to adopt QAR, where most airlines still only operate the black box - 'post mortem' approach. As one air crash investigator said - ***"Waiting for crashes to happen has not made flying safer".*** Lets keep this in perspective, however, as worldwide, every year, about 15,000 aircraft serving nearly 10,000 airports, transport more than 1.2 billion people with relatively few accidents or incidents. Whether this safety record can be maintained remains to be seen. *"Under competitive pressures, many airlines are foregoing the extra margins of safety that they maintained routinely when they could pass the extra costs on to customers,"* says ***Fortune*** magazine. The Federal Aviation Administration, charged with the task of ensuring air safety in the United States, is *"underfunded, undermanned and, badly managed,"* the magazine reported. Good press about flight safety obviously does not get through to everyone as it is estimated that 1 in 6 of the adult population in the U.S. is afraid of flying.

Can We Beat The Odds?

So, if we are conducting our 'risk assessment' and believe that airline choice must have a part to play in our risk reduction strategy, how would we go about it. In fact even before we set about the process is there, in fact, any purpose to be served at all by practising an 'evasion strategy' when it comes to safety in flight. A study carried out by an **Arnold Bennett**, a professor of management science, at the **Massachusetts Institute of Technology** together with a student analyst **Alexander Wang**, would seem to prove that the exercise has little, if any, impact on mortality figures.

This conclusion was drawn from airline data for 1986-96. Bennett concluded from the figures that, amongst established U.S jet carriers, fatal crashes were completely distributed at random among the airlines. In fact the chance of each carrier suffering a crash was broadly in equal to it's proportion of overall flights. In other words it is a complete 'lottery'. Discriminating among airlines to improve survival odds is a fruitless pursuit according to the Wall Street Journals summary of Bennetts research.

According to Bennett his findings made a mockery of safety tables and U.S Airways was a good example of this. From having one of the highest, observed risk levels in 1987-96 it had one of the lowest for 1977-86. In the States there has always been criticism about the post de-regulation airlines, yet, with the exception in 1996 of the tragic Valu-Jet disaster, there were no other fatal accidents amongst the newcomers in the period 1987-96. (Recently criminal judgments have been found against the company responsible for the Valu-Jet servicing). This is set against the expectation that, from experience (based on the fatal accident rate for established airlines), the probability was greater than 40% that the new entrants would have had at least one major crash over that decade from the millions of flights carried.

Prop Jets

An area which seems to meet the a higher risk expectation is commuter propeller and prop-jet flights. Bennett did, however, believe the increased mortality could possibly be laid at the door of other factors. For example, commuter planes, unlike big jets, land at remote, smaller airports without control towers. Remote fields, in high alpine environments may all contribute to an increased mortality, but as prop-jets and big jets serve different routes the traveller has no room for manoeuvre - the prop-jet is probably the 'only show in town'.

A clear divide exists, though, between the West and Third World airlines, which do have a higher passenger death risk. Bennett advises that, staggeringly, in domestic operations the overall difference is a factor exceeding 10. Internationally, the statistics show very little difference between the Third World and First World airlines on similar routes. Mortality rates for the period 1987-96 were essentially the same.

Bennett concluded from his figures that there was no way to exploit the statistical differences in risk so as to improve safety on a given trip. He also states that, fortunately, there is, in reality, no menacing risk levels that would drive us to want to conduct the exercise in the first place. The figures showed that a passenger who took a First World domestic jet flight would, on average, go for 21,000 years before succumbing to a fatal crash. The same data from 1987-96 gave 14,000 years for travelling internationally, 5,000 years for propeller/prop-jet U.S commuter flights, 2,000 years for jet flights between First and Third Worlds and 1,500 years for Third World domestic jet flights.

Safer by Car or Air?

In one year about half a million people die on the roads of the world. Contrast this figure with the number of airline deaths in 1996, which were some 1,945, with the figure falling to 1,226 in 1997. According to statistics released by Boeing, "commercial jets crash less than 2 times for every 1 million flights." A very interesting statistic is the comparison Bennett made between car journeys and flying. The data is thought provoking, to say the least, and brings in a new factor to the equation - distance you intend to travel!. We constantly hear the statement that flying is safer than car journeys - according to Lloyds of London, it is 25 times safer to travel by air than by car. The real truth is, however, that as the overwhelming majority of aircraft accidents occur during takeoff and landing, the flight's risk is, broadly, independent of it's distance.

By contrast, travelling by vehicle means the risk is roughly dependent to the distance being travelled. Thus shorter trips by car are statistically safer. Bennett used the example of a business traveller in his 40's who wears a seat belt and does not drink alcohol before driving - concluding that his death risk is lower in a car than in a jet, but only for distances up to 150 miles. This is a non-working example, though, as little time would be saved flying this distance. Focussing on longer journeys, Bennett invoked a 'rule of thumb' that *"for every hour saved in travel time taking a jet rather than a car, there is a bonus and that is a 70 second rise in life expectancy tied to choosing the safer form of travel".*

Extending this concept to other forms of travel e.g. First World intercity trains and buses, the threshold distance for equal safety with jets is roughly 500 miles. Thus, mortality risk is lower by land at, say, 400 miles. It is necessary, however, to add another factor to the equation and that is non-fatal injury, which is considerably more likely on land than in the air and that especially in the West with levels of traffic congestion the trip will take several more hours. So a mortality risk that is one in 40 million doesn't seem so bad after all.

Avoid the Obvious!

Despite what we know about not being able to beat the odds, we would certainly want to avoid the obvious dangers, should any exist. They do and these are domestic flights in the former Soviet Union, all flights with China Airlines, most African airlines and South and Central American ones. A South American and African airline is 10 times more likely to have an accident involving fatalities than a North American or European one.

A 'bush plane' in Central Africa - the only show in town.

Clearly there are unacceptably wide variations exist in airline safety. For example if we compare airlines based in Africa and Latin America, with those registered in the U.S and Europe, statistics show that in the former there were 0.52 crashes per million flights between 1980 and 1996, while in the latter there were 0.37. In 1998 the inter-governmental **International Civil Aviation Organisation** agreed that national safety regimes should be subjected to compulsory safety audits. It sounds good, but we must remain skeptical. The safety recommendations which followed the tragic crash and fire which engulfed a British Airtours Boeing 737 at the U.K's Manchester airport and which killed 55 people in 1985 have still not been implemented. Because in the panic to escape passengers became jammed in the opening between two forward bulkheads, the UK's **Air Accidents Investigation Branch** recommended, amongst other things, a widening of the minimum gap. Some 15 years later there has been no change. Widening the gap to the recommended 30 inches would have forced airlines with high-density seating to carry fewer passengers on some types of aircraft. For the British authority to legislate would have placed British carriers at a commercial disadvantage, so it didn't happen.

"Frequent Flyers Survive"

A point of comparison with regard to airline safety, is that in 1993 the world's air travellers made just over 1.3 Billion flights. During this 'average' year for flight safety, there were 33 fatal accidents to civil airliners of all kinds, including domestic, short-haul propeller powered craft. The world total of airline deaths was 1,020.

Interestingly, in the 'average' fatal accident more than half the people on board survive. Also it has become a fact that frequent flyers have a better chance of surviving an accident than do occasional travellers. No hard facts support why, but it is probably due to an increased familiarity with the aircraft and a decreased inclination to panic. Whilst we previously looked at the futility of trying to beat the odds with airline selection as a risk reduction strategy, where we can help ourselves is in the very unlikely event of being in a crash.

For information from the Web try AirSafe.Com which gives an overviewof the travel safety records of international carriers.

Survival Advice

First, do not ignore the safety briefings. Note the exits and picture how you will get there when the panic starts. You will read later in the book about how to survive a fire in a hotel and, broadly, it will be the same in an aircraft. There will be blinding smoke, panic, limited visibility and you may be reduced to operating by touch. Know where your seat is in relation to the emergency exit and count the rows - you may have to count them by feel at a future point in time. **Sit near an exit**, must be the primary advice. Secondly, **sit near the rear** - the last 10 rows are often the part of the plane most intact after a crash. Somewhat of a problem if you want to travel first or business.

Don't believe everyone will panic in the accepted sense of the word. Evidence from survivors of major disasters tell of people frozen into immobility. A woman who survived the air crash and subsequent fire at the U.K's Manchester airport in the1980's, tells how as she was fighting her way to the emergency exit she passed people who were getting their luggage from the overhead lockers - this as the cabin filled with smoke and flames. She was sitting at about the middle of the plane - nobody survived who was seated behind her and only about 50% of people survived who were seated in front of her.

A British man who survived the sinking of the Herald Of Free Enterprise, only one of less than 200 survivors out of 1,000 passengers, recounts how he passed small groups of people who had gone into 'committee' to plan what to do rather than just obey the emergency hormones which were driving him to survive at the time. You must fight to survive and avoid what is known as 'paralysis by analysis'.

'Black Star' Awards

This is the blacklisted award system given by airline pilots to the very worst airports with serious safety failings. These were contained in a dossier,'leaked' to the U.K's Sunday Times in summer 1998. The dossier named more than 150 airports with safety failings with San Francisco, Hong Kong and Nice being labelled as 'critically deficient'.

High tech. meets Third World. A Gulfstream G4 waiting to take off from a Kenyan airstrip.

Delegates were presented with this list at a closed meeting of the International Federation of Airline Pilots Associations (Ifalpa) in Montreal earlier in the year. It is the official 'wish list' of places you would rather not fly over, take off from, or land at, as one pilot described it. The 15 with black stars are San Francisco, Nice, Hong Kong, Wellington in New Zealand, Fornebu airport at Oslo, Buenos Aires, Leticia Rio Negra and San Andres all in Colombia, Maiqueitia in Venezuela, Hauru in the Solomon Islands, Lagos and Port Harcourt in Nigeria and Kabul in Afghanistan.

Even closer to home pilots report landing problems at popular tourist destinations such as Greece, where there are inadequate lighting and no air-traffic controllers on the ground. In fact delegates at the convention were asked to consider whether Greece air space should be given a black star award. Many tourist destinations have inadequate radar systems, poor approach lighting and poor quality radio communications.

San Francisco is listed because planes land in pairs on parallel runways and it has been known for planes to drift across to the other runway. Also in the event of an abort the 'published' route out can take one plane into the path of another.

At Nice airport planes are now often forced to make a circular approach final approach using a navigation system that can be inaccurate by hundreds of yards. Whilst in Amsterdam noise restrictions mean planes are being forced to land in strong crosswinds rather than use safer alternatives. So far there have been two accidents where crosswinds played a crucial role.

The IFalpa executive director, Cathy Bill said, "if airports and airspaces are listed, it means they have serious deficiencies, not that they are unsafe". British Airways, as usual took a more relaxed view about such operational hazards and talked about safety not being compromised.

Radiation

Unfortunately what Bennett in his studies didn't take into

account is another unseen hazard - radiation. Over the past few years there has been increasing press interest in the fact that frequent fliers are exposed to more background radiation than those of us who may be more earth bound. In Chapter 3 there is a specific section on this together with the increasing problems of air quality on planes.

Conclusions

As with life in general, the risks associated with travel are unavoidable. This doesn't mean though that we can ignore planning and precautions. It does mean we have to accept the risks, but first we need to know what they are, estimate their likelihood, assess any 'impact' factors which may aggravate matters (e.g. personal health problems linked to a higher Third World health risk), assess how the happening of a particular event will impact on yourself and the business and then plan avoidance and/or support procedures.

Avoidance may amount to simply maintaining awareness and practising some *'risk reduction strategies'*. Support may be adequate insurance, corporate rescue plans, security support (people) and possibly kidnap and ransom cover. All we do comes at a cost. This may be time, inconvenience, restricting where we go, what time we avoid going somewhere, or financial expenditure and any risk assessment must make the balance work. As a tourist it may be that you decide to take a cheap, 'compact' camera instead your thousand dollar Nikon. As a businessman it may mean the inconvenience of not taking your 'notebook' computer with you and it may mean restricting you social activities and not dressing in your usual, possibly flamboyant and expensive manner.

It's all your choice, but to make an informed one you need just that - information. It's out there and it's available, often at little cost and there is no excuse for travelling in ignorance.

CHAPTER 4

Travel Health and Safety

In the same way that the security issues around the world are increasingly important and it is becoming a more not less dangerous world in which to travel, so it is with health issues. World poverty and standards of hygiene get worse in relation to population growth, producing worsening living conditions for millions of people.

The horror, and it is literally that, of seeing the conditions in which people live in Delhi or Bombay is as clear an indication as you will ever need of the problems facing many nations in the years to come. It becomes annoying, I'm sure, to be reminded that it is to these and other poor, underdeveloped countries that tourists and the business traveller are now making increasing number of visits. In the search for thrills, excitement, challenge, extremes and different cultures, the international traveller is journeying to the furthest and poorest corners of the world. Often they are ill-prepared for such journeys, either due to a poor understanding of the true nature of the conditions, a lack of adequate equipment, no cultural appreciation, poor health, fitness and lack of the necessary medical prophylaxis prior to departure.

Don't think that the average business traveller is any better prepared. Few who travel abroad have any suitable emergency first aid training, yet in these remote parts of the world it is a 'self help' society in more ways than one. In Russia and many Third World countries, if you have a medical emergency, your chance of survival rests on the hope that an emergency ambulance does not turn up. If it does, you may not survive either the journey, nor the medical attention at the hospital to which it takes you.

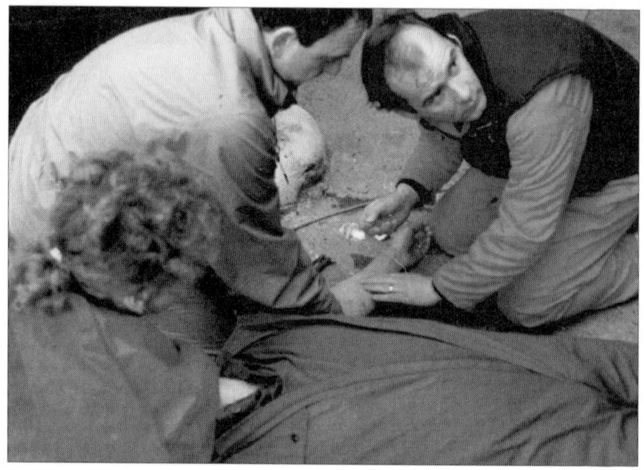

The more remote the location, the more you will need to rely on your own skills. Here, soon to be ex-pats get hands-on emergency First Aid training.

This is not to decry the excellent abilities of medical staff, it is simply a comment on the, often, complete lack of even the basic essentials, such as a supply of new unused needles, blood and basic hygienic conditions. Often medical facilities are run down and in crumbling buildings, underfunded and overstretched with little sympathy for the plight of rich foreigners. Your plan, in the event of illness or serious accident, should be to leave the country as soon as possible. In the meantime, prior to evacuation you should know that you are able to in some way assist those who help you and this may be in the form of clean needles you have brought with you (see medical kit).

Statistically, we are always more likely to suffer illness or accident whilst abroad, than we are to be attacked, robbed or kidnapped. Few of us could probably could remember and then with only with some difficulty, those occasions when we have returned from abroad and not had some stomach upset, however minor. Even the process of air flights has a negative effect on our bodies equilibrium, both in the form of 'jet lag' as well as causing a general disturbance to our systems.

Environmental Hazards

In addition to the crossing of several time zones and the disruption that has on our sleeping and waking cycle, international air travellers are subject to various forms of stress that may reduce their resistance to disease: crowding, long hours of waiting, disruption of eating habits, changes in climate, are all factors which, may in themselves provoke nausea, indigestion, extreme fatigue and even insomnia. Travel stress is seen as resulting from the above linked with such issues as cultural differences, frustrations and even religious problems.

Even in European countries, such minor things as the change in the type of water, or richer foods than we are commonly used to, can have a disturbing effect on our digestive systems. The further afield we travel, particularly to the Third World, the more the risk increases of our falling foul to, what is now, a fairly horrendous array of diseases and viral infections.

The **WHO (World Health Organisation)** recommends up to one week's recovery time for very long haul flights, which is patently impossible for the already time pressured businessman. There has been much press coverage about the poor conditions aboard most aircraft these days, particularly relating to the transmission of infectious diseases and even blood clots. The latter is attributed to the overly cramped conditions and the reduction of individual space.

Be aware of physical hazards. The Yellow Pages guide to St. Petersburg in Russia gave a warning about 'unmarked and unprotected sidewalk hazards'. *"Be careful when walking on sidewalks for open stairwells, deep holes, iron bars sticking out from the walls and other hazards"*. Most street construction (holes etc) are poorly marked.

Moscow streets and sidewalks are often in a poor condition and snow only makes matters worse. Six or even eight lane roads and the speed of traffic only increase the safety issue.

Following the privatisation of British Airways (BA) some years ago, seat size went from 34 inches to 31 inches. Even young people are now reported as having blood clots resulting from flying. BA cabin staff, frightened to report their own health problems to their employer, also tell of increasing respiratory illnesses.

Fortunately travel sickness is rare in the case of air travel, but people who are having to travel in boats, especially small ones, and who have little boating experience are advised to take supplies of anti-seasickness drugs. Travel sickness drugs and others required on a regular basis should be carried in hand luggage and not stowed.

Heat and Humidity

Excessive heat and humidity, or over-exertion in these conditions, may lead to exhaustion from loss of fluid and salts leading to severe heat-stroke requiring medical attention. The answer is to keep one's fluid intake up in such conditions and I personally find that one doesn't need any rule of thumb as to how much fluid you should take in, as your body tells you - if you feel thirsty drink. If you are in hot climes never set out on any journey where you are not resourced with more than adequate supplies of bottled water. Dehydration has warning signs and include:

- extended periods without the need to urinate
- passing very dark, yellow urine
- lightheadedness and severe headaches

Remember you do not simply lose fluid, but also vital minerals and salts. Fluid replacement is best with drinks that are high in mineral salts (fruit and vegetable juices, clear soups etc). These are all recommended in cases of exhaustion. Unless contraindicated try and add a little table salt to food or drinks which can help to prevent heat exhaustion, especially during the period of acclimatisation.

In hot, humid conditions try and shower regularly to prevent any fungal skin infections taking hold. Loose cotton clothes and applying talc or Mycota type powder to sensitive areas will help to prevent or control the effects. Also be aware of sharp contrasts in temperature between day and night and prepare your wardrobe accordingly. Inappropriate dress can result in a susceptibility to colds, through sharp temperature fluctuations.

Altitude

This is not usually a problem for the business traveller and is usually an issue which needs consideration by the mountain trekker. On a mundane level altitude can give rise to insomnia and may be distressing for people with cardiac or pulmonary conditions. At high altitudes the risks increase dramatically with the possibility of acute pulmonary or cerebral oedema. These can cause a sensation of extreme faintness, accompanied by difficulty in breathing, dizziness, headaches and vomiting. Death can result unless the patient is removed to a lower altitude. Gradual adjustment by stages so as to acclimatise, is advised for any high altitude exposure.

A popular tourist destination, but one at altitude and one which can demand a degree of physical exertion to get around - not good combinations for the unfit or people with heart or respiratory problems.

Sun

There is enough warnings in the popular press about the cancer risk from over exposure to the sun's rays. Exposure to ultra-violet rays can produce severe and debilitating sun-stroke, especially in light skinned people. If you do want to expose yourself to the sun's rays, do it progressively, use a filter sun cream, wear sunglasses and don't ignore wearing a hat. There has been a growth in popularity of the sun filter shirts. It is not always the case that covering up prevents the damaging rays getting through and there is now clothing on the market which has a complete sun-block capability.

Traffic Accidents

Forget malaria, bilharzia and beri beri - traffic accidents are the leading cause of deaths among travellers. The more remote and poorly resourced the area the accident occurs in, the more likely it is to be fatal. Also regulations governing traffic and vehicle maintenance vary considerably from one country to another and that may be from poor to non-existent.

Setting Out

Before setting off on a vehicle journey, which may be to a remote or difficult region, carry out a Route Reconnaissance. You will not be able to physically 'Recce' the route but you can do it with maps and other resource data. You need to know hospitals, safe havens (police posts, army barracks), accident black spots, unmade sections, fuel stops, rest areas, general road state, proposed weather and whether there are any risks of banditry - if so, are these activities restricted only to the hours of darkness. Before setting out there should be a detailed vehicle and kit check.

Before you set off on your travels, try and find out whether doctors and hospitals will require immediate payment in cash for treatment, as many in fact do. Also establish what, in terms of medical kit, you should take with you e.g. syringes. If you will be abroad for some time, especially if you are accompanied by your family, then both you and your spouse should get some first aid training under your belts. It is a self-help society in many parts of the world.

If you do have any special medical condition get your Doctor or clinic to summarise the condition and to type it out for you on their letter head and sign it.

Prophylaxis ("preventative treatment against diseases").

Preventative treatment may take the form of vaccination or medication.

Vaccination

It is possible for travellers to be immunised against a certain number of diseases. Whether a person should be vaccinated will depend on many factors e.g. duration of stay, overall state of health, destination, type of travel and likely exposure risk given the nature of travel once 'in country'. Also critical is the time available to be vaccinated. If you are 'fast balled' to go abroad and could depart in two days then immunisation against some diseases will not be practical as they need ten days or two or more doses before becoming effective.

Don't be confused with vaccinations required in some countries by law for entry to their territory, vaccinations recommended by the WHO for general protection against certain diseases and other vaccinations which may be advisable in certain circumstances. Can I say, better to be safe than sorry. I adopt a 'belt and braces' approach to preventative treatment.

For many years international travellers would have been familiar with the International Certificate of Vaccination. Essentially this allowed one to have recorded one's vaccinations for say, smallpox and cholera, as well as yellow fever, but now the only certificate required would be The International Certificate for Vaccination or Revaccination in respect of Yellow Fever. Yellow fever is currently spreading in South America with suspected cases in Surinam and there are fears it could have reached the Caribbean.

What about the other two. Well the WHO officially confirmed, in the early 80's the eradication of Smallpox and that smallpox vaccination was "no longer required". With regard to Cholera this still remains a problem and will be looked at later in the chapter.

In the U.K. I would have to recommend you going to your General Practitioner (GP) for the necessary immunisations if it were a decision solely based on cost. Many of the treatments such as Polio, and Tetanus are free, contrasted with British Airways Travel clinic at £11 per treatment for these two. Commercial clinics will argue that your GP may not be up to date on the latest recommendations, but I have not found this to be the case. From your GP most vaccinations will simply cost the price of a prescription, yet a commercial clinic could be ten times this, as in the case of Hepatitis A. Often if vaccines are held at the GP's surgery there may not even be a prescription charge. The main advantage is that the GP has your medical records and can see at a glance what may be due or not.

Acting Sensibly

Two instances spring to mind. I read an account of the death of an Englishman who disappeared one night, whilst camping in the African bush. He was last seen by his African guards, who had gone off elsewhere, leaving him alone and cooking a meal next to the river they had camped alongside. They heard a scream and returned to find only one of his shoes floating in the river. The article went on to give the name of this body of water which was the 'Crocodile River'. Now maybe his guards didn't pass on the name of the river, but even so!

A second tragic death occurred in Australia, this time when two American female tourists, whilst on a boat trip some years ago, decide to go for a swim!. They were aware of the name of the lake they were on which, as with the first incident, was called 'Crocodile Creek'. One girl was taken under by the crocodile and killed.

I mention these incidents only to make the point that stupidity and ignorance are close bedfellows. A lake or river needn't have such an obvious descriptive name to be dangerous and essentially apply the rule - **High Risk** or **Unknown Risk** - ignorance is no excuse. In Africa, there are few bodies of water which are safe to swim, bathe or wade in. Not because something with big teeth has eyes on parts of your anatomy, but rather something which is very small, in the form of a parasite, has designs on your intestines, liver and urinary tact.

This is the Bilharzia parasite and it is a worm which penetrates the skin and causes damage to your internal organs. There is no vaccine, although the disease can be treated. Bilharzia is a widespread infection in Africa, the Middle East and parts of the Far East and S.America. Do not accept local advice that the water 'is safe' -don't wade, wash or swim even in the deepest parts of a lake. The cause of the problem is a blood fluke, which is passed in the form of eggs by human urine or faeces and which, in turn, infect snails in the water. Eventually these are released as larvae which penetrate even unbroken skin exposed to infected water.

Food Sense

In 99% of the Third World and 95% of the developed world avoid eating food from street vendors, cooked, raw or otherwise. Certainly in most Third World countries you should not entertain food which is not cooked in either your hotel, which I have to assume is of a reasonable standard, or from any cafe or restaurant which has not been recommended. If somewhere has been recommended, only accept that recommendation from someone you trust and exclude taxi drivers from this list.

Do not eat fruit unless you can peel it, as the water it has been washed in is likely to be contaminated. This applies to even 5 star hotels in some parts of the world. In St Petersburg in Russia, I will not even brush my teeth in the hotel tap water despite assurances as to the efficacy of their filtration system. The Guardia Lamblia virus which inhabits the water in St P. is virulent and extremely problematic if contracted. If water quality is an issue, then drink only bottled water, brush your teeth in the same and don't have ice in your drinks. It never fails to stagger me when I look around a bar in some places and see the number of people who have ice in their drinks - they seem not to have made the vital mental leap.

"**Be careful what you eat**", sounds simple, but few people today truly understand it's implications. Diarrhoea affects an estimated 20 -

50% of all travellers according to the WHO. It can cause everything from embarrassment and inconvenience through to the disruption and complete abandonment of travel plans. For vulnerable people it may be fatal - remember, in the last chapter we talked about 'impact factors' such as our general state of health prior to travelling.

The appearance of food is no guide to its safety and even contaminated food can appear appetising. Eating safely when travelling means not always being able to eat when, where and what one wants. Short lived episodes of diarrhoea effect up to 50% of travellers.

The WHO says that the main personal precaution is to consider unpasteurised milk, non-bottled drinks and uncooked food, apart from fruit or vegetable that can be peeled or shelled, as likely to be contaminated and therefore unsafe. Ice cream and home made mayonnaise also frequently constitute a danger. Even with cooked food, the traveller should ensure that the food has been thoroughly and freshly cooked i.e that it is piping hot! Cooked food which has been held at ambient temperatures (15 - 40 degrees) for some time (4 - 5 hrs) constitutes one of the greatest risks of food borne diseases, since contaminating bacteria may multiply in it.

Unpasteurised milk should be boiled and if at all possible drinking water, if suspect, should be boiled or chlorinated and filtered. Avoid ice unless you can guarantee it has been made from pure water. Wine, beer, hot tea, coffee and carbonated soft drinks or fruit juices that are bottled or otherwise packaged, are usually safe to drink. If you know in advance that daily water may be suspect, then go equipped with water disinfectant agents.

In certain places in the world at certain times of the year, various species of shellfish and fish contain poisonous biotoxins, even if cooked well. If you are ever in doubt about any food and are forced to consume it, then do so in the smallest proportions possible. Our stomach's gastric acid has some protective effect .

On a security point never accept food, sweets or drinks from strangers, particularly in places like Kenya as it could well be drugged.

Air Quality

Air quality is also important for those who suffer from respiratory illnesses, particularly asthma. I was recently working in Naples one summer and the air quality was simply dreadful. If you do have a problem make enquiries.

Drugs

The U.S.Department Of State - Bureau of Consular Affairs reports that in 1994, 2,500 Americans were arrested in 95 foreign countries. Of these, 880 ended up in jail abroad, many labouring under the incorrect assumption that they couldn't be arrested for drug possession . What they also soon realised is that there is very little anyone could do to help if caught with drugs. Some countries do not distinguish between possession and trafficking. People have also been arrested for possessing prescription drugs, particularly tranquillisers and amphetamines. Arrests have been made for prescription drugs in quantities which authorities suspect were for commercial use.

Any traveller must have a reasonable working knowledge of the drug laws of a country before they visit. At this point, if you are reading this in the U.K., don't believe that the British are any less ignorant of their position if arrested for drugs, than their American cousins and the last few years has produced a regular flow of Britons arrested in South East Asian countries for smuggling drugs. Irrespective of your nationally what every traveller must realise is that their respective consular office will be powerless to help. For example, any U.S consular office will visit one of their citizens in jail, ensure that the person obtains local rights under that country's laws and are treated humanely. All it can do in addition is give a list of local recommended lawyers and notify family and friends and relay requests for money - that's it.

Penal Systems

The Consular section of your Embassy cannot demand your release, act legally for you, represent you at trial and, in the case of the U.S. Government, cannot pay any fees or finds. What anyone who is thinking of transporting, buying or carrying drugs when abroad needs to know, is that the judicial systems of many Third World or developing countries, bears no resemblance to how we know it to be in the West. In Russia, many people who have been arrested, can spend longer on remand than the sentence would demand if and when they are eventually tried. They exist in overcrowded conditions which would horrify even the most hardened observer.

Even in a highly developed country like Japan, the penal system is one which brutalises it's inmates, where solitary confinement can mean staring at a brick wall in a cell for years, not just days. Recently, Japanese former prisoners have made claims for human rights abuses. Interrogation in many Third World countries amounts to torture and many have no bail allowed for drug offences, with sentences sometimes including life and the death penalty. This applies, for example, in such places as Saudi Arabia, Malaysia, Pakistan, Turkey and Thailand.

If the film 'Midnight Express', is anything to go by, then the death penalty would seem the 'sentence of preference' rather than spend some years in a Turkish jail. In general, trials can take years to happen, evidence collected illegally may be used against you and many countries do not have the luxury of trial by jury. Those countries which do not impose life or death sentences usually have a mandatory - without parole sentence for drug offences of 7 years.

So be advised **NEVER CARRY PACKAGES FOR ANYONE** where the contents remain unknown. Small amounts of proscribed drugs, even Marijuana may mean a sentence, equivalent in the West, to that which a large scale trafficker would receive.

Unintentional Possession

Don't forget the medicines you routinely use carry with you may be treated as illegal drugs when abroad. I repeat, when you are planning a trip abroad, do some research to establish whether there are any restrictions on taking the drug in and out of your home country and, of course, the country you are to visit. Check with the relevant Embassy or High Commission, or in the U.K the Home Office Drugs Branch.

Don't carry medicines loose in your toiletries bag. Keep them in a correctly labelled container which was issued by the pharmacist. Personally, I keep receipts for proprietary medicines I may be taking with me. If you are on prescribed drugs and you have some concerns, take a letter from your Doctor or a copy of your personal health record card in case it becomes an issue at Customs. Bear in mind that some medicines available over the counter in your own country may be controlled in other countries and vice versa.

I'm quite happy to go along with the first instruction and so should everyone, but what if you want that shower whilst lying in bed?!
A notice in the Galle Face hotel - Sri Lanka!

Lets look at some specific problem illnesses we may encounter on our travels:-

Cholera

Cholera is an acute diarrhoea type disease caused by the bacterium vibrio cholera. You can be infected by ingesting contaminated food or water and the risk is heightened if you are eating raw or improperly cooked food, raw fruit and vegetables and seafood. On occasions you may have been a victim of cholera without realising, as minor symptoms may be mild diarrhoea. At its worst, this is an acute diarrheal disease.

Often in the Third World, whole communities are subject to the debilitating infection where overpopulation, inadequate sanitation and polluted water supplies all contribute to the infection taking hold. Some people are chronic carriers and these may be the very people who you are tempted to buy some little morsel from.

If you have very watery and severe symptoms of diarrhoea and vomiting then matters can go from bad to worse pretty quickly. The large amount of fluid loss can take hold leading to severe dehydration and death, even as quickly as three to four hours, if suitable treatment is not sought or available where you are.

Cholera Vaccination

Whilst vaccination for cholera is available it gives at best only a half chance that it will provide some protection and only for up to three to six months. It was for this reason that in 1973 the WHO amended the International Health Regulations so that cholera vaccination should no longer be required by international travellers. Vaccination had done nothing to stop the spread of the infection from country to country and no country now officially requires a vaccination certificate from travellers. Beware though of the 'extortion' demands for unofficial jabs at borders. It may be worth considering having the jab at home so as to obtain the certificate.

If you have had a cholera vaccination do not for one minute let your guard down and labour under the incorrect assumption that you can eat and drink with impunity. Personaly, I do not have a cholera vaccination for that very reason. I rely on good sound, common sense and ensure that I have left these shores with a good supply of rehydration salts. Dioralyte or a chemist's own brand are ideal and come in one of my favourite flavours blackcurrant.

At the slightest sign of diarrhoea I will take some salts to keep the fluid balance. If you do have problems and symptoms are severe seek medical attention, but in the interim get plenty of fluid and salt replacement down you. Severe cases will require an intravenous rehydration, but if it is going to be some time before you can get to help then help yourself. Antibiotics can shorten the illness, but anti-diarrhoea medicines such as loperamide are not recommended by the WHO. The common name is **Imodium** or **Arett.** Long term use of **Loperamide** should be avoided, but anyone who has planned a long car or bus journey, with little prospect of relief and has any diarrhoea, will welcome the blocking action of this and other drugs such as **diphenoxylate (Lomatil).**

The problem is the long term build up of toxins within the system with prolonged use of these drugs. Do not be tempted to buy anti-diarrhoea drugs abroad. There are preparations which have been linked with severe side effects. Take advice from your Doctor or travel clinic and take any medicines recommended with you.

The Rules :-

◆ Avoid ice, unless you are sure it is made from safe water

◆ Eat food that has been thoroughly cooked and is still hot when served. Cooked food that has been held at room temperature for several hours and served without being reheated can be a serious source of infection

◆ Avoid raw seafood and other raw foods, except fruit and vegetable that you have peeled or shelled yourself. Remember **Cook It, Peel It or Leave It !**

◆ Boil unpasteurised milk before drinking it. Apart from cholera drinking unpasteurised milk can be the cause of some very serious intestinal problems.

◆ Ice Cream from unreliable sources is often contaminated and can cause illness. If in any doubt avoid it.

◆ Be sure that any meals bought from street vendors are thoroughly cooked in your presence and do not contain any uncooked foods. If you have any doubts about the hygiene of the vendor or the operation pass by!

One doesn't have to have Cholera to experience diarrhoea type illness. Every corner of the world has it's own little indigenous, loose bowel speciality. If one is away on business for only a few days there is not the license to spend two days in bed whilst the problem runs it's course. If you are prone to such problems then you may need to consider a prescription for antibiotics to take just in case. This would not be recommended under normal circumstances. We mentioned proprietary treatments earlier on and again they should be used sparingly. Fluid and salt replacement and, if possible, rest are the primary means of treatment. Prolonged use of medications can cause an unhealthy build up of toxins in the body.

Tuberculosis

Not many years ago the West was prematurely, as it turned out, patting itself on the back for it's eradication of tuberculosis (TB). Now, though, we are being told it is the most potent of threats to our health. In many rural Russian towns TB has reached epidemic proportions, with whole families victims of this debilitating condition. TB in a family means isolation for the parents from the children and loss of employment for the breadwinner. The subsequent loss of income means a falling living standard, poor diet, poor sanitary conditions, falling local levels of taxation resulting in ever worsening health services and supply of medication and with it the loss of an individual's ability to break out of the downward spiral. Travellers to rural areas of Russia need to be aware of these conditions and the possible problems.

TB is likely to become a scourge of Western nations, carried by business travellers, holidaymakers, immigrants, refugees and asylum seekers. It is reported that 20 of the 27 countries in Central and Eastern Europe and the former Soviet Union are seeing what has been described as an 'uncontrollable resurgence' of TB. Later in this chapter we look at how the deteriorating quality of air in aircraft cabins is a cause of the spread of this infection.

In Chapter 3 we looked at the importance staying out of foreign jails and if there was ever a compelling reason for staying out of a Russian jail it would be TB. More than 20,000 prisoners are reported to have died of TB in the last 2 years, with some 100,000 sick with the disease. They are dying form a highly contagious and virtually incurable strain caused by only rudimentary health care and inadequate treatment. Prisoners take antibiotics until the symptoms are reduced, but fail to complete the course and barter the remaining drugs, leaving them with a highly contagious, multi-drug resistant TB (MDR-TB). It is reported to be one hundred times more expensive to treat than normal TB.

Eradication is only possible by treatment under the DOTS (Directly Observed Short Course) protocol, but as a practise this protocol has not been adopted by the Russian health authorities and is only practised in a few, trial areas by Medicins Sans Frontieres. It is said that TB thrives on poverty and it's spread throughout Russia, outside it's prisons is, therefore, assured. It is estimated that some 200 million worldwide could contract the disease by 2020 and some of the worst affected areas will be those popular business and holiday destinations. They will include regions of Brazil, Mexico, India, Indonesia and South Africa. Don't think it will be a Third World problem. From its eradication nearly 40 years ago it is expected that in 1999 there will be some 6,000 cases in Britain with London showing a 100% increase in the last decade.

Malaria

Malaria has, over the years resisted all efforts to eradicate it. Not only has it resisted efforts to eradicate it, it has fought back by adapting to and becoming resistant to anti-malarial drugs. There has been a marked rise in the number of visitors returning to the U.K from East

Africa having contracted malaria. Set against an average number of 29 for the first quarter for the past four years, 1998 saw some 154 cases in the period. This has been laid at the door of a reluctance to prescribe **mefloquine (Larium)**, particularly to short-term travellers. Of the cases reported, 68 people took no prophylaxis, 39 took **proguanil** and **chloroquine** and 3 took **mefloquine.**

If you're planning on a Safari style trip, be prepared for some very basic conditions........

A protazoal parasitic blood infection, transmitted by the bite of the female Anopheline mosquito, mostly between sunset and sunrise, it is a common and serious tropical disease. This mosquito can smell human blood form about a range of 200 miles or so it seems. It is nothing if not single minded when it comes to seeking out and biting humans.

Malaria itself seems almost intelligent in it's ability to change and survive all that modern science has thrown at it over many years.

..............particularly when you get inside the tent!!

It is still the single most costly infection with indigenous populations in those areas where it has a strong grip - Central Africa, Asia, S.America. In many areas such as the Eastern Mediterranean, some countries of Asia and South America where there is Malaria, it is not usually to be found in the urban areas, whereas this is not true of India and many urban areas of Africa. Broadly the malaria mosquito is not to be found above 1,500 metres, although in very hot, climatic conditions it has been known up to 3,000 metres. The particular season of the year has a lot to do with the potential to contract the infection and take advice before you go.

Human malaria is caused by four species of Plasmodium - Plas falciparum, P. vivax, P. ovale, P. malariae. For people who travel to infected areas there is a high risk of contracting the infection. The WHO advises that in excess of 10,000 people fall ill with Malaria each year upon returning home and about 1% of people who contract P. Falciparum die. In Britain between 5 and 15 people die each year. It is believed that most of these deaths could be prevented by earlier diagnosis and treatment.

One problem with malaria is it's incubation period which, after a bite, may vary from 8 to 10 days, but cases have been known to emerge months after the return, at which time it is hard to relate feverish symptoms to the trip abroad many weeks ago. Often at this time scale the symptoms are incorrectly diagnosed as flu, stomach infection or the like. Headaches, fever, non-specific aches and pains lead the diagnosis away from the cause if information is not provided by the patient that he or she has within the past twelve months returned from a malaria area. If you have and you have a fever, then you need a blood test. The other three forms of malaria are seldom life threatening, although the incubation period could be as long as 24 months. The problem of malaria is getting worse and both prevention and treatment are becoming more difficult due to the resistance of the parasite to drugs. This resistance is spreading.

Protective Measures

The first step in the battle with this and any other tropical disease or infection is knowledge. Knowledge about the level of the problem in the area of your intended trip. You need to know the malaria risk - that is the type of malari and, whether it is one of the benign varieties or the malignant falciparum and any information as to the resistance the infection has developed in that region.

For example the WHO reported on:-

Sudan: malaria risk - *predominantly in the malignant (P. falciparum) form - exists throughout the year in the whole country. Highly chloroquine-resistant P.falciparum reported.*

Sri Lanka: malaria risk - *predominantly in the benign (P.vivax) form - exists throughout the year in the whole country excluding the districts of Columbia, Kalutara, and Nuwara Eliya. Highly chloroquine resistant P.falc reported.*

So you can see the level of information available, both with regard to the areas, types and resistance. The next example gives even more detail.

Thailand: malaria risk - *exists throughout the year in rural, especially forested areas of the whole country. There is no risk in cities and the main tourist resorts e.g. Bangkok, Chiangmai, Pattaya, Phuket. P.falciparum highly resistant to chloriquine and to sulfadoxine-pryimethamine reported. Resistance to mefloquine and to quinine reported from areas near to the borders with Cambodia and Myanmar.*

Your Doctor will be able to find out which vaccination is best for you and the circumstances.

1. The first line of defence against malaria is - **not getting bitten.** Easier than it sounds, but as a first rule try and avoid going out between dusk and dawn when mosquito commonly bite. This is not a rule, as you can be bitten at any time of the day.

2. Any exposed skin should be treated with an insect repellent and one which contains **diethyltoluamide (DEET)**, or the more modern eucalyptus based e.g. ***Mosiguard.*** A new range of anti-mosquito sprays and creams are available called ***Autan Active***, containing a new non-DEET formula using **Bayrepel** - a new ingredient that claims to offer greater protection and lasts for 8 hours. It comes in body spray, pump spray and stick formats.

3. Wear long sleeved tops and long trousers when going out at night and, generally, the advice is to avoid wearing dark clothes which attract the insect. Clothing can also be treated with repellent

4. Sleep in properly 'screened' rooms, which itself should be well-constructed and well-maintained in the most developed part of town. If there are no screens over the windows then all doors and windows to be closed at night.

5. If there are no screens use a good quality net over the bed, well tucked in and impregnated with **permethrin**. Both the net over the bed, if there is one, should have no holes as with the window screens.

6. If you are in any doubt about the room use an anti-mosquito spray, or the mains or battery type regulated dispenser. The slow burning pyrethroid coils work, whilst the electric buzzers are ineffective.

Anti-Malarial Drugs

No anti-malarial drugs give complete protection and the price paid can be very uncomfortable side effects. I was told the story whilst in Uganda of a very senior female business representative who whilst making a trip to the region wrecked her room in the hotel and attacked staff in a near berserk rage. She had to be evacuated from the country, much to everyone's embarrassment. The cause was found to be the anti-malarial drug she had been taking, generically - **mefloquine**. The common trade name you will find as ***Larium*** or ***Mephaquin*** and it has developed somewhat of a reputation for it's range of side effects. Broadly it should not be prescribed for those people who have a propensity to depression, anxiety attacks, or mood swings and by people who have a history of epilepsy, or where there is a family history of the illness. Pregnant women in the first twelve weeks, people with high blood pressure and anyone whose work will demand a high level of co-ordination.

Always start your treatment 2/3 weeks before the trip so you can measure the extent, if any, of the side effects you may be susceptible to. Apart from going berserk, Mefloquine can cause nausea, diarrhoea, dizziness, abdominal pain, rashes and skin itching, with possible headaches and sleep disturbance.

Personally I find little side effect with mefloquine, save a very demanding thirst, which passes after a while. I find the discipline of only taking the tablet once a week a boon, unlike some other prophylaxis, which is required daily. People should not be scared away from taking a course of mefloquine if they are travelling to areas where there is widespread chloroquine resistance, which would include most of Sub-Saharan Africa, the Amazon basin and many parts of South East Asia.

The oldest and most frequently used drugs have been the generic named **chloroquine** and **proguanil (Paludrine)**. They are certainly more benign to take than the mefloquine based anti-malarials, but there is now considerable resistance to these drugs in many parts of the world. There can be a reaction to this combination in the form of nausea or stomach upsets. Normally they will be prescribed together. Proguanil, has less side effects than mefloquine, but there may be occasional problems with anorexia and there can be nausea, diarrhoea and mouth ulcers. Chloroquine can cause nausea and diarrhoea, but the effects can be reduced by taking it after a meal. Itchy skin, rashes, headaches and blurred vision are sometimes reported and if these occur consider changing the type of tablets. Years of use is known to cause eye problems.

Treatment Regime

All anti-malaria treatment should be started one week or more before the trip and continued for four weeks after the return to cover the period of incubation of the parasite in the Liver. Following a bite by an infected mosquito the process is that the parasite will travel to the hosts liver via the bloodstream, where it will incubate, later to emerge and attack the red blood cells, hence the need to maintain the treatment following return from abroad.

Some anti-malarial prophylaxis, such as chloroquine, may also be prescribed as a treatment for malaria once contracted, although not proguanil. Other treatments are sulfadoxine-pryrimathemine, doxycycline, quinine, and also mefloquine, but as you can see from the extracts of the WHO advisory on Thailand, resistance has not only developed to prophylaxis, but also to the range of treatments.

In fact in areas of Thailand near the border with Cambodia, P. falciparum infections do not respond to treatment with many drugs and failures of over 50% with mefloquine are being reported. In areas of chloroquine resistant P falciparum you may also be advised to take **pyrimethamine-dapsone (Maloprim)** plus chloroquine or doxycycline as an alternative to mefloquine.

The whole area of obtaining suitable treatment is complex and fraught with choices, so get advice and make sure you are certain that the advice given is correct. If in doubt double check. I have found many General Practitioners are sometimes ignorant of the complexities of the issues involved, particularly in areas not commonly travelled to.

Things That Bite

Insects

Many anthropods transmit communicable diseases such as: malaria (Anapholese mosquito), yellow fever, dengue and dengue haemorrhagic fever (Aedes, Haemogogus and Sabethes mosquito), viral encaphalitides (Culex and Anapholese mosquito, ticks), including Japanese encaphilitis (in China, India, Japan, Laos, Myanmar, Nepal, Phillipines, Korea, Sri Lanka, Thailand, Vietnam), African trypanosmiasis (tsetse flies), plague and tungiasis (fleas), typhus (fleas, mites, ticks, lice), and Lyme disease (ticks). The list goes on and it pays not to be too narrow minded when it comes to the insect repellent and the common sense use of clothing, as mentioned earlier.

Don't think that you need to be somewhere exotic to catch insect transmitted diseases. Tick-borne encephalitis can be contracted by ramblers in certain forested areas of Scandinavia, Central and Eastern Europe and Russia. Lyme disease has effected forestry and estate workers in Scotland for some years now.

Mosquitoes can be a problem in other less suspect places such as Australia. Although there is no malaria in the country there has been a growth in the range of viral diseases spread by mosquito. Known as arboviruses, they may cause dengue, Japanes encephalitis and murray valley encephalitis. Although incidents are quite low, take the usual precautions so as not to get bitten.

Dengue Fever (DF)

The World Health Organisation reckons that the incidence of DF has exploded from 30,000 cases reported a year in the 1960's, to a staggering 20 million today.

The growth is in the urbanising areas of Asia, particularly in the increasingly popular holiday destinations of Laos, Cambodia, Vietnam, Malaysia (42.4% increase in 1998). This caused people to store water in containers, making an ideal breeding ground) with cases in Haiti, Puerto Rico, Cuba and even Cairns in Queensland, Australia. Even the clinical Singapore has reported 4,300 cases in 1997. In the first four months of 1998 there were some 1,786 cases reported almost double that in the same period the previous year.

The disease peaks in the wet season (usually June to November). It is viral so antibiotics are useless and a vaccination is years away. It has a short incubation period and those who contract it will usually do so while they are abroad. It used to be called 'breakbone fever' with painful joints, a rash, headache and high fever. The treatment is painkillers and inactivity. The malarial anti-avoidance routines of not getting bitten that were described above apply equally in the prevention of DF. The only difference you should be aware of is that the Aedes mosquito doesn't just bite at night, but is active just after dawn and before dusk, but will lie in wait in any shady place. They thrive in unsanitary and squalid Third World urban sprawls, where they breed in stagnant pools of water.

The good news is that DF is rarely fatal, however the variant dengue haemorrhagic fever is and involves serious bleeding and very low blood pressure. Again the cure is not to get bitten.

HIV/AIDS

It has to be said at this juncture that there is no evidence that **human immunodeficiency virus (HIV)**, the causative agent of **acquired immunodeficiency syndrome (AIDS)**, is transmitted by insects. We will look at this subject in more detail later.

Things Bigger Than Insects

It is sensible to keep out of the way of anything with teeth and fangs. Most animals will avoid contact with humans but it can't be guaranteed and I strenuously recommend when abroad that you keep well away from animals, domestic or otherwise. In areas of endemic **Rabies**, dogs and cats should not be petted and contact with wild animals, especially bats, foxes, jackals, skunks, raccoons and mongooses, as well as domestic and wild monkeys should be avoided.

Find out which animals are likely to be Rabies carriers in the areas you will visit and no animal bite should be ignored and after cleansing the wound with soap and an antiseptic, professional opinion should be sought as to the possibility of Rabies in the area. Rabies infected animals may be encountered in all countries, with the exception of the following: Australia, Bermuda, many of the Caribbean islands (but not, Cuba, Haiti, Grenada, Puerto Rico or Trinidad), Gibraltar, Iceland, Japan, Malta, New Zealand, Norway, the Pacific Islands, Papua New Guinea, Portugal, Sweden, and the United Kingdom.

It is possible to have a pre-exposure immunisation, before you travel but this is only recommended for those who may be exposed to a higher than normal risk e.g. spending more than one month in a country where rabies is a constant threat, travelling in such a country in a remote area for an extended period and away from medical care, such as trekking.

Be advised that pre-exposure vaccination does not eliminate the requirement for prompt treatment if bitten by a Rabies suspect animal, it simply reduces the post-exposure regimen. When you get to medical help ask for 'human diploid cell vaccine'. If in the case of difficulty contact the British Consul. If the animal was domestic inform the authorities who should keep the animal under observation. Endeavour to obtain the name and contact number of the owner so that if you are to come home you can keep in contact to establish whether the animal becomes ill or not.

Hepatitis

Viral Hepatitis is an infection of the liver which can cause jaundice and we are all probably aware that there are, in the main, three distinct forms we should be aware of. These are hepatitis A,B and C. **Hepatitis A virus (HAV)**, is a water-borne infection and is usually caught by taking in contaminated food or water. It can also be passed from person to person as it is present as a virus in faeces. Anywhere that basic sanitation is a problem you are exposed to the risk of hepatitis and after an incubation period of between three to six weeks you could suffer from the jaundice like conditions for many weeks.

One needs to be scrupulous with personal hygiene in such locations, particularly after visiting the toilet. All the rules we covered earlier in the chapter about the protective measures for cholera apply equally as well for the prevention of hepatitis. The prophylactic measure for many years has been through the process of immunisation with a gammagobulin injection, although the effects are short lived - approximately three months, protection is not one hundred percent and supplies may not be available unless you have organised matters well in advance of your trip.

If you are travelling to problem parts regularly or you will be away for some time then vaccination will be more appropriate with the HAV vaccine which became available in Europe in 1992. With a booster after one year, protection can be for up to ten years. It takes ten days for the vaccine to be effective so plan if you can. There is also a combined new vaccine called Twinrix, which provides protection for both hepatitis A and hepatitis B.

Hepatitis B, is, like AIDS, a sexually transmitted virus and the spread would be through:

- sharing a contaminated needle
- sex
- a contaminated blood transfusion

The symptoms are similar, but more severe than hepatitis A and can lead in some cases to liver damage. There is a specific vaccine for hepatitis B, but it can take up to six months to be fully effective and requires three separately spaced injections.

Anyone who is planning to be away for some length of time would be well advised to go for the vaccination. Don't ignore, however, the application of good common sense. That having been said, hepatitis B is the only sexually transmitted infection for which there is a protective vaccine.

As a cautionary note about sex abroad, many bacterial infections, such as gonorrhoea and syphilis, are showing increased resistance to penicillin and other anti-microbials for sexually transmitted viral infections e.g hepatitis B, genital herpes, or genital warts, treatment is inadequate or non-existent.

Finally in the case of **hepatitis C**, there is no vaccination for the virus, spread in the same way as HIV/AIDS and hepatitis B. The only way to be safe is to be cautious.

The list unfortunately goes on and any traveller to Sub-Saharan Africa and parts of India and Asia will need to be vaccinated for **Typhoid, Tetanus** and even **Meningitis.** The latter may only be required if you plan to stay for some time in the area where infection is indicated. **Poliomyletis, Japanese Encaphalaitis** and as we mentioned previously **Tuberculosis**, you will also need advice on as well as **Yellow Fever.** Typhoid has been identified as one of the biggest killers in Papua New Guinea and is most common in the Highland region.

A **Yellow Fever International Certificate** is provided following vaccination at a designated Yellow Fever Vaccination Centre and in the U.K. this includes many G P's. Contracted in areas of Africa and South and Central America the virus is transmitted by the bite of an infected mosquito and can lead to a lethal form of hepatitis. The certificate is valid for ten days from vaccination and lasts for ten years and will be required for entry in numerous countries if you have travelled from an infected area.

The vaccine has almost total efficacy, while the case fatality rate for the disease is more than 60% in adults who are not immune and tolerance to the present vaccine is excellent. Take advice on the requirement for the vaccination if you are travelling to countries designated as yellow fever endemic zones. However, it is recognised that the risk of yellow fever for international travellers is low, particularly for those who limit their travel to urban areas. However, in recent years, fatal cases of yellow fever have occurred in unvaccinated tourists visiting rural areas, due in the main to actual areas of infection not being reported.

HIV/AIDS

In a nutshell, don't have sex with anyone other than your usual partner. AIDS is a worldwide problem, but in places like Africa it has reached the most dreadful proportions. In fact, most of the world's 33.5 million Aids cases are in Sub-Saharan Africa, with an additional 4 million infected each week.

In 1999 the U.N. revealed that AIDS causes more deaths than any other infectious disease and the epidemic, almost of plague proportions, is still not at it's peak. By January 2000 the AIDS epidemic will have claimed 15 million lives and left 40 million living with the viral infection that is slowly eroding their immune system. Some countries in Africa where populations were booming only a few years ago, will soon see such growth cease, as death rates from the disease soar. We are told that in some countries, one quarter of the population are HIV positive. Don't believe either that these are the people at the poorest end of the social spectrum as the problem increasingly includes the middle classes and professionals.

The U.N. report by the WHO, revealed that in the past year AIDS had replaced TB as the world's most deadly infectious disease. In fact, it is now the world's fourth biggest killer after non-infectious heart disease, strokes and acute respiratory diseases - leading to nearly 3 million deaths worldwide in 1998. It is now the biggest single cause of death in Africa. Even in South Africa there is estimated to be some 580,000 new cases each year and a life expectancy reduced to only age 38 by the year 2010.

There are some 2.2 million AIDS orphans in the country and companies are losing 3% of their work force to the disease.

One quarter of the population of Zimbabwe and Botswana are HIV positive and one in five of the population suffers similarly in Namibia, Zambia and Swaziland (in the U.S. the figure is 0.7 percent, while in Europe it is 0.23 percent). Another report by the Worldwatch Institute in Washington says that death rates are rising so fast in Zimbabwe that the once rapid population growth will come to a halt over the next 3 years. Some 2 million out of 11 million - one in four adults in Zimbabwe is HIV positive, with 1,200 dying each week.

According to the World Bank, by 2005 half of all skilled people in Malawi's towns and cities will have perished and nearly 15,000 teachers are expected to die from the disease in Tanzania by 2010. The epidemic in these countries is now beginning to rival the Black Death which killed 20 million people in Europe in the 14th century.

The big problem to watch out for now is Asia and the Far East e.g China. The rate of growth of the problem in East Asia and the Pacific has grown by 460% from 1996 to 1998 with Eastern Europe and Central Asia not far behind at 440%. That having been said East Asia and the Pacific have approximately 560,000 recorded cases against 22,500,000 in Sub-Saharan Africa.

It remains to be seen what will happen to the massive populations of India and China, as India now has some 4 million HIV positive cases and China some half a million now infected. A massive explosion could take the figures to astronomic proportions.

You can ignore these chilling facts at your peril. If you do have sex with a stranger in certain geographies it is roulette and simply put you are playing with your life as the stakes. Tourists and business travellers from the U.K have been infected during short trips to Europe and other overseas destinations.

There is no vaccination nor any cure for either HIV or the full blown AIDS which may follow from it. It is a lifetime illness and can be passed in four main ways:

- unprotected sex with an infected person
- through infected needles, such as medical and dental or tattooing needles.
- transfusions of infected blood
- from an infected mother to her baby.

If sex is on the menu then you are embarking on Russian Roulette if you do not use a condom. Take them with you and don't rely on Third World quality control, by buying them abroad.

Screened and Couriered Blood

We have mentioned earlier the advisability of taking both sterile needles and syringes, within a medical pack. Be aware, though that many countries will frown on these unless they are part of a suitably marked HIV/AIDS prevention kit. Travellers should consider obtaining membership of the **Blood Care Foundation** (through **MASTA**), a charity operating a courier service, supplying screened blood world-wide in the event of an injury or illness. Call the **MASTA Travellers Health Line** on **44(0)9068224100**. They also have a range of travel health products and to find out more telephone **44(0)1132387575.**

As a broad summary of the vaccinations, it is a good idea, if you have not previously been immunised against **diphtheria, polio** or **tetanus,** to have these done, irrespective of where you are travelling to. For those areas where you know hygiene and sanitation standards are below par, the hepatitis A and typhoid are recommended. For infected areas yellow fever and anti-malarial tablets and protection against insect bites. With everything else carry out your own research to confirm what your doctor or travel clinic advise.

Medical Kits

On some occasions whilst running Executive Protection details, we may determine it is necessary to take abroad with us, a fairly comprehensive first aid bag. For the average traveller something of this size and complexity would be excessive, but if you are stationed abroad and in a Third World environment then you should try and build up a reasonably comprehensive medical kit, without it being unmanageable.

If evacuation is likely to be an issue then you should maintain 2 first aid kits. It is no good if you suddenly need items from an evacuation kit only to find it has been appropriated for general use. Wherever we travel and for however long we should always take a minimum amount of first aid equipment. This may only amount to some plasters, analgesics, travel sickness tablets and some rehydration sachets. The kit, in it's basic form should contain aspirin or acetaminophen for pain or fever, antibiotics, re-hydration salts, insect repellant and sunscreen. Antihistamine can be used to ease insect bites or stings and can also be used as a decongestant for colds, allergies and to prevent motion sickness. In the U.K., the most common brands are piriton and triludan.

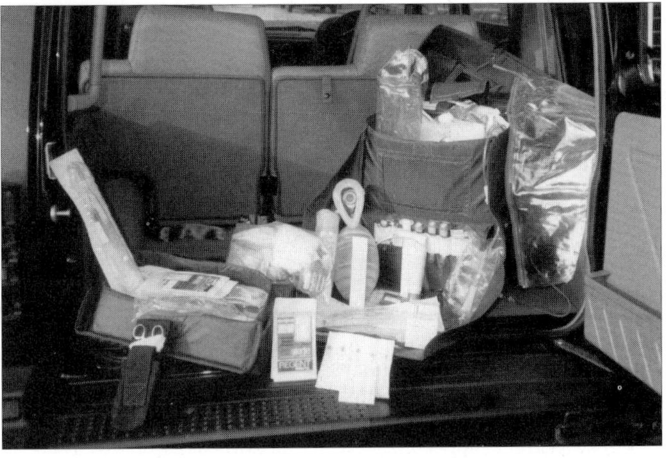

A very comprehensive vehicle medical kit which would be required if you were in a remote location. It contains, amongst other things, endo-trachial tubes, fluid and an intravenous giving set.

Obviously, the extent of the kit you put together will depend very much on what your research tells you about your destination, what you intend to be doing and the length of your stay. There are two aspects to the kit - what you take and how you pack it. If you are planning on taking a comprehensive one you may need to split it into two. If part of your kit is designed for hepatitis B/HIV prevention, so that medical staff have clean needles to use you will need to have this with you at all times, particularly if you have an accident. It is obviously not possible if you are seriously injured to make a detour back to the hotel to pick up this bit of your medical kit. So what choices do you have.

The first choice is to buy a prepackaged kit. There are many available and in the U.K. most are available from the better outdoor/camping shops. The second option is to put your own together, the only downside being you also have to find a suitable carry bag. If this latter option has appeal, then try using one of the complimentary toilet bags you may have received over the years in business class. Most are fairly durable, about the right size and often compartmented. The 'off the shelf' kits can be either general or specifically AIDS prevention ones.

Don't ever carry any loose, unidentified pills. Always have pills either in blister packs or in prescription bottles and make sure you keep the cotton wool or tissue in the bottle, so that they don't break up.

Consider the following as options you may feel you should have with you:

Adhesive plasters, antiseptic wipes, micropore tape, paracetamol, wound dressing, triangular bandage, rehydration sachets, loperamide for diarrhoea, an antihistamine (chlorpheninamine), fungal infection (miconazole), lacto-calamine, iodine tincture for water purification, spoon for rehydration solutions, crepe bandage, suntan cream. One of the best anti-fungal creams is canestan and can now be obtained over the counter.

Taking the contents a stage further, you may also want to include items for anti-infection. Remember others are likely to be using this kit and there is a presumption that they know how. One of the proprietary brands provides with their kit an instruction card in eight languages. The following are what you may need to pack in addition to a basic first aid kit:

Syringes (at least 2), needles (at least 5, including a dental one), an intravenous cannula, silk suture, injection swabs, skin closure strips, non-adhesive dressing and tape. Additional items could be, **latex gloves, scissors, fine forceps, antiseptic spray and gauze swabs.**

Depending on how you will pack the kit you need to ensure if you have needles that these and the other anti-infection items are contained in a plastic or other firm container. Kit and the absence of training do not go well together. Even if you only have some basic first aid training then it's better than nothing. If you are planning on some remote location then you will need more. If your employer is planning on sending you to some far flung corner of the world then demand they put you through a course on wilderness first aid, if the process is not already in place.

In the U.K there are a number of very good schools available, but selection of the most suitable is a difficult proposition, particularly for companies. For advice telephone **Chase Consultants Limited on 44 (0) 113 2443109, 51- 53 Unity Business Centre, 26, Roundhay Rd, Leeds LS7 1AB, UK.**

Air Travel & Health

Remember if you are going to fly and you have any pre-existing medical problems such as heart and chest problems, recurrent blood clots in the lungs or legs, recent strokes, uncontrollable blood pressure, epilepsy, chronic sinus or ear problems then consult your doctor.

If you have any complaints such as a metal hip replacement you should carry a doctors certificate to show customs officials, as the hip will set off metal detectors. Pacemakers are not likely to be effected by detection devices, if they are of good quality and well maintained (the detection devices that is). If you are not sure ask for a body check, but have the certificate to back up the request. On a general point, if you do have a chronic illness, wear a 'medic-alert' bracelet .

Blood Clots

Deep Vein Thrombosis (DVT) would seem to be an increasing, despite what airlines like British Airways may state. They reject any link between seat size, space and blood clots. An inability to move one's lower limbs can result in poor venous return which can cause a clot, in other words - prolonged inactivity. At it's worst the clot can move through the body and lodge in the lungs causing a pulmonary embolism, resulting in severe chest pains and possibly death.

We can take measures to help ourselves and one of the first is to try and be somewhat active. Take the pressure off your thighs from the seat and occasionally squeeze the muscles, rotate the feet and move about. Avoid getting de-hydrated as in this condition your blood thickens, which may mean restricting your intake of alcohol. Always drink plenty of water on a flight. There are some experts now who estimate that one in 20 passengers can be affected by DVT.

Often, in the past, referred to as 'economy class syndrome', it is now recognised that a person can also be at risk in any other section of the aircraft. In October 2000 a British woman Emma Christofferson, 28, died shortly after taking a flight home from Australia and another woman in her 40's suffered a fatal pulmonary embolism during an 11 hour flight between Johannesburg and London. A consultant at Britain's Ashford hospital, which receives emergency cases from Heathrow airport, was reported in Time magazine as estimating that DVT may affect as many as 2,000 travellers in the U.K each year and that some 15 die from DVT developed on long-haul flights. It will come as no surprise that airlines refute the connection between cabin conditions and DVT, but the WHO is convening a meeting of scientists and industry representatives to study in detail all evidence.

It should be mentioned that those people who have a predisposition to developing DVT whilst travelling, will be those who have suffered from previous incidents of thrombosis. Age is also a factor and doctors suggest for those people who are most at risk that they consider an injection of anti-coagulant within 24 hours prior to flying, whilst a lesser preventative action may be to take aspirin prior to take off, unless you are pregnant. Movement is the key, however, when you are in your seat and some limited exercises all help, as does keeping your water intake up and alcohol down.

Radiation

It is reported that airline crews and passengers receive bigger doses than the general population and exposure can rise from 100 to 300 times that at sea level. In simple terms this is because at high altitudes the Earth's atmosphere is thinner and offers less protection. The radiation dose also varies with geographical latitude. The further north the aircraft and the closer to the Poles, the higher the radiation doses. New research into the biological effects of ionising radiation is continuing, but, as yet there is no firm thinking from airlines or regulators about a solution, although from 2000 all passenger aircraft will be legally required to measure cosmic radiation levels and crew will have regular medicals.

The problem is thought so serious that the **European Commission**, which initiated the research will run education seminars with the **Aviation Health Institute in Oxford** to alert large corporations to the health risks to executives who fly regularly. A **Professor Dudley Goodhead** who runs one of the world's leading radiation and genome units, reports that ions can cause a wide spectrum of damage to the

DNA, cause genetic mutations in human egg cells and sperm cells. Cancers occur in single cells that experience multiple changes and as radiation problems are dosage related, the more one flys the greater the risk.

The average person in the U.K. receives an annual, background dose of 2.6 millisieverts (mSv) of ionising radiation a year. By contrast, air crew and some frequent flyers, are at the top of the tree of the occupational exposure league at some 4.6 mSv a year, compared with workers in nuclear plants who receive 3.6mSv. The annual limit for nuclear plant workers in Europe is 20 mSv a year, whereas 6mSv is the limit for air crew. A frequent flyer on conventional transatlantic routes between London and the east coast of the States may spend some 700 hours in the air. It is estimated this person will receive an annual dose of 5.6mSv, including the average dose of background radiation.

A **Wallace Friedburg**, of the **Federal Aviation's, Civil Aeromedical Institute**, says this represents 170 x-rays a year (based on 4.1 hours at 37,000 feet, equalling one chest x-ray). By comparison, the average dose received from cosmic radiation on the ground in Britain is equivalent to 13 x-rays a year. Hans-Georg Menzel, from the European Commission's radiation protection research unit says that frequent fliers to New York or Tokyo, who notch up 500 hours will be very close to the recommended dose. Menzel, who was a co-author of a report made following a study with 3 airlines, which covered a wide range of international routes concluded that *"all frequent fliers should be registered in the same way as aircrew, Some businessmen will fly more than crew. Cancers in some people can be instigated by exposure to cosmic radiation".*

One study, carried out by the American government claimed there was a higher risk of cancer for air crews, frequent fliers and pregnant women. In fact, the transportation department predicted that among 100,000 crew members who flew 960 hours a year, about 30 additional cases of cancer would occur, compared with the numbers expected in a typical section of the population.

Similarly, a study of Finnish aircraft crew, who were exposed to half the recommended cosmic radiation dose every year, showed that female workers had a two fold risk of developing breast cancer and a 15 fold increased risk of developing bone cancer. Typically, a British Airways spokesman stated *"there is no medical evidence of any adverse health effects for long-haul flight crew which could be related to cosmic exposure".* The Finnish study was with 1,577 female flight attendants working for Finnair between 1940 and 1992. If that isn't medical evidence, I don't know what is.

In truth there is little airlines can do to improve matters. Ionising radiation can be stopped from penetrating the body only by a thick shield of lead, concrete or water. James Curies the Commission's director general for environment, nuclear safety and civil protection, did suggest that manufacturers could try designing aircraft with greater fuel efficiency at lower altitudes - some hope! (PC).

It is probably up to ourselves and to our employers to design some risk-reduction strategies and the best that we could hope for would be to make some reduction in the hours we spend on long-haul flights. Executives need to be cogniscant of the problem and begin a 'log' of the hours flown and the routes taken. Corporations should also improve the health screening of the executives each year. For more than 20 years **John Hall**, a music business executive, flew regularly between his offices in New York, Paris, Sydney and London. It was reported in the U.K's Sunday Times, in an article on the problem, that in 1993 he was diagnosed with bladder cancer and came to believe that frequent flying was on of the main causes. *"At the craziest of times I could have flown between all of them in the space of a week. There came a point where something clicked and I knew I had to stop",* said Hall 51, who has now recovered.

Booze Away!

Radiation results in the production of 'free radicals' which are highly reactive molecules in the body. One counter-measure to free radicals is to take doses of vitamins E and C, both during and after flights. These vitamins are known as 'scavengers' of free radicals. Despite what I said about alcohol a few paragraphs earlier, you should also know that red wine is also one of the best scavengers of free radicals as it contains high concentrations of enoviton which is supposed to stimulate the body to eliminate the radioactive substances.

Air Rage and Air Quality

We have all known for some years, that the quality of air in airplanes has deteriorated. In the interests of economy many airlines are skimping on cabin ventilation.

A new study found that airlines have switched to recirculating air, rather than providing fresh supplies. About half the air in a cabin that passengers breathe is recirculated, which means it has been sucked out of the cabin, passed through filters and put back in again mixed with fresh air from outside. The reason that a complete change of air from outside is not used is that air brought into the plane has to be warmed which takes fuel. Simply put, by recirculating used air this cuts an airlines fuel bills by as much as 2 per cent, a significant saving on long haul flights. Airlines using recirculating air can save as much as 6 tons of fuel on a typical transatlantic flight.

What now emerges, according to a **Conor Whelan** of the **U.K's Cranfield College of Aeronautics**, is the strong link between air quality and air rage. Incidents of air rage have increased by some 400 per cent since 1995 and incidents have become more serious. The practise of recirculating cabin air cuts costs, but is blamed for passengers increased 'agitated states'. Whelan reported that in some cases, airlines are pushing the amount of recycled air to 60 per cent, but it does have an effect on passengers. Whilst in older aircraft a constant supply of fresh air was forced through cabins, in almost all new aircraft about half is recirculated. Effectively this means that carbon dioxide concentrations can reach 3,000 parts per million - 10 times the level in normal air.

Such high levels, it is reported, can cause mood swings and irritability. At the highest concentrations it can cause blackouts, dizziness, shortness of breath, heart palpitations, which in some passengers can lead to panic. This increase in carbon dioxide can be compounded by the effects of both altitude (cabin pressure) and alcohol. For first and business class passengers there is some relief where, having more individual space, means they get 50-60 cubic feet of air per minute. By stark contrast economy passengers will only receive 8-20 cubic feet per minute.

Whether air rage can be traced to air quality is debatable, but what we know for sure is that incidents are on the increase. B.A reported some 266 incidents up to the end of March 1998, for the previous 12 months. There were a variety of causes, but many would seem to be down to a 'frustration of expectation over reality'!. All the factors which make up this are those we all know well - inconsistent attitudes, inconsistent service, poor air, poor seats, poor space, aggravated by alcohol and the stress of modern day travel, often made worse by the prospect of missing connecting flights.

Air Unhealth!

On a more mundane level poor air quality caused by recycling cabin air is believed to be at the root cause of other health problems. As well as worrying about the health risks of our destination, we now need to be concerned about the effects on our health risks of flying there and back. The use of recycled air is now being seen as the cause of a possible array of illnesses.

Ideally the stale air, prior to it being recycled, goes through **High Efficiency Particulate Air Filters (HEPA)** and, supposedly, these remove the disease causing agents (pathogens). It wouldn't seem to be working though, as evidenced by the increasing number of passengers struck down by colds and chest infections. This was reported in an interesting article by **Farrol Khan** in the travel magazine **Conde Naste Traveller**. The article went on to report of the passengers catching tuberculosis on flights as in the case of the two Scottish businesswomen.

It would appear that it is now common practise to turn off the air conditioning packs and cut the amount of fresh air coming into the cabins and rely on the filtered air. Khan wrote that pathogenic bacteria thrive in high humidity, viruses in low humidity and that both conditions are present in aircraft. Bacteria, favoured by humid conditions at the beginning and end of a flight can cause abscesses, sinusitis, bronchitis and, in rare cases, TB. The viruses, we are told, likely to cause most problems thrive in low humidity and during a flight, humidity levels can drop from an average 40 percent to as little as just 2 percent. In contaminated air this is likely to cause colds, flu, and even pneumonia and Khan states such conditions as ear infections, headaches, allergies, fatigue, nausea, dizziness and irritation/inflammation of the eyes, skin, nose and respiratory tract are all possible.

A **Dr William Needleham of Pall Corporation** which manufacture HEPA equipment says that recirculated air is highly infected and unless high-performance filtration is employed, the millions of bacteria which are generated by coughing and sneezing will circulate in the cabin. Filters efficiency, it was reported, varied from 50 percent to 90 percent. Deep cleaning which decontaminates all the piping and ducts will only happen once a year during a major overhaul.

As we have said earlier on 'up front' is the best place to be and Khan advises sniffing Tea Tree oil (a natural antibiotic) when someone sneezes and using a facial spray to keep the membranes of your nose moist - a safeguard against micro-organisms. We know we cannot expect airlines bent on every economy to redress the balance, but it is another example of the drive for profits balanced against the wellbeing of the passenger.

More Problems

New research reveals that some aircraft are slowly being poisoned by organophosphates (OP) leaking into the air conditioning systems. Despite this U.K authorities are refusing to conduct their own research, according to a report in the U.K's Sunday Times in August 1999.

The article reported that 14 aircraft types have been associated with the problem, including the MD-80. BAe 146 and Airbus 320, also flown by British Airways. The research was carried out by the University of Columbia and it found that due to poor oil seals, toxins can leak into cabins. The research was prompted following complaints of mysterious illnesses suffered by thousands of cabin staff in America, Canada and Australia. A senior Australian pilot , Captain Frank Kolver whilst making a landing at Melbourne airport, smelled strong odours and fumes in his cockpit. He was attempting to land his BAe 146-300 and found himself confused, suffering from vertigo and incapable of making the landing. Fortunately for all concerned his co-pilot, who was not effected was able to land the plane.

The symptoms, we are told, include a headache, burning throat and eyes, disorientation, blurred vision and breathing problems. The problem is an ingredient in most engine oils - tricesyl phosphate (TCP). Despite such reports and staff illnesses, airlines and authorities refuse to deal with the problem. Once again it is an issue of cost and as a consequence they refute the 'leak' theory, quoting some very low incident of oil leak problems.

The facts, however, are cabin crew and, no doubt, passengers are being subject to OP poisoning, where even a low dose can be cumulative and very harmful. Clearly planes do not have to fall out of the sky to be harmful to our health. Maybe the occasional holiday traveller need not be so worried as should the regular business traveller, but such problems as are reported above impact on the health of all of us, particularly as we increase the number of times we fly each year.

Only one week after the tragic crash of the Air France Concorde, a British Concord was diverted to land prior to it's scheduled stop when passengers smelled aviation fuel in the cabin.

And Finally - Stupidity!

When it comes to sex abroad, common sense is often left at home. There has been a dramatic increase of heart attack fatalities and cardiac problems with tourists visiting Bangkok, Thailand. Recently there have been 20 Britons and 40 German tourists who have died and investigations have revealed that the disproportionate number of deaths have been caused by the victims taking a combination of alcohol and Viagra and then having sex.

The problem has been exacerbated by the fact that Viagra is freely available in chemist shops in the city at £15 a pill. Despite the fact that a prescription should be necessary, the drug is sold openly and without prescription. Those people with heart disease and diabetes sufferers are most at risk.

CHAPTER FIVE

Personal Security Overview

So now you have the bad news about a place you intend to visit, what can you do to improve your personal security. Included in the definition of security I want to include safety. In commerce and industry we would necessarily split the two into convenient boxes and refer to 'Health & Safety separately from a company's security issues. As individual travellers, security, as well as health and safety issues, are all rolled into one.

We need to be aware of the health risks, such as the risk of Malaria in, say, Kenya. Equally though we need to know about the security risk of vehicle hijack in this region, as well as the safety risks associated with setting off on a journey up country into what is a difficult and dangerous environment and not to go out on foot after dark, not to camp in lonely places not to walk or sit on empty beaches and not to destroy or deface Kenyan currency as it is a criminal offence. All are a question of mindset and preparation. The preparation is a mental conditioning process, also having a system of improving knowledge, possibly training and acquiring the correct kit for the job in hand.

Often it is us, the tourist or business traveller who are our own worst enemies. A recent European survey suggested that at least 25% of crime and health problems in travellers can be attributed to inappropriate behaviour, simply because people were unaware of the potential problems of a situation - in essence - *'actions based on ignorance'*, but what the survey didn't conclude was how many people, in full knowledge of a problem situation, ignored the warnings and acted inappropriately out of choice - very many I would submit.

This underscores the importance of information gathering, but it made the point that for the tourist traveller the information not only had to be available, but that in addition such information had to be 'specific, effectively transmitted to users, understood, convincing and utilised by travellers'. Fine words, but as we know the information itself is seldom available, irrespective of the form it's delivery takes. However, it is little value having such knowledge if it's implementation produces an overly restrictive regime - it will be ignored.

Personal security is a product of two things;

- **an adherence to some basic procedures and**
- **a level of constant awareness.**

We will start to deal with some of the do's and don'ts, or, in other words, procedures in succeeding chapters and deal with awareness now.

AWARENESS & VIGILANCE

In succeeding chapters you will read about how to conduct yourself in a variety of situations. These are the seemingly never ending lists of do's and don'ts, for ones conduct in the street, hotel, airport and whilst mobile in vehicles or trains and planes. What I know and have developed as a practise over many years, is **that one ounce of awareness is worth 100 pages of do's and don'ts.** How you carry your bag, where to keep your money, how you choose a taxi, count for nothing if you are oblivious to both your environment and the people who are in that environment with you.

There are two broad areas you should be aware of. The first is your **physical environment**, in other words the street you are walking in, the nature of the area you are in, the lighting, the type of shops, or businesses, side streets, or alleyways. Second you should maintain a constant awareness of the **people or vehicles** that are in your vicinity or look like they could at some point be within your immediate area.

We can sum this up as:-

Situation Awareness & People Awareness

As you will read in Chapter 5 street muggers require a victim who is *'switched off'* for the element of surprise to be in the attackers favour and in addition they need a means of escape. This usually results in their victim being identified whilst he or she is walking on a major, busy thoroughfare, but only being attacked when they turn off onto a less well lit side street with further side roads off it as a means of escape. This doesn't mean you are safe whilst you are on the very busy main street it just means your risk has gone up when your environment changes for the worst. Therefore, to know your risk has increased you must be alert to how your environment changes.

Always 'switch on' at popular tourist spots. It is where you may be 'targetted' - Instanbul.

There have been far too many instances of this occurring to tourists in the Florida and Los Angeles environs, when they have strayed off the safe, well lit and heavily trafficked main routes. To compound the the problem, many have stopped to ask directions from the very gangs who will rob them and worse. In Florida the local authorities have now 'waymarked' the routes to prevent tourists straying into areas of danger.

In any personal strategy for improving one's safety, avoidance of threat and risk must constitute 90% of the overall requirement. If you are a person who has physical skills and some combative techniques, this may be useful, but it has to be accepted that to have to use them means something has gone wrong with your other avoidance strategies. Believe me, if you are taken by surprise, it will be over before you can act physically. The definition we use in the Close Protection field for personal security may help:-

"The object of personal security is to reduce the risk of kidnap, assassination, or criminal act, by the application of certain Principles and Procedures to normal daily life"

In the world of Close Protection we apply ourselves to ensuring that all the preventative, proactive measures (Procedures) are in place when we are looking after a VIP. This does not mean that we ignore the eventuality of them not working on occasion and we must therefore be skilled at the defensive, reactive (Drills) which come into play if danger threatens.

So it should be with an individuals own, personal 'risk reduction strategy.' A person must learn to be their own 'Bodyguard' and this means learning all the various procedures that are applied to look after a person of importance, accepting that, to ourselves, we are no less important than the next billionaire. The only difference is that he can pay to have the necessary skill level applied to his situation, whereas you will need to learn and apply how it is carried out yourself.

The first thing is to look at some guiding principles of personal security and those of you who have my book 'The Modern Bodyguard' will be familiar with them and they are that-

THE INDIVIDUAL IS RESPONSIBLE FOR HIS OR HER OWN SECURITY.

THAT SECURITY MEASURES MUST BE COMMENSURATE WITH THE THREAT.

THAT AWARENESS IS THE CORNERSTONE OF GOOD PERSONAL SECURITY.

Lets look at each in turn.

The Individual is Responsible for his/her own security

No one other than ourselves can be responsible for our security, however when I talk to people, they are often of the belief that others are more responsible for looking after them than they themselves. Equally many people believe that their own part to play in security issues is not important. I come across this in work environments where people feel others are looking after their welfare and general office security is not really their concern. They do not believe that their singular actions or omissions can prejudice the many.

When in the street it is ourselves, not the police who we turn to for help. In the office it is us who are responsible for ensuring that we comply with security rules and not someone else's responsibility to maintain a safe working environment. We must learn to lock doors, challenge strangers, wear our ID's, report our suspicions etc. This is particularly important if our office is in some Third World region.

Security Measures

The second principle concerns both resources and attitude. Resources may be improved security at home -locks, alarms, lighting, viewers, CCTV etc or it may be what you invest in time and money on, say, self defence lessons. On a more subjective front the principle also refers to one's attitude to such things as crime and how we react and respond. If we lock ourselves indoors and become too frightened to go anywhere after reading the newspapers about the increasing levels of crime, we have gone too far. If we take every journey on the basis that we will be attacked, we will put ourselves under unnecessary stress and paranoia will set in. So what we do and how we approach the problem mentally, must be in balance with the risks we perceive as possible. This means in some way we need to conduct a Risk Analysis. This doesn't need the appliance of science, but you should better understand the potential problem, to be able to make more appropriate changes. Chapter 3 should have given you some of the mechanics of this process.

Constant Awareness

Our cornerstone and third principle is, unfortunately, the most difficult of all the principles to make work for us. If awareness is absent then every single other issue with regard to self protection goes out of the window. If we draw on the experiences of the Bodyguard industry you can see over numerous incidents where kidnappings and assassinations have occurred, that the success of the attack was singularly down to achieving the element of surprise.

"Security measures should be commensurate with the threat"!

In other words all the pre-attack surveillance, which may have gone on for weeks prior to the attack, the rehearsal and, on the day, the actual ambush setup all went unnoticed by the protective detail, usually resulting in their deaths.

Knowing every rule of personal security, in terms of what to do and what not to do, counts for nothing if you never see the person who attacks you. You may have obeyed every rule in the book, but if you do not 'switch on' then it's all pointless. *"Self Protection is an attitude of mind not something we practise as a daily routine. It is about our attitude to ourselves particularly when we are out on the street. How we look, walk, act and are perceived says more than anything else about our attitude to the world around us. Portraying a positive appearance can go a long way in you not being selected as a target."*

The above quote was taken off an internet site and succinctly sums up where the main effort needs to go in our attempts to lead safer lives - ourselves. Another reference form the Internet was from the Metro Nashville Police Dept

"Self protection is more than learning a few simple yells and carrying spray to ward of attackers. It is a habit of mind. Self protection is the way you think, dress, & walk. You have a traffic light in your head that tells you stuff all the time. When something doesn't seem right about a guy, listen to that yellow light in your head. Self protection is a study of options - whether to reduce risks, run, talk, or fight."

Realise what your risks are by using Risk Reduction Techniques. You have probably thwarted attacks in the past and just didn't realise it, but your old appearance could have been a successful enough deterrent in itself. Many robberies and assaults are unsuccessful. You are most likely to be attacked during TRANSITIONS, where you are going from one place to another. Transitions occur when you go from your car to work, from work to your home, walking to the parking lot, taking the trash out, or jogging down the road. Transitions may increase you risks, but are unavoidable parts of life. There are risk reduction techniques that enumerate things (actions that decrease or increase risks). Walking with a umbrella, child or dog decreases risk of attack. Pairs or more are less likely to be attacked than solitary persons. Remember to look around you. PEOPLE WHO LOOK LIKE GOOD VICTIMS ARE GOOD VICTIMS."

We are told that victims encourage crime! Some people may want to refute that, unfortunately I believe it to be a truism. Target selection, which villains carry out on our vehicles, houses, businesses and us, is based on the level to which we will contribute to our own attractiveness and that solely pertains to how easy we will make it for them. Criminals like things easy - better an easy £100 than a risky £1,000. We may make it easy for them because when we leave the house, we leave a convenient rear window open or when we walk down the street we expose the gold Rolex, whilst at the same time talk on the mobile phone. This is no more true than when we are abroad, as we stand out even more from the crowd, particularly if we display obvious wealth.

To any watching villain he knows he can get a watch and a phone off someone who is oblivious to his surroundings. When a terrorist bomb is 'booby trapped' and constructed in such a way as to go off when the intended victim carries out a particular action e.g. opening a door, turning on the car ignition, opening a parcel, we say that the device is *'victim operated'*. In other words the victim becomes the timing device for the bomb.

So it is with ourselves and our personal security. If we walk down the street preoccupied with our own thoughts we are asking for trouble and in fact we 'invite' trouble. Also what we do contributes greatly to the event of an attack. A mugging is 'victim operated', in other words, there is contributory negligence.

Personal Security is a combination of the following;

Responsibility

Precautions

Awareness and Expectation

Common sense!

During a recent project with a company on the Continent, I had to give a seminar on Security Awareness to a group of ex-pats, who kept managing to get themselves mugged. Prior to the seminar one of the participants came up to me and said *"we're going to be looking at common sense things I take it?"* I asked him what made him ask and he replied that he knew these (the do's and don'ts) anyway. I said we would but even if I gave the assembled throng 1,000 do's and don'ts it patently wouldn't help, because if everyone knew them now anyway and the answer was the application of common sense then they wouldn't have had 11 people mugged out of a total complement of 23 people, in just 3 months.

If we analyse the conversation there are contained in his statement the two classic misconceptions that:

1. That having a common sense list of rules, actually means you follow them and act in a common sense way

2. That intelligence and intellect are natural bedfellows of common sense.

3. That a simple list of do's and don'ts means that the individual, if he follows them has no further role in the process!

From my experience all three couldn't be further from the truth. The group in question was highly intelligent, young, reasonably fit, but had, not to put too fine a point on it, not a clue and were 'walking victims'. Their attacks were 'victim operated.'

Personal Radar

On the street we need to develop our 'Personal Radar.' Concentration, broad-external focus of attention, all are part of this personal radar, but for most people their radar is, to all intents and purposes switched off. The analogy is like buying a new £100,000 yacht and fitting it naturally with radar. As you are sailing along with the tiller in one hand & a gin & tonic in the other you hear a loud crash as you run into rocks and a 'beep' as the radar tells you you are near rocks, I'd submit you'd be less than pleased with its performance, quite rightly expecting it to see the rocks from miles away and so enable you to avoid the danger. Yet that is only as good as our own personal radars which probably operate out to only a few feet. *"they came out of nowhere!"* (the classic of cry of everyone who has been mugged). Your personal radar is effectively inoperable, whereas it should be working out to possibly hundreds of feet, taking in the whole of your visual environment, not just 3-5 feet.

The group who kept getting themselves mugged in Europe were guilty of this and had even been mugged in pairs, but always whilst they were deeply involved in conversation and ambling along slowly, oblivious to their environment or who was in it. The 'nature of the animal' in this case was the route cause of their troubles. They were computer analysts, programmers and technicians and all displayed the characteristics of people who had a 'narrow - internal focus of attention'. They walked around at all times of day and night oblivious to the environment and people in it, whilst concentrating on the problems of their working day.

Staying Alert & Aware

For many years I had the same problems as everyone in keeping a constant state of alertness. Whenever I am training business executives in personal security I know when I get to this part on how to stay aware that the same objection will come up. This is that to constantly be thinking about threats is an act of paranoia. They are quite correct, in that if you tried, to the exclusion of very other thought, to simply devote your conscious brain to look for threats you would soon mentally tire of the process and stop doing it. If you remember, I said at the beginning that we cannot tackle the problem from the aspect of our conscious mind. It has too much else to do and too many other thoughts intrude.

Also it isn't necessary, because we have a 'standby' system that we can employ and that is our sub-conscious. What we need to have, in computer speak, is the ability to 'multi-task.' In other words we need to in some way dedicate only part of our cognitive process to be permanently aware and alert to our environment, but not so that we have to consciously think about the problem. With the executives I train I ask them whether they never stop at a kerbside and blindly walk across or, do they stop and apply some system to check for danger. I then get them to attest to the fact that this is not paranoia, but preventative. As children we were rightly taught to avoid being knocked down not learn how to roll off car bonnets without injury.

They stop because they are 'programmed' to stop and what we must do is put some more programming into the system. For programming, substitute habit forming.

The common sense drill at the kerbside of 'look right, left and right again only has any relevance to safety if a person is conscious and aware enough to remember to stop at the kerb in the first place - many aren't, but are preoccupied, or as we say 'in a dream'. For 99% of people 99% of the time, this is the mental state which predominates. Using the same analogy the 'cross code' is preventative, it's how we teach children not to get knocked down rather than teach them how to survive impact with cars.

There is a presumption by most people, the above group being a classic example, that knowing what not to do actually means that they will carry out the plan. If you were to study kidnap & ransom attempts by international terrorists and organised crime groups, one very glaring fact would emerge. This is that the protective detail (the bodyguards) in nearly every case die and die first. This is not just a consequence of lack of combative skills, but simply as a consequence of being unable in those circumstances to practise those skills - in other words they were taken by surprise. The majority of Police, Military and even civilian Close Protection teams can shoot, fight and have been taught highly skilled anti-ambush skills.

The reality though is that they never got a chance to do any of it. They are simply 'taken by surprise' and the shock, surprise and ensuing confusion and dislocation with the unfolding events results in the classic 'freeze'. Cars run into each other, panic overcomes even trained responses and in seconds it's over before they can even understand they're in it!.

Mental Overdrive

The problem is one of maintaining constant awareness. Whilst we don't walk down the street with our eyes closed, we may just as well, because all we do is **LOOK**, but don't **SEE.** We basically take in just enough data so that we don't get run over, or keep constantly bumping into people. We simply navigate to our intended destination avoiding the most obvious hazards and we do this in our cars, on foot, on public transport and to a similar extent at home and in the office.

Through habitual repetition of events we are able to perform in a mental overdrive where we take a minimal 'conscious part in the proceedings - our minds are elsewhere - and we perform without direct concentration or attention. For example if we actually did concentrate the number of road accidents would fall dramatically. We will expand on this in the next chapter. into a sweat.

Shock & Expectation

Shock and surprise are the weapons in a villains armoury and whilst being aware will help us see trouble coming it still may not help us come 'to terms with it.' This has to be tackled by understanding the problem of Expectation. This we will cover later and expectation, even for people whose occupation puts them on the 'front line' of risk, often suffer as a consequence of not fully understanding it's implications. We all have the opportunity to go into 'denial', that is we believe that because we are careful and cautious that it can't happen to us -wrong. It is often simply a case of the wrong place - wrong time, nothing that we have done wrong or right. This I will put in the correct context later.

One other aspect that we must constantly bear in mind is this: "**that the time we feel most safe, we are most at risk.**" I will keep coming back to that thought throughout the various chapters.

Awareness Is The Cornerstone Of Good Personal Security!

It may be the cornerstone, but, unfortunately, it is the part of the overall structure which is seldom in place. I can teach someone to punch with enough impact to put a twenty stone man down with one shot to the body and I could teach it in a couple of hours. However, to reach a state where I've been able to make awareness a natural part of someone's psychological make up could take two weeks. The problem is the punch may only be needed once every five years, the awareness is needed every waking second.

Therein lies the problem - awareness competes every waking moment for some space in the conscious and sub-conscious mind, whilst at the same time your brain is involved with all the mass of detailed information which it processes all day long. You are busy. Your mind is busy. You are preoccupied and are often concentrating on thoughts and problems which call for your attention to be focussed inwards towards these internal workings. Every so often we surface and take note of our surroundings, then submerge ourselves again with our ponderings. This happens both when we are driving and on foot.

On Autopilot!

When I'm teaching Executives about personal security techniques, I get them to tell me what information they process when they are walking through a busy street. They admit that they do take information in, but when they have actually thought about it for a while they admit that all they process is sufficient information to allow themselves not to bump into anyone.

Don't be so naive to believe that people to where you are travelling abroad will be pleased to see you. When the average wage is $80 per month, as it has been here in Moscow, there can be a high resentment factor to Westerners with money who openly flaunt it. Keep a low profile and dress down - 'Red Square'.

Awareness is a 'situational' thing. By that I mean if tomorrow I dropped you into the back streets of Manila, or the jungle of Borneo you would be switched on and switched on for 24 hours-you wouldn't even want to go to sleep. You switch on because they are bad places to be and, what's more, it is obvious that they are, so you do not let your guard down. Put yourself back in the real world and you believe, incorrectly that it is benign and non-threatening. WRONG- read the liturgy of crime throughout this book to know that even the most peaceful location in the world can be shattered by the most heinous crime. No one and nowhere is safe from the effects of villainy in all its forms and we make the situation worse by creating the conditions which are ideal for them to ply their trade.

Think about awareness as two aspects

1. **Situational Awareness** i.e. surroundings for both threats, dark alleys, wooded areas, hiding places, and for the positives such as escape routes, populated areas, good parking spots, better lit areas, police stations. Good situational awareness will not only help you assess the possible dangers, but also the possible options available.

2. **Threat Awareness** i.e. in terms of being aware of people and vehicles and assessing not only any immediate danger, but the future potential. This relates being on the street to driving the car and before you make any move or turn looking not only ahead but also behind. If you do it on the road it's good on foot.

ABH =Avoid Being Hurt or;

A head

B ehind

H azard/help

When I'm training potential Bodyguards I ask them how they will stay alert and aware. The answer is that once they have 'instructed' themselves to be alert then it will happen. Unfortunately it won't and it won't because the basic human make up won't allow it to happen.

The reason is that our conscious minds are incapable of holding one thought, to the exclusion of all others, for longer than a few seconds. So, saying 'I am now alert' will only make you alert until the next thought enters your mind, in maybe, 5 seconds.

Stress Exclusion

It is not possible to employ our conscious brain for the task as it only seems able to deal with subjects in a 'linear' manner which means that one thought replaces another and so on. Before we look at the answer to the problem we need to know what, in being more aware, we are hoping to process, in terms of additional information. The problem is one of 'LOOKING but NOT SEEING'. It is also the problem of modern day STRESS. We are daily bombarded with information or 'stimuli' and most of it, i.e. the noise, press of people, traffic, pace of life, we now exclude from our 'cognitive' processes because it is stress forming. We shut out most of the information in our surroundings so as to keep the stress of modern city living down to a minimum. People who come into the city from the country find the situation untenable as they have not learned to exclude this mass of stimuli. We haven't done it consciously, but sub-consciously over a period.

This is the hub of the problem - we operate our daily lives at a mental sub-level or sub-consciously where experiences and responses are filed away and occur without our conscious and concentrated effort. There are also other factors at play, particularly with regard to our surroundings. The problem is to do with the amount of information we receive from our immediate environment. The problem is one of receiving the information that denotes threat or risk. The two aspects we will look at are:

Accumulation & Recognition

Accumulation is the amount of data or information that we actually allow into our brains & Recognition is what points of reference we have for determining that a particular piece of information needs careful analysis- e.g. Threat!.

If we take Accumulation first, we are told by psychologists that the human organism is increasingly subject, as we have said above, to stress & stress that is unhealthy. Many physical ailments are now seen as a by product of stress and the pace and pressure of modern life, with all its uncertainties, have now begun to take their toll. Rats when subject to constant high noise levels or when locked in a maze exhibit high stress levels.

It pays to repeat it again, that modern day living does this to us. Noise, traffic levels, pollution, press of people in the streets, aggression all act as uncomfortable stimuli. The consequence is that when we are now out on foot or in vehicles we simply 'shut out' most of the information that we could potentially receive. We are sub-consciously 'tuning out' data that comes to, including unfortunately, those signals that we really shouldn't exclude that convey information about risk!.

We become broadly insensitive to both our environment and people in those surroundings and, more particularly, to changes in those surroundings which may increase threat. We are on 'auto-pilot', which like a real auto-pilot means we are basically blind to our surroundings. We are able to avoid the most obvious risks, but even then that is not always the case as car crashes and pedestrians being knocked down happen far too frequently. Most can be attributed to being 'switched off'. Call it 'jaywalking', or careless driving, it boils down to the very simple fact that people are usually WIDE ASLEEP!

Recognition is what we actually process as important from what little data we allow in. We have internal priorities so that we don't overload the system and what we end up ignoring is are the very subtle references which are important to our safety. The over long, side glance from two youths who pass us in the street. The person who shows an undue interest, the van which is parked alongside our vehicle, the poor quality of the street lighting all of a sudden, alleyways, bushes etc etc. We need to register people, vehicles and our environment, because it is the changes in our environment which we need to perceive so as to be able to raise our 'Awareness'. Our goal is to avoid Risk or Threat, whichever you prefer to use.

When training people in this I use the Threat Pyramid. It helps people to understand the relationships between certain areas which are-

THREAT AVOIDANCE

THREAT EVALUATION

THREAT AWARENESS

Threat Avoidance

This is the Flight or Fight part of the Threat Pyramid and sits on the top of the other two, supporting parts. To be able to escape or to be ready to fight demands that certain things have taken place and taken place in a sequential way. What I mean is that you are able to fight or flee because you have not been taken completely by surprise, that you have had time to evaluate certain changes in your immediate environment that make you uncomfortable. Jumping forward to vehicle security in Chapter 6 the statement "don't be surprised by your own car"- helps illustrate the point here. If you give yourself no opportunity to abandon your vehicle if people near it make you very uncomfortable then avoidance of the threat becomes impossible and you become 'associated' with that car to your detriment.

If, however you park in such a way that on returning to the car you are able to get a good visual from some distance then you have created the right circumstances i.e., a safe reactionary gap, if you have to leave it. On the street you will be unable to avoid a violent robbery if you have no perception of threat as you are approached. One of the principle benefits of avoidance is that you don't have to rely on physical skills- i.e.Proactive!

Threat Evaluation

To see someone as a threat, or to see a situation as unsafe, requires that you have actually had a period of time to be able to carry out an Evaluation of what is happening around you. This is the only part of the pyramid that you are able to make any rational decisions. The Evaluation might have taken a few minutes or just 30 seconds and in many ways it is instinctive. Who can say with any certainty that the three youths standing round the corner are going to be a problem, but good self protection is about not taking chances. Follow your feelings i.e. someone who feels wrong, usually is wrong. People say we can 'smell' danger and some are better than others, usually it is those people who are more switched on who are most perceptive about others.

Threat Awareness

Evaluation though, depends on, or rests on, the third and most important part of the Threat Pyramid and that is the Threat Awareness. It is very simple when you think about it, in that to escape a potential threat you must first have had to have come to a decision that the person is a threat, which means you must have had time to make the Evaluation, which presupposes that you were able to 'SEE' him in your environment i.e. you were AWARE! If you are not aware there is no support for the other two areas and then you have the classic response to the attack - ***"he came out of nowhere"***

What awareness does is to buy time for you to remain in control and take the necessary steps to alter course, or be prepared to fight, but not to be taken by surprise. Surprise is the main weapon in the armoury of the villains you may encounter. They require you to be shocked and stunned with the way events happen - the surprise, speed, swearing and shouting, demands and threats of violence are all designed to keep you off balance and compliant. 'Forewarned is Forearmed' - There is no shock if you have seen events unfold in sufficient time to get to grips with it.

You will still be frightened and have an adrenal rush, but you will be reasonably in control. But how does one stay alert and aware through a normal daily routine? There are a number of systems available to us which can bring all this together, but first I want to relate the Threat Pyramid to a very useful system of having some 'visualisation' to help us in the task.

Colour Codes

We have to thank an American combat pistol instructor Jeff Cooper for his work on what has become known as 'Coopers Colour Codes.' Cooper developed these codes many years ago to help Law Enforcement personnel have an immediate and visual system of reflecting the changes of threat in their environment. Cooper recognised that being skilled in weapon handling was of little use if, at the time you needed to use it you were still trying to make decisions about the level the threat had reached and what your correct action should be.

He used the following colours, calling them 'Conditions' e.g. condition White, Yellow, Orange, Red and Black. We can ignore the last condition Black as that was the 'application of deadly force' Those people who work in the UK for any government agency will be familiar with the 'Bikini Alert' states which are colour states again like Coopers, but these are coloured cards, or written colour states which alert everyone who enters the premises what the security alert state is that day. The colour state alters with the potential for terrorist activities. Workers then know, depending on the alert state, that they must be more vigilant and observant for 'suspect' people and packages, for example. The colour alert state has been a 'visual trigger' which has conditioned them to a particular mind set.

This is how Cooper's colour codes can work for us. I don't use the colour codes when I am in a face to face situation as an action trigger to help me physically preempt assault. An 'action trigger' we will look at later, but very simply it is a 'tool' for replacing decision making with a conditioned, reactive, response. Somehow the symbolic colour effect never worked for me and I had to develop a different system. However, to bring the colour codes to play alongside the Threat Pyramid as situational warnings about environmental changes, has always worked well for me and I use it all over the world in some reasonably threatening environments. They are a visual stimulus which allows you to move smoothly from one area of the pyramid to another, but to understand how, we first need to look at what each condition represents.

Condition White - relates to being 'switched off'. In other words it is where 99% of people spend 99% of their time. This is the victim state and in this condition a person has no awareness and navigates down the street or road, 'looking, but not seeing' and taking no information in. People in this condition have no time to recover from the 'surprise' when an attack takes place.

Later we will look at some statistics to do with violence, but remember that even favourable statistics are nothing to do with 'life' and life never seems to have read the statistics. Don't just believe that the general public are guilty of this, as even police officers are caught unawares and taken by surprise. They can have violence erupt in front of them in the most unexpected places, as evidenced by the injuries they suffer whilst on duty. They, like us, are walking the familiar, peaceful streets on a sunny, Saturday afternoon, with their thoughts elsewhere only to find themselves fighting for their lives in the next ten minutes. So condition white happens below the pyramid, unlike the next colour state

Condition Yellow - This is the 'state we should be in 100% of the time. It is the equivalent of turning the radar on! This is your 'scanning' and 'seeing' state. You are switched on and alert to your surroundings, having good 'situational awareness.' In this state you could describe people and vehicles which passed you some minutes ago. This is the alert state where you 'play the game' of people watching and if we related it to the field of Close Protection what you are doing is practising your 'anti-surveillance drills.

You will look and see people and try to pigeon hole them, even if you have to make a game of it i.e. " solicitor, mid 40's, not married, having a bad day! or - villain, late 20's, housebreaker, twice in jail, single, left handed. If you were to stop and ask them you probably find you were perfectly accurate just that you had the two people the wrong way round. Don't laugh it happens to the best. Three armed, but plain-clothes policeman in a car stopped a vehicle with, as they thought, three suspicious people on board and ordered them out at gunpoint. It turned out that the three they stopped were also plainclothes policeman.

The spin off from being in a permanent alert state is that you send out the signal that you are. This happens because to 'see' people properly you must look at them, however fleetingly and it means to them you have acknowledged their presence. Don't forget the most 'switched on' person in any street is a villain- one because he's on the look out for opportunities and two he's looking for the police. He knows when he's been seen and once that has happened his opportunity for surprise has gone. If he now appears again you will have recognition and be very suspicious. Should that happen then your colour state would change

Condition Orange. Any change in your environment produces a change in the colour code. Condition orange relates on the pyramid to Threat Evaluation. Seeing that person a second time, if he was someone you didn't like the look of the first time, means you must evaluate and make a decision. This is what being switched on buys you - time to stay in control.

Condition Red. The 'trigger' colour for us to get out of the situation and in enough time. It's the *"Flight or Fight"* response. Just as we don't stop to weigh up the pro's and con's of stopping at a proper red light when driving, so it is here. Our action should be a 'conditioned response', not a considered decision.

This shot of New Delhi! with its wide roads, grand buildings and lack of people would not prepare you for the experience of Delhi.

'Traffic Lights'

What happens each time you move colour states is to visualise the new colour. When I first adopted the colour code I found it impossible to visualise the colour states as I had no internal field of view where I could place them. Eventually in one of those flashes of inspiration it came to me and that was the traffic lights. What I do is to have my three lights, but instead of having the traditional green, amber, red, I work up from yellow, orange and red. I find it not too difficult to keep the visualisation of a traffic light signal, but it would be impossible to do it all the time. It isn't necessary to keep the image there all the time just when a situation changes. What is essential is to keep the awareness at work all the time. So what we need is some system for being permanently aware, without paranoia and to use the colour codes to signal changes.

So if I am walking around Moscow and I'm on one of the busy main thoroughfares I am very aware, but in condition yellow. If though it is necessary for me to have to use one of the underpasses to cross the road as I prepare to go down the steps the mental traffic light appears and it goes to Orange. This acts just like the colour code alert state for workers in government buildings. They don't carry a colour coded alert card in front of their nose all day long, seeing it once in the morning by the lift triggered their minds for the day and so it is with the way we should use the system. As I'm walking in the underpass I now see four men with obvious ill intent and the lights appear in my minds eye and turn to Condition Red. My choice is now very simple - turn and get out or get ready for problems. Not to keep you guessing for too long what I would do, but it goes something like 'heels and dust!

So the colour conditions do two things One they can act as 'situational' warnings, when our environment is about to change for the worse. This may be simply turning off the main drag into some quieter, less well lit. less well populated part of the city, because we know that this is now where we are likely to be mugged, not on the main drag. Second the codes act as an action trigger and this is when you have condition Red. As the light turns Red in your head its action not thought which should have the ascendancy. The thinking happened in Orange, its now reactive, whereas the other states were all proactive.

"The best place to be when a crisis occurs is nowhere near it"

Use the same common sense approach overseas that you would at home. Be especially cautious in or avoid areas where you are likely to be victimised. These include crowded subways, train stations, elevators, tourist sites, market places, festivals and marginal areas of cities.

Don't use short cuts, narrow alleys or poorly -lit streets, Try not to travel alone at night.

Avoid public demonstrations and other civil disturbances.

Keep a low profile and avoid loud conversation or arguments.Do not discuss travel plans or other personal matters with strangers.

Avoid scam artists. Beware of stringers approach you offering bargains or to be your guide.

The beautifully constructed tomb of the unknown soldier, outside the Kremlin walls, Moscow. This and the statue of Yuri Gagarin represent what Russians do well.

This gives a whole new meaning to 'room security', as you would need a small gun boat. 'Over the Water' hotel rooms in Bora Bora.

A sudden and violent sandstorm in the Algerian desert. You must be prepared for such eventualities, both in respect of clothing and kit.

This is Sadam! - so named by his keepers in Entebbe zoo - Uganda. In fact, as a consequence of the wildlife slaughter during the Amin years, Sadam actually came from Tanzania.

My armed guard for a reconnaissance into the foothills of the Rowenzori National Park. This was a time of terrorist activity and the park was closed. Despite this, articles were still appearing in U.K. travel magazines about camping and walking in the park..

A gathering of indigenous tribesmen in the Masai Mara region of Kenya - performing for the tourist market.

Dodging escaped domestic animals is just another hazard on African roads - Uganda.

Machu Pichu - Peru. Altitude and difficult conditions underfoot could mean problems for people who are less than reasonably fit.

Beware of pickpockets who will:

- jostle you
- ask you for directions or the time
- point out something spilled on your clothes
- or distract you by creating a disturbance

A child or even a baby can be a pickpocket. Beware of groups of vagrant children who create a distraction while picking your pocket.

Wear the shoulder strap of your bag across your chest and walk with the bag away from the kerb so as to avoid drive-by purse snatchers.

Try to seem purposeful when you move about. Even if you are lost act as if you know where you are going. When possible ask directions only from individuals in authority.

Know how to use a pay phone and have the proper change or tokens on hand.

Learn a few phrases in the local language so you can signal for help, the police, a doctor, fire, your hotel and the nearest Embassy or consulate of your country.

Protection Against Terrorism

Terrorist acts occur at random and unpredictably, making it impossible to protect oneself absolutely. The first and best protection is to avoid travel to unsafe areas where there has been a persistent record of terrorist attacks or kidnapping. Chapters 1 and 3 should have given you some food for thought about these areas. The vast majority of foreign countries have good records of maintaining public order and protecting residents and visitors from terrorism. Later we will look at more specific problems as they relate to air travel and terrorism and long term stays abroad.

CHAPTER SIX

Security on the Street

From experience a businessman will spend less time actually on the streets of a foreign city than will, say, a tourist. There may have been a time when our 'typical' businessman first visited a city, that he did the tourist 'bit' and saw the sights. Now he will jet in, do his business either in his hotel, his company's offices, or at other locations and travel by his company's or another company's vehicles. Seldom will he be on the streets and as such is less of a victim to the constant hassle that would be visited on tourists in many cities around the world.

The average street criminal is also attracted to the tourist market because he knows they will be carrying cash, cameras and videos, but, more importantly, they will as a breed, be 'switched off', relaxed and not on their guard. A good point made by a Tod Hoffman, following on from this point is that if you are a businessman abroad, avoid looking like a tourist. This is where all your training and thinking about the concepts we have discussed about - **Awareness** - come into play.

I make the above point as one of comparison between the tourist and the businessman, not only because of the purpose of being on foot and vulnerable is different but also because the body language emitted tells a different tale to the whole range of people who will have it in their mind to approach you on the street. These range from the genuine beggar, potential guide, the street salesman - be it currency exchange or tourist items, to the con-man and street thief or worse. I watch the different attitude adopted by this assembled throng to three or four people in suits walking in a street to a similar number of tourists. They are by far more cautious in approaching those on business. This is not a function of dress or any other objective aspect that rules a businessman out as a potential sucker, it is a question of the subjective impression and non-verbal signals. A businessman is invariably on the street with a purpose, that is to get somewhere, whereas by comparison the tourist is there to see sights and soak up the atmosphere.

How You Walk

The actual pace of progress as they walk is markedly different and the slow pace of the sightseeing tourist makes him or her vulnerable to approaches and a victim of their environment. Tourists also walk about with their 'holiday heads' on, meaning they are relaxed, trusting, don't want to give offence and are equipped with both a budget and a mental resolve to spend it. It has always been my belief that in certain parts of the world the tourist is far more at risk than the businessman will ever be. Also, as has proved the case a terrorist attack on a group of tourists, which are a soft target can have catastrophic impact on that country's tourist industry. Also, tourists find themselves in groups either being transported somewhere or actually somewhere with other tourists. This gives a terrorist the possibility to hit a group of people with considerably more impact. Egypt, as a tourist destination has still not recovered from the attack on the tourists at Luxor.

A group of businessmen doing the tourist bit - The Russian Space Control Centre - Moscow.

The important point here is the non-verbal signals you exude. The businessman probably has the "don't mess with me" look, together with an assertive demeanour, a dark purposeful suit and a general manner which will brook no approach. Unfortunately, as an aside, even the most powerful businessman when he goes 'native' and dresses as a tourist manages to look like he is in need of a 'fashion graft' and loses every shred of dignity and bearing. In an instant he becomes someone who could never be taken seriously and whose personal, character weaknesses become patently clear.

However, what you should know is that the person who has some ill intent in mind is looking for one thing in a potential victim and that is opportunity. Opportunity for a robbery, pick pocketing, or simple theft is created not by the offender, rather by the victim. This is the awareness factors coming into play. They require someone who is 'switched off' and someone who seems willing to acquiesce to an approach.

"Tourist Shot Through The Heart In Bahamas"

Two years after the murder of tourist Mr Jonathan Porton, the Royal Bahamian Police have reported to the British coroner that they have no clues as to the identity of the two men who shot and robbed Mr Porton.

The victim had been out for a meal with his wife and another couple when, on getting into their rented car they were attacked by two hooded men. Mr Porton struggled with one of the assailants, at which point he was shot through the heart. The gunmen still demanded money from him and ripped a gold chain from his neck. They attempted to drive off in the hire car, but the keys had been removed and eventually they fled on foot. Mr Porton was pronounced dead at the hospital.

It is impossible to foretell how we will individually react to a robbery, but you have to come to some predetermined course of action should it happen. The basic rule, which we have said elsewhere, is do not turn a theft into a violent assault. If, however, it looks like there will be violence anyway then you must resist. The situation where you are under a gun and being assaulted nobody can advise you about - it is down to you at the time to act, once you can determine what will be the best. If you do act, do it quickly and do it violently. If you have to go for peoples eyes or throats then do so, but commit yourself or do nothing at all. A half hearted effort will only worsen your situation. If you are outnumbered you may have to try your best to talk your way out of serious harm and equally if you have no combative skills whatsoever, your chances of being effective with physical action is likely to be nil.

Beware The Busker!

You must decide very quickly about how you will deal with an approach in the street. Remember that most street traders, in most parts of the world are allowed to operate as a consequence of paying a local villain a 'tax' in exchange for the 'license' to work. They are often under pressure to work in unison with 'scams' or outright theft. Street traders or buskers who gather crowds around them, may be doing so to enable pickpockets to operate amongst the crowds.

In Red Square you will be approached by Street traders, photographers and all manner of opportunists - don't get involved if you sense anything untoward. Don't show your purse or wallet in public.

Whether you are a tourist or someone on business, you need to decide before you step foot outside your hotel or vehicle or emerge from the customs at the airport what your attitude will be.

As a consequence of my work I have a policy of politely, but firmly saying no to everyone, even if the approach is innocent and benign. Don't make the mistake of believing that you will be able to distinguish between the nefarious individual, who is out to rip you off and the innocent street trader or enthusiastic, amateur guide - you won't. A conman is a conman because he is good at it and doesn't look, or sound like a conman. In fact the person who has the least evil intent probably looks more threatening.

If I am on the street looking after a client, we may have a purpose in that we are en route somewhere or we are actually on the street looking at stores, property or his companies products which are being sold.

At times we can attract hangers on, from small boys to large thugs and we ignore them all. We ignore the large thugs after we let them know we are aware of their presence and this is by means of eye contact. Not contact which in itself is both provocative and challenging, simply an acknowledgement that we are aware of their presence and that we are no longer people who can be taken by surprise, therefore, not opportunistic for them.

The same applies to where you live now. Whichever country you come from all major cities around the world, with one or two exceptions have domestic street crime. The modus operandi of street robberies is broadly the same. Victim selection, the initial approach and shock tactics to keep the victim off balance and frozen into immobility and compliance whilst the theft is carried out . The key element to this is 'surprise'. If, however, this is lost, so is the main plank of their selection procedure.

As skilled amateur psychologists, street thieves know that 99% of people 99% of the time are 'switched off' and walk about in a dream like state. They can identify someone who is unaware at a mile away.

The first thing is 'Switch On'. Start the 'game' of people watching and 'situation awareness.' When you leave your hotel on a sunny morning to walk 300m to the beach or leave your office at lunchtime to walk around town you do not expect to end up in hospital stabbed or dead! - some people never return. Forget the statistics for a moment, they will give you no comfort nor assistance if tomorrow it's 'your turn'. When you make a 'transition' from one environment to another the 'Traffic Lights' in your head must be clearly visible.

Demeanour

I've mentioned non-verbal signals previously and if you can cultivate some of the more positive ones you will be half way there to avoiding many street confrontations. Whether we are on the streets of London, Manilla, Mexico City or in some seemingly benign sleepy backwater, we need to look self-assured. We need to maintain an erect carriage, purposeful stride and exude an aura of alertness. Easier said than done, but these are fundamental prerequisites before we even look at some do's and don'ts and avoidance planning.

How You Are Perceived

So switch on and, more importantly, look as if you are switched on. Body language is the most important, subjective self protection message that you emit. You should send out signals that tell others you are aware, confident, in control, know where you are going and will be difficult to take by surprise. Walk Aware, Briskly and with Purpose - don't display vulnerability.

Always walk with speed. When I'm giving seminars I ask the people who they would think is the most difficult type of person to mug. The answer which we eventually come to is 'a deaf person on the run'.

With someone whose deaf it's impossible to use a question as a deception and it's impossible to run alongside whilst you demand their wallet. The converse then, as to who is easy to mug becomes easy to appreciate. Someone who is stopped, looking around, obviously lost, holding their wallet, or a map, or walking slowly in a dream.

Unknown Risk

Remember, most street crime is opportunistic and for this to happen a number of factors have to be in place. First you have to be chosen as a target. People who look wealthy or display that wealth on their wrist in the form of a gold watch are a target economically.The final piece of the selection is down to you and how you appear. Look switched off and you have put the pieces of the picture into place for you to be a victim, you are now also a target 'opportunistically'.

Street criminals, either robbers or sneak thieves, have a process of target selection. It is simple and based on two factors and two alone - **commercial potential** and **opportunity**. Taking them in order, if you were to walk everywhere in a bathing costume you are unlikely to be mugged as you patently present no commercial potential. Opportunity has more facets to it such as **lack of witnesses**, **escape availability** and finally the **element of surprise.** It is this latter aspect that we in fact create the opportunity for someone else to take advantage of.

Thieves are people who want the easiest possible life, which, fundamentally, is why they are probably thieves. They want a 'target' who looks to have economic prospects for them, but equally as important a target who can be taken by surprise or who has, unknowingly, created the ideal circumstances for the would-be thief. This is achieved by putting your bag on the floor, or on a counter and then becoming occupied with some matter or other, flashing money, a wallet, credit cards and helping the process by disclosing to all and sundry the pocket you carry it all in.

These are the objective actions that betray us, but even more dangerous is disclosing our mental state, in particular the fact that we have no clue what is going on around us.

Every person who has been mugged in the street says one thing - "**they came out of nowhere**"-, when in fact the mugger had been on the same street, in view and watching the victim for minutes. They came "out of somewhere" and the feeling of them appearing as if by magic is created by the shock and surprise. This is the circumstance street thieves work hard at creating. Whether they are sneak thieves or muggers it is you who creates the ideal opportunity for them to ply their trade.

So three main rules - reduce your economic attractiveness, opportunity and reduce the possibility of being taken by surprise.

1. The first of these is easier to do than the second and third. If at all possible don't carry a briefcase or handbag. Don't be on your own, Don't flash money around, separate money into workable smaller amounts, no jewellery, no cameras, videos or binoculars. (This is very difficult when you want a record of you trip, but the advice, as always, is related to the risk). Recently I have been on holiday in Europe and carried an expensive digital camcorder with me, but I am conscious of any interest in me at all times

2. Be aware of your surroundings. Think if you had to mug someone where you would ideally carry it out, then see if where you are fits the bill.

3. By sending out the signals that you are alert you reduce the main plank of an attack, because you reduce the element of surprise.

If A Car Stops

Take nobody at face value and if you are asked for directions by anyone in a car, preferably do not stop, but if you have to keep a good six feet or more away and don't be drawn towards the car, particularly if you are asked to look at a map or piece of paper with an address on it.

◆ If a car stops and you are threatened scream and shout and set off your personal alarm if you have one to hand. Get away as quickly as you can - don't run in the direction of the traffic as he can follow you easily, so back track and get into a shop or similar. If you can make a mental note of the number & description of the car and occupants, write them down as soon as possible after.

◆ So that you cannot be surprised by a vehicle, endeavour to walk towards the oncoming traffic, this way a car or van cannot draw up behind you. I don't want to differentiate between male and female, but certain situations do hold more danger for the lone female.

Muggings (Street Robberies)

These can take place day and night but, generally they will take place in 'secondary areas, to the main shopping and business areas of major cities, although attacks do take place in even the busiest and best areas. The perpetrators of street robberies are the disaffected and violent youth of today.

They exhibit three things:-

NEED
GREED
HATRED

Lets look at some of the general pointers as to how a street robbery occurs:

Progression of The Event

1. Observation and selection

   - based on vulnerability

   - ease and escape

2. Test for Opportunity

- any witnesses
- are you paying attention
- how are you reacting to distance gap closing
- the contact approach method

3. Your immediate response determines whether they discontinue OR

4. Assault progresses to physical contact

Approach/Closing Distance Gap

How to recognise an 'assault approach'

◆ Loiterer conversation stops

◆ Any verbal calling or comments

◆ Very close walk-by and reverse

◆ Followed or flanked

◆ Some innocuous request

◆ Personal space violation

◆ More than one approaching

◆ Your time to decide diminishes quickly!

Immediate Response Necessary

◆ Sound off and give a directive- if you have not seen the incident develop with enough time to alter course and seek safety, your first weapon is your voice

◆ Be specific when yelling for help

◆ Run/spread the distance and find people

- Forget your doubts
- Forget the embarrassment factor
- If you don't do these things the event will progress and you will need Part 2 of this book sooner than you thought, and if it progresses anyway what have you learned.

Reaction To Physical Contact

- Listen to what they want if they tell you
- Don't turn a theft into a violent assault
- Give up the item

With **Compliance/Cooperation** options- there are positives and negatives. They may still inflict violence gratuitously or they may take the items and leave and at the point you accede to any request you do not know. If it's simply a theft then comply.

With **Resistance/Fighting** options- there are positives and negatives. You may lose and suffer greater harm than if you had co-operated or you may win the day with little or no injury. There is also the degree to which the other party may suffer injury. One point to remember you can never resist you can only fight. To simply resist would get you seriously hurt. If you are being assaulted or being kidnapped, then fight.

As you will read throughout this whole book I keep emphasising that at the time of the event this is no place to be making carefully balanced decisions about the pros and cons.

There is much you have to take in, does he have a weapon? perceived physical capabilities, is anyone around to help, is he changing location, is he hurting you? now- it all becomes a question of priorities.

General Reaction Guidelines

- Don't let them transport you elsewhere

◆ The sooner you notice the approach the more options you have. Awareness factors.

◆ Consider temporary cooperation which may assist in reassessment and better positioning- in other words can you buy some time

◆ If able to break and run - do so

◆ Ineffective defensive manoeuvre will make matters worse

◆ If you must, fight to escape - Timing, Technique, Tenacity

You are more vulnerable when;

◆ You are isolated (safety in numbers)

◆ You are in darkness (stay out)

◆ You are near areas of concealment (hiding places)

'You must consciously plan to avoid these'- **Security (vs) Convenience**

Worst Areas

◆ Subways at night

◆ A deserted station or bus depot

◆ lonely, narrow and poorly lit streets

◆ Short cuts through parks, wasteland, back streets or alleys and lonely beaches.

◆ Walking alone - the later the worse, particularly in a known dangerous area

Other Specific Problem Areas

◆ Parking areas - shopping centres, sports events, transportation terminals

◆ Stairwells, elevators, toilets

◆ Automated teller machines (ATM's)

- Public recreational facilities - Parks
- Any 'Drive through' service area

Pre-Incident Indicators

a. Unnatural impediment to your movement

b. Correlation of third party movement to that of yourself

c. Sudden changes of status of a person or persons near you. Predatory movements i.e. circling & two or more moving in from opposite directions (pack actions)

d. verbal exchange initiated by a stranger

e. Target or escape avenue glancing

f. Person or persons approaching at an oblique path that will intersect with that of yourself.

g. Hidden hand or hands that cause an unnatural walking posture

h. Bumps, pushes, shoves or grabs

i. Relative absence of locals or authorities

j. Automobiles stopping alongside, slightly to the front or behind

k. Any obviously intoxicated person or persons

l. Any second pass by a vehicle

m. Obvious attempts at 'Baiting'

n. Glances between apparent strangers as they approach, impede, hail or otherwise interact

o. Undue attention to your presence or vehicle.

What signs can we look for in the demeanour and body language of others that will indicate to us that they are building themselves up for either aggressive dialogue or worse?. Also how can we tell that the point has been reached where they may be about to move to physical violence and escalate the threat. If we are going to preempt this occurring we must be sensitive to mannerisms and the signs along the way.

In my book ***Streetwise***, there is considerably more information on target selection, warning signs, verbal and non-verbal clues about assaults.

General

Some Points or Do's and Don'ts

The following list of Do's and Don'ts are applicable not only in respect of street robberies, but as points of general street security:

Carry yourself with confidence; even when you are lost, walk as though you know where you are going - which should of course be the case.

◆ If you need directions do not ask a stranger on the street, rather ask staff in a bank or similar institution, but in certain geographies avoid the police e.g Colombia, Cambodia, Mexico.

◆ Stay on the main streets and streets which are well lit and well populated at night.

◆ Don't show expensive jewellery

◆ Anything valuable should be in the front, inside pocket, not in your back pocket or the side pockets of a jacket.

◆ Carry your handbag in a 'self conscious way - let it fall in front of you not behind - flap in toward you so it can't be snatched from behind - one method of attack is the fast hit and run from behind. Also carry it in a way that makes it easy to let it go. There is an argument for wearing the strap on the same side as the bag so that if it is grabbed you will lose the bag without suffering a potential neck injury.

◆ Carry belongings in a nondescript bag. Camera bags, aluminium cases and laptop computer cases are asking for trouble.

◆ Cash and passport etc should be in a concealed money belt or neck pouch.

◆ Do not retrieve items in public, but prepare for what you may require well in advance.

◆ Avoid protests, demonstrations and any social disturbances.

◆ If you are in a high kidnap region, vary your daily routine.

◆ Don't attract attention to yourself by speaking your native language loudly.

◆ People should know where you are going.

◆ Carry some form of identity with you at all times.

◆ Use the gap between cars if someone runs at you.

◆ Don't run whilst you are still in full sight of the person or persons that concern you. If someone does cause you concern make your alternate move in a calm way.

◆ Dress conservatively and remove all 'brand' names and labels.

◆ Don't use a phone box to phone for help. Even in London an office worker in was dragged from the phone box and raped as she phoned for help.

◆ One ploy is for one person to stop you and ask for change of a large denomination note - if you pull the purse or wallet out a second attacker will snatch it . The first can deny any involvement even if he doesn't run. They may use an alley off the main road you are on to wait in - so raise your awareness etc.

◆ Distribute your money around your person divide notes and keep some old credit cards in a top jacket pocket. These are 'give aways'

◆ Consider carrying a 'bluff' purse or wallet to give away.

◆ Before going into a shop to buy something, carefully try to prepare the correct amount to pay for the item don't sort it out in the shop as you can be targeted there and they know in which pocket you keep what they want.

◆ Never stop in the street for any request or 'Question & Answer' session.

◆ Don't take shortcuts.

◆ Never pass through a subway until you can utilise a full escort of other people.

◆ Never walk close to buildings, past unlit doorways and alley-ways, keep well out from the building to avoid being jumped.

◆ Walk facing traffic - this prevents a vehicle pulling up to you unseen and deters 'kerb-crawlers'

◆ If a car stops use your voice

◆ Never accept a lift from a stranger, even if he claims his car is a taxi.

◆ Don't talk to anyone in the street. They can be like glue and will often prey on politeness - be rude.

◆ If you are wearing high heels take them off before you run.

◆ If you think you are being followed move away or change direction, then go to the nearest occupied area and call the police

◆ Walk quickly across the road and cross it again if necessary

◆ Walk to a busier area where there will be other people - a shop, a garage, well lit house, pub, cab office etc.

◆ If you go into a shop for help BE CALM don't scream or shout, or they will react against you and take you as a threat be rational, reasonable in your request for help

◆ Don't flash expensive jewellery

◆ In most countries it is an offence to carry any item for the sole purpose of self defence but it may be possible to improvise, but the reality of this we will look at later.

◆ Foreigners have been drugged in bars, hotels and even buses - it may be from bottled drinks which were already opened, sweets and cigarettes - so refuse all offers.

Avoid crowds and the usual 'higher risk' crowded places such as:

◆ Subways

◆ Rail/Bus Stations

◆ Elevators

◆ Tourist Sites - we know you can't avoid them, because they are why you are their, but raise your awareness level suitably.

◆ Market places

◆ Festivals

◆ Street vendors, particularly when they operate near pedestrian 'bottlenecks' e.g at busy street crossings.

Out & About

◆ NONE OF US IS INVISIBLE! - It is folly to think we go unnoticed and it won't happen to us

◆ Trust your intuition - if you feel scared or uneasy - don't ignore but act on it

◆ Be Alert when out and about.

The covered market in Istanbul. All the usual precautions should apply. In essence, simply 'switch on' and don't fall into the trap of ignoring people and their interest in you.

◆ Don't be out on the street if you have had too much to drink.

◆ Moderate your intake if you know you will be walking or ensure you have a known taxi company picking you up.

◆ Walk tall keep your feet slightly apart for good balance, keep your head up and your mind focussed on your surroundings. Keep your hands out of your pockets.

◆ Know where you are going & how to get there .

◆ Look confident without appearing arrogant.

◆ Good posture, stamina, strength are all positive aids to good self protection.

◆ Walk down the middle of the pavement. Keep clear of alley-ways, shrubbery and dark doorways. Try and think where someone could be concealed e.g. behind the rubbish skip you are walking towards.

◆ Don't stop to help at a road accident, if necessary go for help.

◆ If you are an expatriate always have your keys ready when you arrive home so as to minimise the time you are stood at the door fumbling in your bag or pockets. In London in 1997 there was a gang operating in wealthy residential areas which targeted people outside their homes to steal their watches.

◆ At your front door be even more cautious and aware than you have been all night. In Russia the lighting outside apartment blocks is usually non-existent.

◆ Avoid long eye contact with strangers as it can taken as provocative. Remember your eyes show any vulnerability or weakness.

◆ Don't hitchhike.

◆ Keep your personal possessions like a briefcase or handbag close to hand in public places, make it more difficult to snatch. You should always be able to see or feel it.

◆ Keep your cheque book in a different place to your cheque card.

◆ We repeat, cover up expensive jewellery and tuck any gold chain into your top or collar.

◆ Try to avoid reading in the street, particularly a street map as it indicates you are not familiar with your surroundings. If you must do it try and keep walking.

◆ If someone asks you any question and you feel you have to reply keep at least two arms length away, better still try and answer on the move. Regarding a request for the time - don't stop!!

◆ Be firm with beggars say "NO" and keep moving. Remember in Europe pickpockets operate in twos and threes - one will distract you, possibly begging and touching, the second will take you valuables and pass them to the third who will be off.

◆ Be very aware of approaches from the rear when standing looking at tourist monuments.

◆ Do not get involved with strangers in the street. Pickpockets usually require you to be distracted and you may be:-

- jostled

- engaged by another in conversation

- or otherwise distracted

Do not let anyone touch you, however innocuous, as even a light touch with the ends of someone's fingers has told them where you keep your wallet. Pickpockets are professional magicians and just like in a magic show, watches and wallets will disappear as if by magic.

◆ Leave little exposed to view and remember even a woman with a baby can be a pickpocket.

◆ Don't speak about any private matter in public and within earshot of stranger, particularly details of travel arrangements.

◆ Whilst you need to avoid crowds you equally need to avoid desolated side streets, there is safety in numbers.

In St Petersburg in Russia you can be mugged by a gang of youths in the main street where the youngest assailant can be twelve or less.

The use of force is only to be recommended in a self defence situation after you have exhausted certain other options. If attacked 3 options - **Flight, Compromise, Attack**

Flight - Get away as fast as you can . Don't stop to think ACT. Run to a place where there are people or a security - most large stores.

Compromise - If you can't get away scream yell, set off your personal alarm and throw it out of reach. Remember though that resistance is not the same as defence!

Attack- Hit hard and break away to run. Be furious and throw your weight into him and break away. Don't stay to fight, your tactic is 'Hit and Run'.

Automated Teller Machines (ATM's)

ATM's are an exposed location. Whilst you are unlikely to be attacked at the ATM if other people are around, you can be targeted there. The following advice applies to using an ATM at home equally as it does abroad.

◆ Keep a good look around you and don't take your card out until the last minute.

◆ Don't withdraw anything other than small amounts, which means you don't have to stand around exposed whilst you count it.

◆ Don't use the machine if there is anyone there you don't like. Play the game - remember the face and watch out for it again.

◆ Don't let people stand directly behind you.- they have been known to mark your coat with chalk which identifies you to their cohorts!

◆ Also avoid dispensers when the street is very quiet.

◆ Make sure no-one can see you enter your PIN.

◆ If at all possible try to avoid using dispensers at night - they can be very dangerous. Drive through ones are regular venues for robberies.

◆ Generally avoid handling cash in the street.

◆ Avoid pedestrian and vehicle shortcuts

◆ Beware of graffiti ridden areas and obvious changes to dilapidated streets etc.

◆ Avoid trying to find shortcuts, stick to main routes.

◆ The appearance of the populace tells you whether you have

strayed off the safe, tourist areas. If you dig for money in a public place move away from people, but watch to see if anyone follows you.

"Walking around money"

Keep money you need for the day in a small wallet, clip or small purse. In a front pocket - a rear one can be slashed. If a skirt without pockets sew one into the inside.

If you buy travellers cheques whilst away, keep the receipt elsewhere from the checks and also write down the cheque numbers. Do the same with airline ticket numbers. Do the same with Visa numbers and if possible photocopy visa and vaccination certificates.

Bogus fare collectors on buses collect fares and disappear. If you pay for a fare GET A TICKET. In taxis stay and see that your luggage is all packed in the boot. don't get in and leave someone to it. On Trains padlock your rucksack to the luggage rail if you have to leave it and there is no one to look after it.

Whenever you are on crowded public transport keep your cash and valuables in front of you and not behind. Place your hand over any pockets in which you have valuables.. Always look behind you when you get off, it is easy to leave items behind

Railway stations are good places to be stolen from e.g. bogus porters, bogus taxis.

- Never walk close to the curb and watch out for 'ride by' bike or motor cyclists who will grab items from you as they ride by. Keep any 'over the shoulder' bags away from the roadside. This is a common practise in such places as Naples.
- keep your wallet in a front pocket.
- In subways be especially careful. Never stand close to the tracks, keep a wall to your back, move any bag you are carrying to the front as you board a train and as you board be very wary of anyone

who is close to you. Remember, though that if someone jostles you he or she may not be the thief. The jostling is likely to be the distraction which enables their accomplice to take something from you.

◆ If you stop to talk in the street with others do not do it in the open if possible, better to stand close to a building.

◆ When you are out in the street do not stand and study a map or street guide. It identifies you as a stranger, unsure of where you are and makes you a static target.

Eating and Drinking

In certain parts of the world restaurants and cafes are places where a variety of crime takes place from pick pocketing, to drugging and robbery. You will find drugging a practise in Russian nightclubs and in cafes in Turkey, Brazil, Colombia, Thailand and the Phillipines.

◆ Try to keep an eye on the food at all times, although this will be difficult.

◆ When ordering drinks ask for bottles and cans to be unopened and watch them being poured.

◆ If you start to feel woozy and think you may have been drugged do not accept a lift to the hospital or hotel from a friendly stranger. Instead, call the hotel and explain your situation, or call emergency assistance. This is where a cell phone comes in very useful. Have all the numbers you need programmed into the phone in advance.

◆ If you are in a street cafe, make sure someone in your party is facing the street. If you are on your own do not accept a position which puts your back to the street.

◆ When sitting in restaurants, outdoor cafes or the like always have the strap of your bag wrapped around your leg or that of the table or arm of the chair and keep it in view at all times.

◆ If possible resist alcohol and certainly do not get drunk. If you are in a party arrange that someone will not drink. Your sense of danger dulls in relation to the alcohol consumed as well as it dulling your general awareness.

◆ watch for sudden disappearance of locals.

Female Travellers

Women have special problems in certain parts of the world and need to ensure they are familiar with the cultural and religious ways of the people they will encounter on their journey. Like it or not, many countries of the world are male dominated societies, the religion, often supporting the secondary role of women in the society. The Taliban in Afghanistan has reduced the role of women in society to that of slaves. Be that as it may there are some basic rules to follow .

◆ The more remote the region the less safe it becomes to travel alone.

◆ If you are going out at night be particularly cautious and never go out alone.

New Delhi.

◆ Be aware of dress codes and comply. In the Middle East dress should be such that it covers bare shoulders and ankles. It should not be provocative.

◆ It may help also to wear a wedding band as some countries frown on single women with the freedom they enjoy in the west. To avoid hassles consider wearing a gold ring and giving the impression that your husband will be meeting you later.

Beware of the Police

If you are attacked or robbed whilst abroad, consider very carefully your actions with regard to the local police.

The Times, in March 1999, reported the case of a British woman who claimed she had been raped by four policemen in Bangladesh. She had gone to report a theft to a police station in Dick. Human rights lawyers claim that police regularly attack women in custody. The British Consul in Dick advised that " women should not go into police stations or similar agencies", however, the Foreign Office's travel advice gave no such warning about the potential to be assaulted.

Under a law dating from the days of the Raj, Bangladeshi's police can put any woman behind bars under the pretext of "giving safe custody". Local newspapers have reported many incidents of rape and deaths in custody. If you have to go to a police station never go alone and ensure your Embassy knows.

CHAPTER SEVEN

Security on the Road

Anyone who has read The Modern Bodyguard, or who is familiar with Close Protection procedures, will be equally familiar with the distinction between '**Vehicle Security**' and '**Mobile Security.**' The former is to do with the security of the vehicle, essentially when it is static and your own personal security in relation to the vehicle, whereas Mobile Security is concerned with the problems we may face during a journey.

Much of this chapter deals with issues closely related to being resident in a country, where routine and route procedures must be attended to. Much of what is written though will equally apply to someone on holiday in a rented vehicle, particularly in a more remote or non-compliant geography. For more detail on this subject read ***The Modern Bodyguard*** and ***Streetwise***.

On a very general point you should take advice as to whether you drive in some countries or not. Remember that in many countries being involved in an accident and as a foreign car driver, irrespective of fault, can mean absolute liability and with severe penalties. Your risk of having a serious accident may be almost guaranteed in some countries of the world and the rising incidence of attacks and carjackings in African countries make unaccompanied car journeys simply too dangerous to contemplate.

In many places frequented by tourists, including areas of southern Europe, victimisation of motorists has been refined to an art. Where it became a problem for US citizens, the embassies and consular officials worked with local authorities to warn the public about dangers. In some locations these efforts at public awareness have paid off, reducing the frequency of incidents. You may also wish to ask your rental car agency for advice on avoiding robbery while visiting tourist destinations.

In city districts car thefts, of and from, are as common abroad as they are at home so:

◆ Don't leave briefcases, carrier bags, groceries, computers, clothing in view and be aware of people who may be watching you put items in the trunk.

◆ If someone suspicious approaches your car while at a traffic light or in a traffic jam, honk the horn and, in some cases, consider driving through the red light.

Lock your doors the moment you are in the car.

◆ Car jackers and thieves operate at gas stations, parking lots in city traffic and along the highway. Be suspicious of anyone who hails you or tries to get your attention when you are in or near your car.

◆ Criminals get your attention by either trying to drive you off the road, or causing an "accident" by rear-ending you or creating a "fender-bender'.

◆ Don't stop to be a good Samaritan, it is likely to be a 'staged' accident or breakdown to get you to stop. In some urban areas, thieves don't waste time on ploys, they simply smash car windows at traffic lights, grab your valuables or your car and get away.

◆ Keep an eye out for potentially criminal pedestrians, cyclists and scooter riders. Be that as it may you should always drive with your windows closed to keep thieves reaching in and stealing any valuables in sight. Always hire a vehicle with AC, particularly in hot climates.

You are at risk in many parts of the world e.g. Kenya, South Africa, Mexico City, San Juan, to name but a few when you are stationery, particularly at lights. In the places mentioned above the practise of carefully rolling through red lights is common, but it is far better if you judge and pace your approach to the lights so as to reach them on green.

◆ If you are held up it is likely your assailants are armed and the advice must be to not resist. Sadly this will not guarantee you surviving unharmed.

General

Travel by vehicle has it's own very specific risks. Depending where you are in the world there are three broad areas of risk. In certain locations all three vie for ascendancy, whereas in others one may be prevalent and they are.

1. Vehicle Accident

2. Criminal Assault

3. Terrorist Attack

1. Vehicle Accidents

We need to keep matters in perspective, both with regard to accidents abroad and the possibility of attack. We are advised that only 750 Americans died in traffic related accidents overseas compared to some 42,000 at home in the U.S. What the figures do not tell us though is the number of accidents nor the injuries and major problems that can ensue from a traffic accident in the Third World.

It comes as no surprise to those of us who have driven in India that it tops the list, with vehicle deaths at roughly 35 per 100,000 of head of population. Interestingly, though, Egypt comes out on top if we look at deaths per distance driven, with 43 per 100 million kilometres driven, Kenya at 36 and Turkey at 22.

However, the dangers of road travel were tragically brought home in September 1999, when a coach skidded off a mountain road in South Africa killing 26 elderly Britons and severely injuring 7 others. The crash happened in the country's Mpumalanga province, near Lydenburg, in the Long Tom Pass. It would appear the brakes failed.

It's either drive in the dust of a petrol lorry or.............

......a white knuckle overtake on a bend -
Uganda - Kampala to Fort Portal road and a local driver!!

Despite S. Africa having the most extensive and modern road network in Africa, it has one of the continent's worst records for accidents. More than 15,000 people are killed on the roads every year at a cost of some 10 billion Rand (£1 billion). Speed is the biggest killer, with an estimated 69 per cent of accidents due to excessive speed, although 47 per cent of drivers and pedestrians killed on the road had blood alcohol levels above the legal limit.

The recent road accident was the fifth bus crash in less than two weeks. Accidents and fatalities in the Long Tom Pass are frequent as many drivers exceed the 60 kph limit in force. The driver of the bus was subsequently jailed.

2 & 3. Criminal and Terrorist Attacks

I should make the point here that it is of little value establishing a motive for the last two. A businessman could be kidnapped in Columbia for ransom by a terrorist organisation as he could by a criminal gang. The guidance given in this Chapter regarding 'Awareness Drills' have a considerable bearing on the prevention of both accidents and attacks.

Broad Rules

◆ Travel in a group whenever possible.

◆ Never overload a vehicle.

◆ Vehicle in good repair.

◆ Good security for the vehicle when not in use - alarm, steering lock etc etc.

◆ Avoid parking on the street overnight.

◆ Inspect before entering.

◆ If the car breaks down open the bonnet, tie a white cloth to the door handle and if anyone stops to offer help ask them to phone for assistance - doors locked.

- Never pick up hitch hikers.
- Know the route and of any secure locations along the route.
- Cell phone or CB.
- Executive tracking- others must know.
- Mentally rehearse your actions in the event of an attack.
- Alert to surveillance.
- Be suspicious of local blockages to your route.
- Travel plans restricted on a need to know basis.
- Keep in touch.

Vehicle Security

Kidnappings, as an example, occur in or near the vehicle and usually close to the home. This is as a result of a number of factors favouring the attackers. First, they will 'track' your routine i.e. travel timings and routes. Second, your route probably presents some good opportunities, but third and most important you will be 'switched off' in the relative safety of your car, having just left, or about to reach the comfort of your own home and when you feel secure. Mornings are worse as people usually take the first mile or so to sort things out e.g. radio, misted screen, seat adjustment, car phone, etc. They mentally 'surface' about 5 blocks away and then concentrate on the journey. This is why so many accidents occur close to the domestic residence.

Basic personal security, as it relates to vehicles, concentrates on one basic issue- attitude. I went on at some length in Chapter 5 , about all the reasons we 'switch off' and this is more applicable when in a vehicle than anywhere. We have a mistaken belief that we are secure in a car. The concern is basically concentrated on two aspects:-

1. How we leave our vehicle

2. How we return to our vehicle

This sounds simplistic and quite rightly it should be if we can get our subconscious '3rd eye' to work for us and not to lapse into 'Condition White'. **Stage 2** -*'how we return to our vehicle'* is almost solely dependent on the intellect and forethought we have applied to **Stage 1.**

If we get the first part wrong you will see shortly, how we can create some 'nightmare scenarios' for ourselves when we return to the car.

Think & Plan Ahead

These days in the age of 'Health & Safety' legislation, we talk about a 'safe working environment.' What we are trying to achieve here is, very simply, a 'safe parking environment.' To achieve this we need to Think Ahead! Our 3rd Eye, should become schooled in the 'risk analysis' of trying to imagination the circumstances which will obtain when we return to our vehicle.

You should know your own foreign town or city well enough to be able to identify those areas where you would not want to leave your car under any circumstances- either because you could expect vandalism and theft from or of the vehicle. Also most people are shrewd enough to know a 'bad area' i.e. one you would not like to park in and then walk through. This isn't difficult, but if you are unsure or the city is new to you then endeavour to find out -use your intuition if you cannot be certain. There are 'no-go' areas in all major cities of the world. If you park your vehicle in a side street and walk passed broken glass on the floor, you know you are in an area where car break-ins occur.

Once again our main problem is not the patently unsafe areas, one because we rightly avoid them and two because as we know them to be bad we adopt a more considered approach to what we do there. It is, to repeat once again, 'the place we feel most comfortable that we are most at risk!' What do we need our 3rd eye to do for us? Very simply it needs to analyse what our vehicle and it's surroundings will look like on our return to it. If it is 2 o'clock on a sunny, Tuesday afternoon when you park and you are going to come back one hour later, things will look pretty much the same.

The Omissions

However, as you return at 8pm the place has become a 'desert.' There are few if any people around and those that are now may seem a little unsavoury and the area has taken on a very 'secondary' feel about it. You now begin to realise some very significant mistakes, or omissions you made earlier. At 2pm in the sun you took no cognizance of the street lighting, although you now realise it is poor to nonexistent. You also realise that your car is not parked under one of the few lights in the street and is almost in darkness.

More importantly some more serious factors may have a part to play, As you look at your car you suddenly realise that you have parked next to what is a very dark and threatening alley on the same side as your drivers door and you will have your back to it as you get in. It may be that there is no alley, but there is a large builders skip alongside your vehicle, and again you will have your back to the unknown as you try and get in. For the skip or alleyway, substitute a wooded area alongside the road, bushes, dark doorways. Essentially you have created 'an unsafe parking environment.' To create the opposite you need to have a few simple things in place.

These are that you have:-

1. Ability to have a 'visual' of your vehicle at a good distance as you approach it.

2. That your vehicle is well lit

3. You have not created the opportunity for hiding places close to your vehicle.

4. You have created the opportunity to abandon your vehicle should your awareness create suspicions as you approach

5. Be aware and suspicious if people and other vehicles are close to your car (a lone car parked next to yours when the rest of the street is empty should make you suspicious), particularly if there are people in it.

Lets expand on some of the points. A good 'visual' means that you are able to obtain an 'all round' view of your vehicle. This is as much to do with your method of approach as how you park it. When you return to your car, the following golden rule must be paramount.

'DON'T BE SURPRISED BY YOUR OWN VEHICLE'

For example if your approach to your vehicle on foot requires to turn a corner from one street into the one where your car is parked, then the above rule demands that the car needs to be parked some reasonable distance down the street you have turned into and not just around the corner. If the vehicle is only 10-15 feet away when you first get a visual you are too close. A hiding place for people who are waiting to rob you or worse on your return to the car may be on the ground at the rear or at the side of the car, practically underneath. This will be the preferred place if you have also parked in a corner e.g. a multi-storey car park .

Distance Creates Time!

At 10-15 feet away, the one area you have no view of is underneath. To be able to get a good view of this area you need to be at least 30-50 feet away. At this distance or further you have perfect 'inter-visibility' all round. At this juncture let me jump to point 4 above, because points 1 & 4 interrelate. The purpose of achieving your all round view of the car is so you can 'evaluate' potential threats. You know that after 'evaluation' the next stage up on the 'Threat Pyramid' is

Flight. By creating a good 'visual distance' you buy time! and time you must have for both the evaluation period and escape. So you see someone under your car from a good distance you can abandon it and seek help. Find a populated area and phone the police - do not return to your vehicle alone.

Approaching Your Vehicle

Given the broad guideline about a good visual distance, you still have to stay 'switched on' as the approach to your car continues. Your risk increases as you close with the car and are about to enter it.

◆ Things you should take into account are any other people or vehicles nearby.

◆ Be especially cautious about vans parked alongside your car, particularly if they have a sliding door and it is alongside the drivers side. It is the most common method of snatching someone off the street and you could be dragged into it in seconds.

◆ If you are unhappy, but not to the extent that you wish to abandon your car then think laterally. This advice applies with the dark alley, rubbish skip, bushes etc and this is 'get in the car through the passenger side!. This way you can keep your eyes on the area of concern and can lock the door the moment you are in.

◆ As you approach try to see if all your tyres are sound. Tyres can be punctured so as to make you stop and leave the vehicle at some point further on.

◆ Look for tamper marks on your vehicle. Make a quick inspection of the vehicle, but do not touch suspicious items. Check the exhaust pipe, tyres, fuel cap, wheel arches and bonnet latch. Always park in such a way that the underneath of the vehicle is visible as you approach - you need to be able to see someone lying down and anything left under the car.

◆ Always have your keys ready when you are close to your vehicle and use the remote to unlock it if your car is so equipped. If not have your key ready and try and 'know' instinctively where the lock is - don't end up 'fumbling' for the lock with the key which over-occupies you.

◆ Don't put parcels or a briefcase on the roof or bonnet while you open or close the door.

◆ As you reach your car you must include a visual scan of the interior, in particular the rear footwell, as someone could be lying flat out of sight in the dark. A small 'Mag light' type key ring torch is ideal to assist in this inspection.

◆ You should have remote opening so you don't need to occupy yourself with finding the lock and getting the key in it in the dark.

◆ As you get into the vehicle make sure you get in backside first. Bodyguards are taught to do this instead of putting one leg in first which people commonly do. One leg first orientates the body into a forward facing profile, so breaking visual contact with what may be coming towards you from the side. Backside first, keeps you facing the direction of any possible threat and keeps you with both feet on the ground longer. You can also use both feet to kick out if necessary.

◆ The moment you are in LOCK THE DOORS as your very first action. Now comes the hard part- which way have you parked? By that I mean have you 'nosey parked' which means you have gone in the lazy way when you parked which is nose in first, or did you do it correctly and park rear end first which probably took more time. Nosey parking is lazy and a dangerous habit. One, it is possible in restricted parking spaces to actually get stuck going in nose first when you want to get out. Two, if someone approaches your car as you get into it you want to be able to get out of there quickly and with the least amount of fuss. In a panic, trying to back out of a tight space can be problematic and dangerous. Women are the worst offenders in this regard and also the most at risk.

The following are some of the Do's and Dont's, but I will say it again knowing them doesn't mean you will automatically apply them unless you stay switched on and plan.

◆ Never leave your house keys in your car, particularly if there is an address and identity as well, e.g. vehicle log book. Whoever steals your car can also break into your home, because he knows you are not at home. He will phone to see if anyone else is. He may not do it himself, but phone an accomplice.

◆ Check petrol, oil, tyres prior to all long journeys. Always check in daylight in a safe place. If used regularly check oil and water once a week.

◆ Always have ample fuel, at least half a tank.

◆ Check tyres before every journey.

◆ Listen to the engine, If it doesn't sound right have it checked.

◆ Make sure the brakes are working efficiently. If you need to brake to avoid a threat better braking gives more distance which gives more time.

Preparing For Your Journey

◆ Plan your route and if it is a long journey that you would not commonly do, prepare a route card and leave one behind with family, friends or colleagues. People must know your estimated time of arrival (ETA) and they must also know to expect a call from you to confirm your arrival.

◆ Not only plan your route, but know the route as well as any safe locations en route.

◆ Travel with other people if possible.

◆ Everyone to wear seat belts.

◆ Try to avoid deserted country roads, choose the widest, fastest route.

◆ Always carry a torch in the car.

◆ Carry change and phone cards in the vehicle as well as a mobile phone.

◆ Try to avoid travelling alone at night.

Even the professionals get lost! A Close Protection team in Spain near the Prime Minister's residence - actually not lost - more disoriented!

◆ Have your car keys ready as you approach the car. This allows you speedy access to your vehicle, but equally as important it stops you fumbling in your purse or pocket and so taking your eyes and therefore your attention off your surroundings. It can also serve as a reasonable improvised weapon if attacked.

◆ Check the back seat & rear foot well.

◆ Lock all doors immediately you are in the vehicle before you do anything else.

◆ Keep a visual contact with your surroundings as you get into the vehicle - don't lose contact with what's behind you and get transfixed with simply the interior of the car.

◆ Don't leave your handbag or briefcase on the seat, put it in the boot or put it well out of sight. The same goes for your mobile phone. You can be attacked when stopped for any valuable item in sight.

◆ Keep the windows closed when you are stationery or in slow moving traffic.

◆ Always park your vehicle in a busy, well lit street. Not only will you reduce the risk of personal attack but also the risk of your vehicle being targeted for theft or vandalism.

◆ Avoid multi-storey car parks. If you can't - then heed what we have said already.

◆ Make sure nothing is left on display in the vehicle. It has been known for a vehicle to be broken into for a child's anorak & a plastic carrier. Apart from the mess and cost it could make you more vulnerable. Before leaving it make sure all doors are locked and windows closed.

◆ Check the surroundings, BEFORE getting out of the car. Take a moment or two to 'scan' the surroundings, particularly in multi-storeys.

◆ If your journey takes you into a remote area then conduct a 'Route Recce' in terms of a risk assessment. Seek the latest intelligence about the safety of the route and the areas you are passing through. Establish the physical condition of the road as well as the weather, services available and emergency /safe havens. Also, ascertain whether buses and trains are safe on the route you propose. Your first port of call for this intelligence should be your Embassy. If there is an English language newspaper available always read it. Often they are a good source of local problems

General Mobile Security

We looked at some 'pre-departure' preparations. To these we can now add the following. We are now safely in our car and travelling down the road. We have a choice to make and that very simply is to switch off or stay in control and use the opportunity to get some 'commentary' work done. You will be surprised about how much of an improvement the practise will make to the standard of your driving. You will be more alert to both other road users and also the actions of pedestrians. You will see situations developing well ahead of you and you will feel that much more in control.

You would think it would be safe on a wide desert road but.........

Commentary Driving

What is primarily required is to apply the awareness training we have highlighted in Chapter 2. I adapted 'commentary driving' training for use in the street and elsewhere, so lets export it back to where it came from - the car. Commentary driving is the verbal articulation of what we observe is happening in our 'environment' when we are driving and that encompasses a complete 360 degrees, in a logical and methodical way.

.... with drivers who overtake on blind bends and hills whilst leaving their fate in the hands of Allah - it's not that simple.

... so a solid roll cage is a must if your risk assessment puts traffic accidents high on the list of hazards.

That evironment also includes also the interior of the vehicle, eg. - the gear we are in, the speed we are doing, revs., oil pressure and what we are intending to do e.g. *"approaching traffic lights on red at approx. 200 metres, I intend to slow down using the gears, now checking the mirror and changing into third to 'pace' my approach to the lights and looking ahead I see two cars stopped at the lights. My speed is now 20 and I am still slowing with the gears and moving down into second, to my sides are parked vehicles and a few pedestrians who show no intention of crossing the road. Looking ahead I see a group of youths waiting to cross at the lights and looking behind I see a car coming up at speed which will box me in if I have to stop etc etc."*

The important thing here is that the 'commentary' work has created enough awareness to make you think about pacing your approach to the lights so that they just change as you get to them and you are not stopped and boxed in, so making yourself helpless should the youths turn out to be a threat. A vehicle's security is best when you are able to go somewhere in it, that is move. All other times, when you are stopped, it is a security risk. Any sequence you use to create a pattern of commentary is OK, but '**AHEAD, BEHIND, INSIDE, SIDES**', is a good working way of creating the full 360 degrees. This way you have a sequence which conditions you to move from looking ahead, to behind, to the vehicle state from your instruments and gear position and then both sides and back to ahead. Commentary work is often referred to as 'Read Ahead' driving. The better you get, the further ahead you will start to analyse what it is you are approaching. More importantly you articulate the process by which you are forming decisions about what to do as the journey unfolds.

What you can do the next time you drive is to try it yourself, but don't do it during a 'rush hour' period, otherwise you will overload the system - i.e. you! Try it during a quiet period and see how you cope. Commit yourself to do it the whole journey, but don't pick a journey that is 200 miles - pick one that will last some 10 minutes at first. You will also want to do it when you are on your own - simply due to the high embarrassment factor. You will quickly understand how difficult it is - one, to be methodical and two, to decide what is 'important' data to highlight in your dialogue and what is not. Lets take pedestrians - ten pedestrians who are walking toward you on the pavement, some ten feet from the kerb, probably need no commentary reference. In contrast, one pedestrian who is walking with his back to you and whose direction would seem to be toward the kerb needs 'reference to' as he or she could have the potential to step off the kerb into your path without looking and intuition will then tell you the appropriate time to sound the horn.

Be selective - on a busy road with many vehicles and pedestrians there is too much happening for you to describe everything - so you must select items which have potential to cause you problems . This may be one car in a line of six coming towards you who 'gives off' all the signals of impatience to overtake i.e. a sports car. As you approach trucks and buses, look underneath the front to see feet.This may be the only piece of someone's anatomy you see before the rest of their body ends up on your hood. You must learn to do this some distance away as the closer you get the less inter-visibility you have underneath. Commentary driving and commentary walking for that matter solve the problem of *"looking, but not seeing"*.

As an objective aid to better sight you may need to be more conscious as to how you position the car. Remember you've paid to be on the road so use it. This book is not the place to teach advanced driving skills, but without weaving all over the place you can probably make better use of positioning to make prior observation of potential risks happen sooner. Read Ahead commentary doesn't mean that your sole concentration is directed ahead. Ahead, Behind, Inside, Sides, conditions you to avoid the fixation with the end of your bonnet to the exclusion of all else, but also ensure that you are bringing into the commentary important 'environmental' detail. Not least of these is weather and the condition of the road. Sufficiency of natural light and changes as you drive along should also be included and the general changes to the type of physical environment. This is where you move from urban to rural, to built up high street to wooded area, to climbing or descending. In anti-kidnap drills, the changes in the physical environment are critical to be aware of as an attack will happen in quieter, more remote locations, with few witnesses and little room for you to manoeuvre or where you are slowed by hills, or constricted by narrowness or forced to stop e.g. railway crossing.

You will soon notice how your attention is directed to the task in hand - your environment and it's potential to 'bite' you. You will also begin to feel like Wellington on his country rides, being able to tell what the road will look like 'over the hill' and 'around the bend.' On unfamiliar roads where you do not know the sweeps and bends the road will take, then look for clues i.e. tree lines, telegraph poles, street lighting- where they go there is a good chance the road will also go.

Surveillance

This next section is equally applicable when you are mobile in a vehicle, on foot, leaving your home or office. We have talked elsewhere about surveillance in general. Surveillance is not just the preserve of international terrorists or criminal kidnappers.

Anyone who takes an unhealthy interest in you as a person has begun a 'surveillance mission'. Be it a street mugger, carjacker, rapist, stalker, they all have to embark on a period of watching you.

So why is it done;

- Target selection Who, Why! What is it that makes you a victim
- To pinpoint vulnerability

Surveillance Detection - Why/How

- Make them select another target
- Make it difficult to pinpoint your vulnerabilities
- Be alert, aware, and OBSERVANT
- Be less predictable & avoid patterns
- Reduce their probability of success.

Being able to detect someone who is watching you is the key to personal safety. If you can spot people or vehicles which make you unhappy, then you must, by definition, have been 'switched on' which is good.

Even the opportunist has need to identify you as suitable for his purposes, so remember, **if he can see you - you can see him**, it is just a question of being alert and intuitive about people. Someone who is following you on foot or in a vehicle will do things which cause him to be vulnerable. In ***The Modern Bodyguard*** I go into some detail about surveillance vulnerabilities, but here, suffice it to say that you will only spot people if you are conditioned both to look and see.

Anti-Surveillance

For 95% of the population intentional attacks on the road will be a rarity. For those people whose wealth is more obvious - cars, house, jewellery, media exposure, then the risks increase. You are identified as a potential target by what you drive, wear, and where you live and what you represent. To get these it may be that their plans are based on your vulnerability whilst you are on the road. You may not though have to qualify as wealthy to have your window or windscreen smashed or your door pulled open whilst you are stopped at lights, to have your purse, briefcase, shopping or mobile phone snatched and you punched and manhandled. You should also have seen it coming. If, however, you are effectively 'blind' due to being mentally elsewhere as you approach the lights, you will not have seen the two, unsavoury characters by the kerbside.

If you are switched on you will not only look at them 50 meters out, but you will 'see' them as well. As you are then in 'condition orange' you should pace your cars approach so as to reach the lights or the back of the queue as they change. What if it just isn't possible to slow down that much, that far out! What you should then try to achieve is to ensure you leave enough room when you stop to manoeuvre. Some very simple rules on this 1. Always look for an 'escape' turn off which is close to the junction or lights. 2. It is within your control not to get 'boxed in.' To prevent this you need room to be able to move and you know that the car behind will close up to you within a few inches. It is therefore up to you to not similarly close up to the car in front. If you cannot see the very bottom of the tyres of the car in front you are too close and will be unable to move away. Stop far enough away so that the bottom of the tyres are visible and you will have enough room to turn out of the line of cars.

Mobile

◆ Make sure that your cars fuelled and regularly serviced. Each week check, Oil, Battery, Water, Tyres, Screen washer fluid.

Seasonally check Antifreeze and Screen De-icer. Before a long journey, double-check that windows are clean, all lights are working, fuel level, oil level etc.

◆ Always have at least 1/2 tank of fuel.

◆ Select well lit, busy, clean service stations.

◆ Carry a mini-flashlight.

◆ Plan your routes and alternatives.

◆ You should be a member of a motoring or breakdown organisation with international agreements.

Choose the correct vehicle for the task in hand. An all wheel drive Chevy van seen here outside the Grand Hotel Europe - St. Petetsburg and used for an Executive Protection detail.

◆ Carry the number of an approved taxi firm with you.

◆ Make sure you have coins and cards to phone but always carry a mobile phone if possible in the country you are in.

◆ Let people know where you are going and ETA etc.

◆ Don't pick up hitchhikers male or female.

◆ If you are approached at the lights by a group of people or two people, you may need to make a decision to run the lights - if you do take great care and do it slowly.

Some more Do's & Dont's

◆ Be prepared to crash -at slow speed- if kidnapped in a public area.

◆ If forced to go somewhere act SOONER rather than LATER.

◆ If someone or something is blocking your way, stop well before the obstruction to assess how you can safely drive out of the situation without putting your personal safety at risk.

◆ If it appears to be a road accident or breakdown it may be safer and more practical to drive to the nearest safe parking spot and phone.

If you think you are being followed:

◆ Stay calm and in control of your vehicle. Do not let yourself be forced off the road.

◆ Alert other drivers - flash your lights and sound your horn.

◆ If necessary keep driving until you can get help. Head for a busy, well lit area with people. Obviously an open police station, fire station, hospital A & E.

◆ Avoid leading a following vehicle to your own home even if you do not live alone.

◆ If you are followed home lock all doors and attract attention with the horn or car alarm.

◆ Don't be forced to stop by someone in another vehicle who tries to indicate your vehicle has a problem. Even if you feel it is genuine drive to the next petrol forecourt.

◆ Never, though, force a confrontation.

◆ Use your 'communications' to alert others.

◆ Attempt to remain cool - injecting fear is the first thing your attackers want to achieve.

◆ Do not try to out-run them - it will end in disaster.

◆ In a crowded area stop, press your horn and alert others.

◆ Try to get another vehicle between you and the following vehicle.- Do not attempt jumping the kerb unless you are trained and competent at such a manoeuvre.

Carjacking

This is not a prevalent crime in the UK, but there have been incidents both in the U.K. and in the States and it is growing. In some African countries like Kenya and South Africa it has reached epidemic proportions. The following are some aspects of the problem:

1. Carjacking is an easy theft method, particularly with the sophistication of todays alarms.

2. What is the carjacker looking for -

◆ Nice car maybe.

◆ Vehicle is stopped and isolated.

◆ Occupant(s) are no threat.

◆ He will need an area of concealment if he is to wait for your return.

◆ Unlocked door or fully open window- doors locked at all times and when stopped open only 2″.

A top down in certain parts of any city in the world is potentially dangerous and invites carjacking.

◆ He needs an escape probability- his best time is when a person is entering or leaving the vehicle.

3. Typical approach scenarios.

◆ Tap from rear, whilst you are getting into the car.

◆ Walk-up approach at a junction, lights or your driveway.

◆ Get you to stop by deception or faked accident.

◆ Tampered vehicle - punctured tyre, blocked exhaust.

◆ Don't put down convertible tops at night or in crowded pedestrian areas.

Taxis

Taxi journeys around the world range from safe to suicidal. In some parts of the world i.e Mexico and Peru you should make alternative arrangements such as a chauffeur driven vehicles. The common practise in St Petersburg, Russia, with locals is for them to stand by the side of the road with their arm out. This is the sign for anyone to stop, not a taxi, but simply a motorist, at which point a deal is negotiated for the driver to divert to to the required address. This is not a practise which can be recommended to tourists, however. Some basic precautions:

◆ Transfers from the airport organised in advance.

◆ Do not not get in a taxi with others already in it, should always be the general rule. In Russia you do so at your peril, but remember that cultural differences will apply as in the case of, say, Morocco where it is common practise for a taxi to be shared.

◆ Don't always take the first taxi in the line, which is easier said than done as you are likely to cause a fight.

◆ Avoid using unofficial or unmarked taxis.

◆ Distinguish between licensed and touting taxis. Only take taxis with clearly identified official markings.

◆ It is a good idea to use taxis arranged by your hotel.

◆ In Russia never give your home address to a taxi driver, Russians never do, just let him know where you want to be dropped off or give him a street and stop him where you want. Often you will be targeted for thieves.

◆ If the rear doors do not lock, sit in the middle of the rear seat.

◆ Seat belt on.

◆ Always negotiate the fare in advance of setting off, if the taxi has no meter and don't get into the taxi until you have. If the fare seems excessive either negotiate or find another.

◆ Don't load your luggage until the fare is agreed.

◆ If you are unsure ask the hotel concierge to both arrange the taxi and also negotiate the fare. Know the currency the fare has been agreed in. Sixty 'local' can easily turn into sixty dollars, which could be ten times the local amount.

◆ Even when the taxi is metered ask the fare. It is only recently that the local administration in Naples Italy, outlawed the practise of taxi drivers doubling the fare shown on the meter. Despite that I had a taxi driver still try it on from the hotel to the airport. Don't be put off by any aggression as seldom will they want the police involved.

◆ If the local language is a problem then have your destination written down as well as your hotel in the local language.

◆ Check that the taxi that turns up is the one you ordered. Ask for a description of the car e.g. make, colour and registration number. If you gave your name when you booked it, make sure the driver can tell you it before you get in.

◆ When you book the cab get the company to tell you the driver's name.

◆ When you are in the taxi stay 'switched on' particularly to the way you are being taken to your destination. If you have a preference as to which way to go then ask and insist. If you are not happy ask to be let out out in a well lit area where there are a number of people.

◆ If you are unhappy make this known, insist on the route you want and always carry a mobile phone with you so you can call the police (have a number) if you are worried that things are taking a turn for the worse and he won't stop. There have been enough incidents of rape and sexual assault by taxi drivers to make any lone female feel less than secure.

◆ Always sit behind the driver, not next to him if you are female.

◆ If in any doubt DON'T get in, trust your instincts.

◆ If you are a woman try to identify a taxi firm which employs female drivers.

◆ If you talk to the driver stay on general topics and give away no personal information.

◆ If you book a taxi from a public phone or in a public place like a bar, avoid being overheard when you give your name and address.

Never get in a taxi with other people and never let the driver stop to pick up anyone else.

◆ Never get out in a deserted area.

◆ Always have small denomination bills with you when you take a taxi - they will never have change for a large one.

◆ Keep all your luggage with you in the car and not in the trunk. If your suitcase is too large for this, make sure the driver gets out of the car to load it for you, otherwise he might drive off.

◆ At your destination the same applies, do not get out of the cab before the driver otherwise he will be off. Moscow taxi drivers are renowned for it.

◆ Pay your fare inside the taxi, not standing outside with your back exposed, your attention elsewhere and your wallet out.

◆ Beware an accident whilst you are in the taxi, which may be staged and not what it appears, as it could be a robbery or a kidnap. Also in some countries if the accident is genuine then you, the paying fare, could be held responsible for the accident. You may consider walking away in the confusion.

The 'Express Kidnap'

A British classical orchestra was giving concerts in Mexico City. It had recruited an American 'tour assistant' who was acting in a support role with translation and logistics. He tells the story of being out one evening and flagging down a taxi to take him to the hotel.

This is just asking for trouble anywhere in the world.

Whilst en-route, the taxi made an unscheduled stop alongside two men standing on the sidewalk. Both men who were armed with pistols got in on each side of their victim, sitting on his arms and effectively immobilising him. They pushed the pistols against his head and body and began issuing threats. He had become the latest in a long list of victims of the business called the 'express kidnap'.

Express, because you will only be held for an hour or two. They demanded his ATM card and his PIN number all the while pushing the pistols into him and hitting him in the chest with their elbows. They relieved him of all his valuables and eventually pulled up at an ATM machine where he was obliged to withdraw cash. They will not simply be put off with a false PIN as their victims are held long enough to physically have to withdraw the money themselves.

He was let out shortly afterwards unharmed. In one way he considered himself lucky, as someone he knew who had suffered the same experience also had his suit and shoes stolen.

Chauffeur Driven

If you have the privilege of a chauffeur there are a number of points to watch:

◆ Establish the chauffeur's identity. Don't be fooled by a pretty face and don't take at face value an unnotified change of personnel.

◆ Enter the car as the chauffeur opens the door of the vehicle

◆ If the chauffeur is not there do not enter the vehicle and, ideally, don't linger on the pavement. Re-enter the building and watch for the drivers return.

◆ Try not to give the chauffeur advance notice of your movements.

◆ On entering, ensure the doors are locked and windows are up.

◆ If possible travel with companions.

◆ If you are suspicious about entering the vehicle, make an excuse for forgetting something and return to your safe, fixed location and summon help.

◆ At night remember poor light conceals a great deal - new driver!, someone in the vehicle!

◆ It will help if new chauffeurs are trained in awareness and security driving. Arrange an approved course.

Car Rentals

◆ Use only the multi-national, big name rental firms.

◆ You need a new, reliable vehicle in good condition, and make it a vehicle which is locally available.

◆ Rental staff are used to being asked for directions and should be helpful and have maps available.

◆ The rental agency should have emergency support and an extensive network of offices. Equally, you need an efficient system when you book the vehicle so as to maximise time. (I've found most airport offices of even the biggest companies often overworked and under-staffed. It may be better to find an office in town than at the airport.

◆ Ask that all markings which identify it as a rental car be removed.

◆ Learn which type of vehicle is most sought after by thieves/ carjackers and choose appropriately. You would not hire a BMW in Johannesburg, for instance.

◆ Whilst nondescript, the car should be large so you will be safer in case of an accident

Two airport points:

◆ Avoid going from the airport to meetings if it means leaving baggage in your car - plan to go to the hotel first. If the room is not ready it can be stored safely.

◆ Always arranged to be met either by a prearranged chauffeur company, reliable and tested taxi company, company representative, hotel car, or client.

◆ Always book a car with air-con, so you don't need to open the windows, especially when you are stopped.

◆ The car should also have central locking.

◆ GPS for cars.

◆ Always book a vehicle with a minimum engine size of 2 litres and with air conditioning. You should not drive with the windows open, particularly in town.

◆ It can often be false economy to go for the cheapest model. You ideally need electronic door locks, electric windows, remote access.

General

◆ Keep car doors locked at all times. Wear seat belts

As much as possible avoid driving at night.

◆ In most third world countries, eg Africa DO NOT drive at night in rural areas.

◆ Don't leave valuables in the car nor any parcels in sight whether they contain items of value or not - people will still break in to find out.

Don't give to gypsy street beggars in former Soviet countires - seen here in Baku - Kazahkstan.

◆ If you have to leave items in the vehicle leave them in the trunk, but arrange this before you stop and leave the vehicle or you may be observed making the transfer.

◆ Don't park your car on the street overnight. If the hotel does not have a parking garage or other secure area select a well-lit area.

◆ Never pick up hitch hikers.

◆ Don't get out of the car if there are suspicious looking individuals nearby. Drive away.

◆ Most places in the world - parking lots and multi-storey car parks are dangerous places.

◆ Pick a well lit and busy street to park in.

Public Transport

◆ Avoid lonely bus stops particularly at night.

◆ On an empty bus sit downstairs in view of the guard/driver-don't sit upstairs.

◆ On the way to work! On a Tube/Subway platform stand or sit near the exit/entrance and always be prepared to retreat from a situation.

◆ On subways choose a middle car, but never an empty car.

◆ Do not, as you see many people do, particularly at the end of the day, fall asleep or doze on public transport.

◆ Be aware of being overheard, particularly on public transport - do not answer any questions about your destination, however innocent they may seem.

◆ On a train the toilets are a safe haven lock the door and pull the cord.

◆ On a train try to sit near the guards compartment and only in a carriage with a central walkway. Always be aware where the communication cord is.

◆ If you are threatened or harassed move to an other compartment. If this isn't possible and there is no apparent assistance you have no recourse, but to pull the emergency cord.

◆ Always be aware of other people who alight from a bus or train when you do.

◆ Tell members of the transport staff if you feel anyone or anything is suspicious.

If a country has a pattern of tourists being targeted by criminals on public transport, that information is mentioned in the Consular Information Sheets under "Crime Information" section.

Sea Travel

Safety is more paramount than security, but nonetheless one must still take reasonable precautions.

Cabin door locked at all times

Read the fire drill carefully and inwardly digest. The evacuation routes will be posted on a wall somewhere near you.

Know where your lifeboat station is - know the ship's layout.

Ask the Purser to hold valuables for you during the voyage.

Keep your luggage out of sight when the door is open.

Trains

Well organised, systematic robbery of passengers on trains along popular tourist routes is a serious problem. It is more common at night and especially on overnight trains. If you see your way being blocked by a stranger and another person is very close to you, move away. This can happen in the corridor of the train or on the platform or the station.

◆ On the train itself again stand or sit near the doors in a carriage with people & check to see where the emergency chain is. If people get on you can get off - even if they get on next to you if you are aware, sensitive to their demeanour or if they are boisterous get off - as they board the train they are actually taking in other people who are probably some distance away and you can slip out as they get on.

◆ Don't sit in an empty compartment of a railway carriage.

◆ Do not accept food or drink from strangers . Criminals have been known to drug food and drink offered to passengers, so never accept food or drink from fellow passengers.

◆ If you are in a country with a high train accident rate try to get a compartment or sit at the rear of the train, statistically the safest place to be should a crash occur.

◆ Criminals may also spray sleeping gas into the carriages. This was a popular practice on the Moscow to St. Petersburg trains. If there is a history of this then sleep with the window open - if it will.

◆ Bring additional security so as to secure the compartment door, such as a bike chain with padlock. On the Russian trains they got round this by levering the whole door of it's runner. These days the problems are less as many trains have special police on board.

◆ Where possible, lock your compartment. If it cannot be locked securely, take turns sleeping in shifts with your travelling companions. If that is not possible then stay awake. If you must sleep unprotected, tie down your luggage, strap your valuables to you and sleep on top of them as much as possible.

◆ Do not be afraid to alert the authorities if you feel threatened in any way. Extra police are often assigned to ride trains on routes where crime is a serious problem.

◆ Always try to keep your property in sight which isn't always easy on a train. Even at home trains can be problematic. In the U.K and in Europe there have been a number of rapes of lone females on trains, on occasions leading to murder. On a less serious note there was also the practise in the UK, of wallets being stolen from the jacket pockets of men who, having hung up their jacket and then sat down prior to the train leaving the station were having their pockets picked. This was carried out by someone in a business suit who sat in the seat behind, took the possessions out of the pocket of the jacket which was usually hanging behind the owner and who then simply left the train. This is possible on U.K trains as there is now no restriction or control as to who gets on the platform or the train. No ticket is needed to get on the train and then get off before it departs.

Buses

The same type of criminal activity found on trains can be found on public buses on popular tourist routes. For example tourists have been drugged and robbed while sleeping on buses or in bus stations. In some countries whole bus loads of passengers have been held up and robbed by gangs of bandits.

Consider very carefully before you embark on a bus ride into the boonies in certain parts of the world. The fatal accident rate can be quite horrific, with poorly maintained vehicles, allied with inadequately trained drivers, unsuitable roads and the homicidal tendencies of other road users. This is before you face banditry, terrorist attacks and robberies by your fellow passengers.

CHAPTER EIGHT

Security in Hotels

Security in a hotel begins with the location of the hotel. It would be convenient to think that location often went hand in hand with the standard of the hotel, but in major cities a five star hotel could still be in the thick of the most dangerous part of town.

The advice given is to choose a hotel that should be in a safe district, with safe parking and with access to public transport. Unfortunately though the factors themselves are contradictory. Any hotel which has direct access to the public transport system is probably vulnerable, due to it's location. As business people we are probably victims of certain imperatives which determine our choice. Where we have to do business and with whom, will often determine the hotels location and often these issues will place us in the centre of cities.

Ideally your hotel should have:

24 hour front desk staffing

A security presence

Electronic card/key room locks

Electronic locks to lifts and floors

Peephole in doors, self-locking, security chain, or bar and double locking facility.

It is now becoming less common to find Western standard hotels in Third World countries which have an 'open house' approach to access. Many hotel chains have moved away from the policy that hotel security started at the hotel bedroom door. It is becoming more common to find perimeter controls e.g. security fences, guards at the entrance gates, lift access control, common door access controls and CCTV. One can even find hotels which have fitted safes in the rooms designed to take notebook computers, which will also recharge them.

Over the years I have observed that the four star airport located hotels are some of the safest. The reason for this is the lack of 'passing traffic'. By this I mean casual, pedestrian traffic we see in most major cities. The airport hotels are usually isolated and accessible only by vehicular traffic. In some instances it is almost physically impossible to reach them by foot and, as a consequence, they are not the haunt of the casual passerby or more critically the casual thief. City centre hotels become the focal point for doing business, in many cases by people who are not staying at the hotel, but who use it as an alternative office. Strangers will go unnoticed and unchallenged, as will villains, whereas with the airport hotels you often see few people in the lounges during the day with the exception of meetings organised in rooms or visiting conventions.

Contrast this with city centre hotels in Moscow. At any time of the day you will find groups of large, expensively dressed, short haired, large men holding meetings. At a nearby table or settee will be two or three larger, less well dressed men. The former are mafia bosses and the others are their bodyguards. They don't go to discuss business in two star hotels, they go to the best. Even worse you may find lawyers and accountants using them (sorry!). So the standard of hotel has little bearing on the standard of people who frequent it. In Moscow all city centre hotels have access to public transport, but you wouldn't use it.

I've also found that city centre hotels are often the most insecure due to their age, construction and lack of modern, architectural security features. The new purpose built transit camp type, out of city hotel is, by contrast, well designed, electronically up to date and, broadly secure. Corridors are often straight with good visibility down their length and no hiding places, whereas in the older city hotels you may have to negotiate a warren of poorly lit corridors to access your room. Evacuation in the event of a fire would be a nightmare and the security aspect is equally poor. A high rise, modern hotel is easier to police and usually has fewer exits.

Tell Tale Clues

You can tell a reasonable amount about the security of a hotel by the type of room key. These days the most secure is the electronic door lock opened with a plastic card, the code being changed with each guest. Should a card be lost the door can be reprogrammed and a new card issued. The more traditional metal key which operates a tumbler style lock is less secure as it probably has the room number stamped on it. The least secure of all is the key which has an attached fob giving the hotel address and room number. If you have the latter type detach the fob from the key.

Another guide to an hotel which has concerns about security is that it has staff badges which include photographs. In some hotels such as Delta Hotels they will provide an escort to your car or room.

Generally, a city centre hotel can be a target for thieves, prostitutes and con artists. In many parts of the world thieves may work in collusion with hotel staff, may be hotel staff or, as is likely to be the case, hotel security is so lax that thieves pretty much have free access to the building. In an ideal world the better the hotel, the better the security and, in general, this is a truism. The problem is, however, that with a better class of hotel goes a better, wealthier, clientele so attracting the criminal elements. I am not advocating staying in a poor standard hotel so as to appear to be poor, rather I want to inculcate the understanding that expensive does not guarantee safe. An hotel with a good attitude to security will never give out guests names or room numbers. If you phone a hotel and ask to be put through to a room they should ask you the name of the occupant which tells you a lot. Also you should not see room keys piled up at the concierge's desk.

An Armed Camp

So where does security start. As it would with your own home, security in a hotel starts with the perimeter. However, unlike your own home there is very little you can do to improve the perimeter security of a hotel if you do not like it. By perimeter I mean fence, wall or barrier which may secure parking facilities, or which may be providing perimeter security for the hotel if it has it's own grounds. In those parts of the world which are truly dangerous all hotels which cater for the Western market have a secure perimeter and guards. Those in Algiers town are a good example. Essentially they are armed camps. In the vast majority of city centre hotels you walk off the street into the foyer and then the door is the perimeter.

In the latter case one's personal security in the hotel is in the hands of either security personnel or in electronic access controls which may be in place. Increasingly hotels are installing access controls for lifts and corridor doors which can only be operated by your room access card. The Baltschug Kempinski in Moscow is a good example. There are uniformed guards on the door, but don't believe they stop the criminal element getting in. You will still see the Russian Mafia, eating, drinking and holding business meetings in the hotel, but at least they are the well dressed element. Access from the common areas, restaurants and bars is, however, restricted in that even if one entered a lift it is necessary to swipe one's room card in a 'reader', before the lift will respond to you pressing a floor button. Similarly, the access doors from all common areas are on a card swipe system and the system does give reasonable confidence. It is not foolproof and anyone who really wanted to get to your room could, but it certainly keeps the wandering opportunist out.

A good example of security at work. The lift needs a room card to be swiped before you can call it to a floor.

Once in the lift, you need to swipe your card again before you can select a floor - Kempinsky Hotel - Moscow

No Stars For Security

There is no security issue taken into account when star ratings are given out and it would be impossible to establish from a hotel it's track record in terms of crime. Speak to as many people as you can who know the geography and the choices and build up a 'preferred list' of your own. In terms of a hotel I like operating from in Moscow I would always incline to the Raddison Slavinskaya, but it is essentially 'open house' despite a perimeter fence, a guard hut at the gate and security personnel on the door. There is total freedom for anyone to wander about the floors and only in 1997 a former partner in the hotel, American Paul Tatum was machine gunned to death in the Metro. Prior to his death he had hardly left his hotel room in the Raddison due to death threats following his removal from the business by his Russian partners. They could have attacked his room, sent him an explosive device and you or I could have been given a room in close proximity to his. He was surrounded by bodyguards and his presence posed a serious threat to anyone staying in the hotel. *(It still has the best gym).*

Floor and Room Choice

So what about the choice of both floor and room. In the Close Protection industry we have guidelines for choosing the most appropriate room for a client. Very broadly we would look for a suite at the end of a corridor, away from the main stairs, lifts and, even fire escapes (service stairs and fire escapes are often routes in and out for thieves or worse). This may seem odd, but remember our object is to be able to control the environment and to do this successfully we need some isolation from the main thoroughfares and also to buy us time to identify someone making their way towards our clients room. It is easier to do this at the end of a corridor than in the middle. Depending on the level of threat, importance of client and security facilities, or lack of them, in the hotel we may have a 24 hour watch on the room either by a physical presence or by means of video surveillance.

The floor we would choose would be above the 3rd and no higher than the 6th. The rationale for this is that being above the 3rd floor, makes it impossible for access to be gained from the outside, as it would be on the ground floor, but it also prevents easy surveillance into the room and makes it difficult to accurately throw an object into the room. Not being higher than the 6th floor means you should not be above the height of a fire engine's turntable ladder - in most parts of the world anyway.

So what, if anything, can we take from all this if we are solitary travellers who do not enjoy the dubious luxury of a Close Protection team. Well, in the first instance, we can take comfort in the fact that we are not a prominent figure whose name is synonymous with wealth or influence and who as a consequence, makes an attractive target for robbery or even kidnap. Most of the rationale on which we base room choice above still has relevance for the solitary, 'unimportant' traveller, whose main weapon in his armoury is anonymity. Or so he thinks until he is observed flashing a wad of dollars and exposing to all who would have an interest an array of credit cards in his wallet.

Don't Be Flash

When in the hotel bars and restaurants sign for everything and carry small amounts of cash -outside your wallet - that you can use for gratuities. Believe nothing else but this - PEOPLE ARE WATCHING YOU!. Also don't be so vain or foolish to think that you have suddenly seem to have grown unexplainably attractive to the opposite sex. If you are a man and women are not flinging themselves at you as you walk down the street at home then be very suspicious if they suddenly start to do it when you are abroad. Some of the most intelligent people seem to leave their brains at home. I keep using the former Soviet Union as an example, but it currently has every example of criminal act being perpetrated against foreigners. Take an unknown woman back to your room and you could end up drugged, beaten-up, robbed and even dead. Don't get involved, whether there is a commercial deal or not.

A few years ago an American man and wife were befriended by a well spoken Russian in a nightclub. Both had their drinks 'spiked' and were subsequently robbed.

Common Sense - Again!

I quote the following tale to illustrate that common sense is not always a bedfellow of intelligence and maturity. It also demonstrates that even in the best hotels there is no truly effective security and that despite what people know about the risks of certain actions, primal drives often override aspects of personal safety. The situation involved a client I was 'looking after' with a Russian colleague. He was a senior European director of a U.S. venture and was staying at the 5 star National Hotel just opposite from Red Square in Moscow. Due to a lack of rooms I was accommodated in a nearby hotel and at night the client was under his own recognizance and best behaviour after I left him. He was in his sixties, married, familiar with country and it's problems and knew all the horror stories.

I met him one morning after breakfast before we set out for the days meetings and he informed me he had had some items stolen from his room when he had been at breakfast. These were a small dictating machine and a small wallet containing airline membership cards, which may at a glance have seemed like credit cards. He said and believed that he thought the person who restocked the fridge was responsible as he knew this had been carried out whilst he had been at breakfast.

My Russian colleague set the wheels in motion with the hotel's Security and on our return near lunchtime they had the facts for us. To his shock what the client didn't know was that every time his room door was opened the time was recorded and the printout showed that at a time when he was in his room the door was opened at just after midnight and then opened again near three o'clock. In addition we were informed by Security that a known prostitute was caught on camera in a hotel corridor and apprehended trying to leave the hotel. She was not searched, but the police were called an an officer took her away. The hotel security had phoned the local police station only to discover that she had never been booked in, meaning she had bribed the policeman not to arrest her.

Unfortunately the client was present as the whole tale unfolded and his discomfort rose in direct proportion to the facts as they were revealed. He had let her into his room and been robbed. He did, however, get off lightly and had she let a male companion into the room after her or drugged him he could have ended up in very bad shape. I discreetly gave him the copy of the printout and assured him that the reference to the filming was confined to the corridor and not the rooms.

I read a great quote on an internet site which seems appropriate and which said, ***"pack your common sense along with your clothes"***.

Don't Invite Danger In

So the very best bolts, locks, chains and door wedges are of little value if we 'invite' danger into our hotel bedrooms. Extending this principle the general rule is never do business with locals in your hotel bedroom. It doesn't matter how well you think you know someone, in reality you don't. A KGB Colonel said to me that the mistake we make in the West is to look at a Russian businessman who may be dressed in an expensive suit, speak excellent English and be extremely well educated and make the dangerous mistake of believing that he is like us, when in reality he is nothing like us. He said Russians have an Eastern way of thinking about things, have little if any business ethics and have no ability to grasp the concept that in a business deal, both parties can come out as winners. Their belief system is that one party must come out worse off and that they have determined it won't be them.

Misplaced Trust

More people who have attempted to do business in the former Soviet Union have fallen foul of this than have come out of it with a positive and profitable experience. By way of illustration I was staying at the Grand Hotel Europe in St Petersburg some years ago when a wealthy Englishman was attacked as he opened his hotel room door one night and robbed of $20,000, some contract papers and his passport, all of which had been in his briefcase which was snatched in the assault.

The person in question had returned from one of the former republics with his Russian business partner having tied up a deal to trade in cotton which would have meant his Russian partner receiving, for his share of the deal, in excess of $200,000 over the next two years.

The shock to the businessman was, that the person he had opened the door to and who attacked him was his Russian partner. The immediacy of the $20,000 today overrode all thoughts of the vast sum he would receive in the future. Again it should be understood that few Russians have any faith in the future however bright. They do not feel in charge, they know the uncertainties of the society and have never been in a position in the past where they were ever the authors of their own destinies. So to do business with them is hazardous to say the least and to let them into your room on an unscheduled visit at night is almost suicidal. The man later received telephones calls which gave him instructions as to where he should go to collect his papers and passport, but, fortunately by then he had learned his lesson.

Security Of Valuables

So what about valuables? If this isn't the first book you have read on travel security then you may have received some conflicting advice. When you read about the security of valuables, the received wisdom is never to leave them in your room, yet when you read about security in the street, broadly you are told not to have anything of value with you. All this would seem to suggest, therefore, that you consign your valuables to the care of the hotel, but even that is not recommended.

I should make the point at this juncture that during all my travels I have never had any item stolen from a hotel bedroom. Equally, though, I should state that given the nature of my work we are usually staying at the best hotel in town, albeit that in some places in the world 'best' is a very relative term.

Also I will repeat what has been said previously in an earlier chapter and that is "**do not take anything abroad you cannot afford to lose.**" Any loss, whilst inconvenient and unpleasant, should never represent a disaster. Physical items such as computers, watches, cameras etc should be insured as should credit cards and cash should be kept to a minimum. If you do feel driven to take your gold Rolex with you then good luck. Even the loss of a passport, whilst highly inconvenient, should not represent a disaster. Don't try to hide items in your room, as you will not find anywhere a thief has not thought of and when you leave the hotel you may easily forget the item.

In reality there may be occasions, through the nature of your job or the country you are visiting that you have with you a large amount of cash. There are still parts of the world where credit cards are not accepted. Whatever the reason if you have currency of any value then, ideally, you should book into a 'Western' standard hotel, hopefully, one belonging to an International chain and, especially one which has the facility of rental safety deposit boxes. In good standard hotels I trust such boxes, even though I would never trust the hotel safe, which is probably anything but safe.

Safety Deposit Boxes

I will use the safety deposit boxes for cash, passport, airline tickets and any sensitive papers. If you do leave your passport in a hotel safety deposit box first establish that if stopped by the local police it is not an offence, as a foreigner, not to be carrying your passport with you as identification. If you don't have the original with you have a photocopy with you at all times. On this point have two copies with you, one on your person and one back at the hotel, together with a number of passport photos.

If there is no safety deposit boxes available for rent at the hotel and you have concerns about the cash then look at the possibility of renting a box at a local bank. I have done this in Hong Kong, when my hotel accommodation was not too salubrious and less than secure. It is not as convenient, but it will be safe. Unless you are able to rent a large box, then you will not be able to safely stow away your notebook computer. Again I have never lost a piece of equipment from a room, but I am very nervous about portable computers, not from the physical loss, as it is insured, but because of the information in it.

Computers

First if you have to leave it in your room, try and ensure that there is no sensitive data within the machine that you would not want others to have. Password protect access and critically, back-up the files and keep these separate, hopefully in the safety deposit box. If you keep any information on the notebook that would prove problematic if it fell into the wrong hands then it shouldn't be on it in the first place.

You have a duty of care towards 'proprietary information' the loss of which would have a damaging effect on your company's business. Notebooks are too easily stolen and it is foolish to have valuable data stored on them. I accept that one purpose of travelling with the notebook is to have available large amounts of data if needed as well as to be productive whilst away and to keep in touch, but I suggest you carry out an analysis before you travel as to how much data you need to take with you. I remember a human resources manager telling me how he sat on a plane next to someone who it transpired worked for the opposition and who proceeded to work on his company's marketing plans in full view the person sitting next to him.

How Safe Is The Safe?

In some of the International chain hotels you may find a small safe in your wardrobe which works on the basis of you keying in your own numeric code for the duration of your visit. I refrain from using them as I am not that sanguine about them, although I have no evidence to the contrary that they are not safe. I always feel as if I am letting others know that I have valuables in my possession by the simple fact that I have locked something away in the safe.

Whilst one incident should not colour our attitude, the following one somewhat supports my concern about the in-room safes. It was reported in a U.K. travel magazine about a family who were holidaying in the Costa Smeralda on Sardinia. One morning the housekeeping staff discovered that the room safe and a sizeable chunk of the wall behind it, together with a suitcase had been stolen. Losses were estimated at some £3,000. Quite clearly the thieves or thief knew of the jewellery, probably through observation and there may have been collusion with a member of staff. The wife described the state of the wall as if the safe had been blown away, although it had probably been levered away from the wall. This is a noisy process and strengthens the collusion theory.

For me it simply illustrates the point that whether you want to believe it or not you are always being watched by someone. The thief knew when the room had been vacated, either through personal observation, or by someone telling him. You are targets when you are abroad so remember that. This was, by the way, a luxury hotel.

Suitcase Security

The same applies to locking your suitcase when you are out of the room. I often leave items within my suitcase, which I seldom completely empty and never lock. In my obscure wisdom I do this on the psychological premise that I am giving the impression that I have nothing of value in the case, otherwise I would have locked it. I'm sure though that my freedom from theft to date is simply good fortune, not good planning.The other school of thought is that you should always lock your case when you leave the room. This is based on the premise that if someone gets into your room do not allow them to use your own suitcase to carry your possessions away. You choose!.

Budget Travel

At the end of the day you will do what you are most comfortable with. For me, if in doubt, I will keep everything with me, even if I am in a less than friendly part of town, but this should not apply for everyone. Much of the advice available, say, on the internet is directed at the backpacking community, travelling the world on a budget and having, necessarily, to stay in the poorer hotels. Often there will be no en-suite facilities and you will require padlocks for your door, suitcase and never leave anything of value in your room even if you go and take a shower.

Galle Face Hotel - Sri Lanka - colonial charm, but 'wide open' hotel with, typically, no security of any note.

If you are travelling on a budget, then choose your hotel after they have shown you your room. Look for solid doors with working locks, windows in good physical condition which are capable of being locked. Take wedges with you and avoid hotels or hostels which have an open house policy, allowing anyone into the building. No locals should be allowed, however inconvenient you may think this is. When you leave your room, in such locations make sure anything of value you have to leave behind is locked away in your case or pack and consider chaining your case to something in the room which cannot be moved.

It is always sound advise not to put temptation in anyone's way, wherever you are staying, so don't leave the Leica in full view when you go out. In poorer hotels never leave anything in the hotel safe. Cash and travellers cheques are at risk.

Elevators

There are some standard security procedures with elevators whether they are in hotels, office blocks or elsewhere.

◆ Never get into a lift with anyone you are unhappy about.

◆ When in the lift always stand by the controls. If the lift fills up don't be squeezed towards the back, but stay near the controls and the doors.

◆ If you are on your own in the lift and someone enters you do not like, get off.

◆ If someone is watching you get into the lift then press several floor buttons so as not to identify your particular floor.

◆ In large cities elevators are frequented by muggers. If you can, get on with several other people.

TIPS

General

◆ If you use the hotels pool, gym or other facilities, never leave keys or personal belongings unattended. Also don't leave magazines behind which may have your company name or your address on them.

◆ Always use the main entrance of the hotel and not some remote side entrance you have found, especially after dark.

◆ Keep only small amounts of cash in your room.

Checking In/Out

◆ Always make a reservation, particularly in a country or city where there is going to be little choice of secure Western style hotels and to be without a room could be highly dangerous.

◆ If you work for a company which is identified with the decadent West then do not let the company book the room in the corporate name. The travel department must be part of the security process. A very prestigious or well known company name can increase your chances of kidnap, extortion or theft. Some companies use unknown subsidiaries to do it through.

◆ If you check in early or your room is not ready, only leave your luggage in a secure locked room. There should be a numbered ticket system in operation so as to identify your luggage.

◆ If the local by-laws require you leave your passport at reception when you check in, obtain a receipt, or better a numbered slip.

◆ If you are a lone female then check in using no title and only an initial for your Christian name.

◆ If you are waiting to be picked up by someone, wait in the lobby not outside and when being dropped off make sure it is as near to the door as possible.

◆ Always keep an eye on your luggage in hotel lobbies. You may consign your suitcases to the bellhop, but keep any light, easily portable items with you.

◆ Beware of pickpockets in busy hotel lobbies, both in queues at the concierge or reception desks and in hotel shops.

In hotel lobbies watch your luggage and your conversation - someone may be looking and listening.

Room security & Key security

Procedures

◆ If you have any doubts about the hotel insist on seeing your room, prior to booking in.

◆ If you are put in an annexe which you feel is somewhat remote from the main hotel building, then ask to be moved. Don't get yourself isolated.

◆ If you are unhappy about your room security ask to be moved.

◆ The door to your room is paramount to your security. It should be solid in construction, be capable of double locking and have a secondary device such as a chain. It should have a peephole which you should use.

◆ As we mentioned earlier don't accept a room which is near a stairwell, elevator, fire escape, ice machine or vending machine. The latter two give people an excuse to loiter near your room

◆ Do not leave luggage unattended when checking in or out.

◆ Deposit the room key at reception when checking out. Do not leave it in the door and don't leave the door ajar when you finally leave the room - any thefts will be down to you.

◆ Know the telephone number and location of hotel security

◆ A computer type card access will not identify the room if you lose it, but what will is the key holder, so separate them.

◆ Safeguard you room key as you would your residence key.

◆ If the room key is of the old fashioned variety I do not leave it with the concierge when I go out. It identifies you are out and can be gained by deception.

The older style hotels are often less secure than those newly built or recently refurbished. You sometimes have to trade off charm for security

◆ If the key is of the old fashioned variety, separate from any tag which has the room number on it.

◆ If your room door is opened with a card and you lose it report the loss immediately to reception and get them to issue a new card and change the locking code.

◆ You may wish to 'test' the security of your room by leaving small change and minor personal items. Personally I believe this amounts to entrapment and is unfair in places with horrendously low wages.

◆ Do not give the room number to anyone you do not know well.

◆ Be 'low key'. Don't 'show out' and don't get drunk.

◆ Recognise if anything is out of place when you come back to the room.

◆ Don't admit strangers to your room.

◆ Avoid using your room for meetings.

◆ Lock, double lock and chain your door at any time you are in the room, even during the day.

◆ Be sure any adjoining room door is locked before you leave the room or settle down at night.

◆ If the door security is poor use a wooden or rubber wedge, or door alarm.

◆ If you are unhappy about the door locking system, place a heavy chair against it so that no silent entry can be made to your room whilst you sleep.

◆ Although most hotel doors will self-lock as you leave the room always get into the habit of checking to ensure the lock has engaged.

◆ If your room has adjoining balconies do not leave any sliding windows open, particularly at night. Also do not leave valuables e.g. cameras out on the balcony.

◆ Unless you are high up and there are no adjoining balconies or wide ledges outside, do not sleep with your window open.

◆ Use your door viewer before you answer the door.

◆ Never open your door to anyone you do not expect. Always visually identify who is at the door before opening it.

◆ Never admit repairmen without checking first with the front desk.

◆ Never discuss plans for staying away from the hotel, particularly in front of strangers.

◆ When absent from your room use some form of 'passive' security like leaving the TV on or place the 'Do Not Disturb' sign on the door. Avoid using the 'Make Up My Room' sign on your door when you leave. It tells everyone you are out. If you leave a light on in your room when you leave, make sure you have closed the curtains.

◆ When night falls, draw the curtains. That way if you enter at night you are not illuminated before you can close them - very important if you are a lone female traveller.

◆ If you see someone 'loitering' or watching you in the corridor near your room then don't enter. Walk on if possible and find some people and report the incident to the front desk.

◆ Always have your room key in your hand as you approach the room.

◆ If you are expecting someone have them call you from the lobby. Don't open the door if someone knocks, just because you are expecting someone.

◆ Make enquiries before you go jogging around the hotels environs. If in doubt about the safety of going out, even early in the morning then confine your activities to the hotel grounds.

Civil Unrest

Depending where you are riots, unrest and armed insurrection can break out at a moment's notice. Often sentiment can turn against Western businesses and people as well as Western style hotels.

◆ If it occurs then don't leave the hotel and contact your embassy or any friendly Western embassy.

◆ If possible try to sleep in an inside room which can provide greater protection from gunfire, rockets etc.

◆ In the event of hearing gunfire or explosions outside he hotel, stay away from the windows.

◆ Also if there is social disorder and shooting taking place, do not get the camera out. Over 60 journalists are killed around the world each year and some 125 detained by local governments.

◆ If you are caught in the open, do not take sides, just 'play the tourist'.

Hotel Room Invasion

A rising crime is hotel room invasion. A variation on the theme of house invasion or carjacking. The object is to catch the occupant unawares, whilst they are relaxed and feel secure.

A traditional burglar looks to houses or hotel rooms being unoccupied, but increasingly, physical and electronic access systems are making such occupations more difficult. Far better to be 'let in' than have to break in. The trend has been to target older people and lone females. Remember you may have been targeted outside and followed back, so don't wear expensive jewellery when out and keep aware.

Once inside you are a victim who can be assaulted and robbed at leisure. They will have all your valuables and can extract your ATM pin number. As you open the door there will be a violent assault so as to gain immediate control. Victims will be bound and gagged and often sexually assaulted. The attackers will not be surprised by the guests as would a burglar. Don't leave patio doors open if you are on the ground floor and move rooms if the patio doors and windows are flimsy and wouldn't resist being forced.

The Method

The methodology is to get you to open the door either by simply knocking on it or by deception i.e waiter, messenger, bell boy etc. So:

- Never open the door to any caller you do not expect.
- Call the front desk to check someone who purports to be with the hotel.
- Don't open the door onto a safety chain, seldom are they strong enough to resist an assault.
- Don't be fooled by someone holding an item like flowers or a parcel when you look through the peephole.
- If you have a suspicious call at the door immediately inform reception. If your call doesn't receive the attention it should phone the police.

We had the case of a British couple on holiday in a U.S hotel who were assaulted in their room literally just as they took occupation of it. It was reported that their attacker, who raped the woman simply walked into the room, the door to which had been left open.

Room invaders are likely to operate at night when they know the rooms are occupied and less staff are about. South Africa's President Mandella commitment to tackle crime followed on from the attack on the Canadian High Commissioner which we have reported elsewhere, but the circumstances are appropriate to relate here. He was in Cape Town to attend the opening of Parliament and around midnight he answered a knock on his door at the Winchester Gardens hotel in the Sea Point district. He was confronted by a robber holding an electric cattle prod.

The robber kicked and beat him, tied him to a chair with bed linen and ransacked the room. He made off with valuables and some £100 cash. It took the victim an hour before he broke free and raised the alarm. Obviously being a High Commissioner doesn't require the attribute of common sense and to open a hotel door at midnight to an unexpected caller is evidence enough.

Staff

Depending on where you are in the world you can expect the hotel staff to be in collusion with the local villains. This may be a willing participation or they may be under duress. In many of the old 'Intourist' style Russian hotels, very shortly after you enter your room there will be a knock on your door and it will be one of the local prostitutes who has been 'advised' an unaccompanied male has checked in. You let them in at your peril as very serious things could befall you. If there is no peephole don't worry, simply ignore the pleas from outside. In such hotels you will also get them knocking on your door at all times of the night.

Some hotels in hotel in Moscow are classic for this. Mafia on the door, mafia inside and prostitutes with a free run of the place. The Kievskya hotel in Kiev, Ukraine has the same problems and it is a common phenomena even in the best of the Western style hotels in this region.

Out of interest one of the hotels in question is physically part of the **Sovincenter** which, with the hotel was the first Western style hotel and business centre in Moscow. In 1999 Boris Gryaznov, it's Director was murdered by unidentified gunmen outside his apartment building. It was a professional hit during which his driver and the Centre's security chief also died. The Sovincenter complex was built by the American industrialist Armand Hammer in the late 70's.

Surviving Hotel Fires

In many parts of the world over the door of hotels should be a government health warning which reads "**This hotel could be hazardous to your health.**" This is not a warning about the level of criminal activity or even about the food, rather it's a warning about the greatest risk to our safety in hotels and that's the risk of fire. Don't, however, believe I'm just pointing the finger at Third World operations. In America, the US Subcommittee on Science, Research and Technology, finds that as many as 85 percent of US hotels lack a fire sprinkler system.

Fire is a very real threat and not just in hotels. It is estimated that each year, some 32.6 million fires strike Americans at home, in hotels, or at the workplace. That's one fire for every second of every day. In fact the US and Canada have the highest rates of death by fire than any country of the world. Fire is the third largest cause of accidental death and injury in the US and total 2 million annually, with one out of every 8 accident deaths due to fire. So we don't have to be talking about the Third World and the consequence of non-existent fire regulations, either as a requirement of the construction, nor as rules for operation. We can be equally at risk on home ground. In the States for example the following is a small sample of the risks;

The Thomas Hotel, San Francisco	**20 Dead**
The Gulf Hotel, Houston	**54 Dead**
The LaSalle Hotel, Chicago	**61 Dead**
Wincoff Hotel, Atlanta	**119 Dead**
MGM Hotel, Las Vegas	**85 Dead**

The problem is that the consequences of hotel fires are a product of having possibly many hundreds of people in a building they are unfamiliar with, who may also be asleep when the fire starts.

One of the most detailed of post-fire investigations was carried out at the MGM hotel and Casino in Las Vegas, following a fire in November 1980 during which 85 people lost their lives with some 600 injured. The hotel had passed a fire examination only six months earlier. The investigation was carried by one man at Harvard University and it was the first time that computers had been used to simulate various scenarios so as to determine the cause of the fire and how it caused so many deaths.

The fire began from very humble origins in the 'Deli', next to the Casino. In the Deli was a wood fibre ceiling which quickly decomposed and released hot combustible gases. In one minute it was ablaze and a 'flashover' occurred, sending a fireball into the casino. At that same time firemen had arrived on the scene, having taken only three minutes to respond to the call, the station house being practically across the road.

As the fireball entered the casino it ignited the plastic tiles in the casino ceiling, creating intense black smoke and in five minutes the whole of this end of the casino was ablaze. Although now we know of the dangers of certain materials, the blaze was fed by flammable, polyurethane seating in the food booths. Although only 7 people died in the casino, some 65 bodies were eventually found in the upper floors of the hotel, where it was discovered alarms did not ring. On the 22nd and 23rd floors there were 5/6 bodies lying, covered in soot, outside the elevators which never came. Smoke and hot toxic fumes had travelled upward via the seismic joints and elevator shafts.

They had not been burned, nor had a further 25 people who had died in their rooms, with no signs of panic, some lying on the floor, the beds and chairs. Strangely there was no signs of soot, but when fire investigators opened the grills to the air conditioning they found the filters for these rooms clogged with soot. These people had been slowly poisoned by the toxic gases, e.g. carbon monoxide and many probably never knew they were dying, they were simply being anaethetised and went unconscious into a deadly sleep.

The smoke and toxic gases had travelled through the upper floors via the lift shafts, seismic joints and the air conditioning system. Hotel engineers had propped open dampers in the air conditioning system which would have prevented, at least to some degree, the spread of smoke. The problem had been that they had been closing themselves due to the desert sun so the dampers had been permanently propped open to prevent this. Even days later smoke was issuing from the top of the building. No fire alarms had rung on the top floors.

A Combination of Minor Errors

This tragedy was the result of a combination of a number of minor errors which conspired to create a major catastrophe. The hotel reopened some six months later, with a $5million fire safety programme and is considered one of the safest hotels today. Even with the best personal preparation many people would still have perished in these circumstances. I have seen video footage of the fire and heard the statements of people who were trapped on the upper floors. Some people, having made an attempt to leave the floor they were on, found it necessary to return to their rooms. Others, knotted sheets and attempted to climb down balconies only to fall off, whilst survivors talked about the desperate feelings of isolation whilst waiting for rescue.

Many broke windows with their furniture in an attempt to attract attention or escape. In fact one of the major causes of injury to firemen was from falling debris from such futile and dangerous actions. We are talking about panic. You must always have a plan in your mind prior to being surprised by a fire - panic will take over if you do not have a plan. Many people have no appreciation about the speed at which a fire can spread. Fire tests confirm that even a small fire in an average-sized room can ignite everything in it in 5 minutes and combustion effects from the fire will start killing people in 32 minutes. The fire investigation report for the Dupont Plaza hotel fire in the US, noted that 97 people died in a mere 12 minutes.

Prior Research

Ask if the hotel you are going to stay in has a modern alarm and sprinkler system installed. If a fire can be stopped before it takes hold it cannot develop a lot of smoke, which is the biggest killer in fires. Also as the water flows through the system it also triggers alarms. Query both your travel agent, if you are a tourist and your travel department if your company is sending you abroad.

Corporate

If you are a company sending people all over the world you should enquire about TIM, which is the acronym for Testing, Inspection and Maintenance. Fire safety equipment is of little value if it is not regularly tested, inspected and maintained and, as a consequence, fails in operation. There may be different legislative and hotel management approaches to this around the world, but if it is your responsibility to place employees in these places you must establish some base standard below which you will not put people at risk.

Whether your company has a travel department, or whether you make the arrangements yourself, if hotels require to be booked you need to know the following:

1. How many floors in the hotel.

2. What kind of fire protection does the hotel have.

3. What inspection facilities are applicable and when was the last inspection.

4. Do the rooms have smoke detectors and sprinklers.

5. How many fire drills are held annually for staff and guests.

6. Does the hotel have non-smoking rooms on particular floors.

Kit List

Consider the following as a fire safety kit list:

1. A torch e.g. a 'mini mag- lite'.

2. A painters or cyclist's smog mask.

3. A portable, battery-operated smoke detector which can be mounted high up in your room or hung on a door nob. Don't place it near an air-conditioning unit or air supply duct as the fresh air may blow the smoke away from the detector.

The Least We Should Expect

Many modern high-rise hotels in the West are now fitted with a comprehensive sprinkler system and an alarm system that renders false alarms nil. In the absence of the latter both management and guests will tend to tolerate and even ignore the problem. Even in the West staff fire safety training is still something of a 'curates egg' - some good, some poor and some non-existent. However it is usually in the Third World where the greatest abuses take place.

Royal Jomtiem Hotel - Pattaya, Thailand

In the late 1990's this hotel suffered a fire in which 78 people died and which was described by the Mayor of Pattaya as the city's worst tragedy. The hotel did not have sprinklers and tourists who were rescued reported that no alarms sounded and no warnings were given.

Local fire fighting equipment only reached the seventh floor and many guests were helicoptered off the roof and harnesses were lowered to others on lower floors. The greatest tragedy, though, was the fact that the management had chained shut the emergency fire doors to prevent guests who used them to leave without paying.

Your Procedure

The first port of call should be to the schematic on the back of your door showing the floor plan, highlighting your room and a marked route to the fire exits. Just to digress, I was in a hotel in Russia studying the plan and attendant instructions which commanded that in the event of detecting a fire one had to contact the reception on the 'Hot Line' - very apt I thought!. The lines may be hot, but don't believe that in a hotel fire it is the fire itself that is going to kill you, rather it is the by-products of fire ie, superheated gasses (smoke), and panic, which will usually be the cause of most deaths long before the flames reach you, even if they ever do, as was the case in Las Vegas. You must, therefore, know how to avoid both smoke and panic to survive a hotel fire.

Where there is smoke there is not necessarily fire. A smouldering mattress will produce great amounts of smoke which the air-conditioning will pick up and distribute from one room to another and from floor to floor. It is estimated that 70% of hotel fires are caused by smoking and matches. The first rule is leave the hotel at the first sign of smoke.

The dynamics of smoke are that being warm, it first accumulates at the ceiling and then works it's way down. The first thing you will notice, or to be more accurate, not as the case may be, is that there are NO 'Exit Signs', as they will probably have been obscured by the smoke and gases. It's probably too late to look for illuminated exit signs if there's smoke and more about this later.

On a physiological front, your eyes will only take so much irritant smoke, then they will close. It's part of the body's defence mechanism and do what you will they will not open. The fresh air you need to breathe is at or near the floor - get on your hands and knees (or stomach) and stay there as you make your way out. Those who don't - don't get far. Many people who are found dead in hotel fires, have panicked, left the room, been blinded, become disorientated and choked to death.

Normal Procedure

As we described above, our normal procedure is we check in, get the elevator, drop the luggage, hang up what's necessary, study what's on room service, check the hotel's films, then go and eat or order in. You may be tired and possibly stressed after a long journey, but your life may depend on taking a few extra minutes to check things out. It helps to get into a habitual routine about doing this and may take a further 3 minutes.

The procedure doesn't end with studying the schematic on the back of the door.

1. You need to go and find the fire exit and, if there's two of you sharing, both of you need to go and locate it. Talk it over.

What you need to know are:

a. How many doors do you pass on the way?, do you turn a corner?

b. Open the Exit door and what do you see, is there another door?. In some countries you may also need to check the fire exit at ground level to ensure that it is not permanently locked or chained.

c. Count the doors on the way back and be precise - you don't want to crawl into a broom cupboard.

d. Are you passing any room with colleagues or family along the way?, in an emergency you can bang on their doors.

e. Is there anything in the hallway that may be in your way? - ice making machine, shoe cleaner, settee, table, etc.

f. Can you locate a fire alarm and if so know how it works should you be able to reach it safely in the event of you discovering a fire.

Now think could you get to the fire exit with a blindfold on?. If you have to do it for real, it could possibly be under conditions which very easily equate to being blindfold. Remember you may be on your hands and knees, with your eyes unable to see due to the smoke and gases so you will only be able to navigate to the fire exit door by touch. What will screw this up is not knowing how many doors, because you are going to have to count them by feel as you pass by and what will disorientate you even further will be coming across an obstacle you had not perceived was there.

We discussed in Chapter 5, the psychology of observation where we all look but don't see and no where is it more important than the thirty or so feet you have to navigate to save your life. One way of learning the route is to close your eyes and 'feel' your way along the corridor, counting the doors and obstructions. There are thousand of hotel fires each year and it is one of your biggest risks, if the country's drivers don't get you first.

Your Room

After you have checked your exit route and put your key on the nightstand - do one more thing -CHECK YOUR ROOM! -

◆ Does your room have an electric bathroom vent?. If it does remember to turn it on in the event of smoke in the room. This will be operated by the bathroom light.

◆ How does your window open?. Is it locked, does it slide, does it have a latch?

◆ Can you open and close your window by feel?

◆ What's outside - ledge, balcony, flat roof, sign etc? Is safe escape possible. Remember trying to jump from anything above 2 floors will likely end in serious injury or death.

◆ If you are disabled, phone reception and let them know.

In The Event Of Fire

General Points

Should you become involved in a fire in your hotel you have

2 courses of action, either to **escape the hotel completely** using the fire exits or to **secure your room** until professional rescue services arrive.

Using The Exit

Should you make the decision to leave your room in the event of a suspected fire, close the door behind you - it is effective in keeping fire out and minimising smoke damage to belongings. Some doors take hours to burn through. They are excellent 'fire-stops' so close all doors behind you. This also gives you a safe haven if you need to get back in if conditions are untenable in the corridor. However, **Take Your Key With You!** It's important that you close the door as you leave, but equally as important that you do not lock yourself out. Waking up in the middle of the night, half asleep and in a panic, with the lights in your room possibly not working, it is all too easy to rush out of the room and not even attempt to find the key or access card. That's assuming you could have found it even if you had stopped long enough to try. Most people leave the key all over the room.

The rule is, get in the habit of leaving the key in the same place in every hotel room and that is on the bedside table (nightstand) nearest the door. You should also have a small (mini mag-lite torch and possibly a smoke mask).

Correct Procedure

If your awakened by or detect smoke, an alarm, the telephone or banging.

◆ grab your keys and get on your knees. Stay low to avoid any noxious fumes which may already have entered the room.

◆ Before opening the door, feel it with the palm of one hand. If the door or knob is hot, don't open it.

◆ Keeping one hand on the door so as to be able to slam it shut, glance outside and assess conditions.

◆ As you exit, stay against the wall on the side the exit is on. It is very easy to get lost or disorientated in a very smoky atmosphere and if you start off on the wrong side you could crawl right by.

◆ Even if the corridor is clear of smoke stay by the wall as you are out of the path of people who may be panicking.

◆ Even if conditions seem benign do not take the elevator

◆ **VIP** - When you reach the exit, **Walk Down and Grab The Handrail**. People running in panic will knock you down if you don't.

◆ On leaving the hotel report to an evacuation point so authorities know you are safe.

Panic - (def.) *'A sudden, overpowering terror, often effecting many people at once'*. Panic is the product of imagination left to run wild and panic is contagious. Panic will also make you do things which will kill you, as we will see later. People in a state of panic are rarely able to save themselves.

Smoke will sometimes get into the stairwell. If it's a tall building, the smoke may not rise very high before it cools and becomes heavy, this is called 'Stacking'.

◆ So if you descend and find smoke - don't proceed!. Turn around and begin walking up - NOW YOU MUST HANG ON. People coming down may be half blind and in total panic and they will run over everything in their way, even firemen. This is why making for the roof in the first instance is dangerous as you will be going against the flow.

◆ Don't panic if you can't get out of the stairwell onto a floor - this is a normal security feature, but you will be able to exit onto the roof or outside at ground level.

◆ If you reach the roof, prop the door open with something. This is the only time you leave a door open, as it will help ventilate the stairwell and you won't be locked out.

◆ Now find the windward side of the roof (wet finger). Roofs have proved to be a reasonably safe secondary exit and refuge area.

Staying Put

If you wake up and there's smoke in your room and the doors hot - DON"T PANIC - many people have defended themselves in their room against a hotel fire.

◆ First open the window and vent the smoke. Open both the top and bottom windows, as this will let air in an smoke out.

◆ Turn off the air conditioner, which could have brought the smoke into the room in the first place. You must decide if you can sleep without the air conditioner switched on. In the Las Vegas fire people died from the toxic gases brought into their rooms, with no knowledge that it was happening.

◆ Cover any vent which could bring smoke into the room.

◆ Don't try and break the window. At a fire in a Ramada Inn, an airline pilot cut himself badly trying to break the window with a chair. You will also injure people below.

◆ If you manage to open a window don't simply stay there and shout and wave - you have to fight back.

◆ If the phone is still working, let someone know you are in the room. You can also hang a sheet out of the window as an alert. It may be you have to phone the police or fire service direct if you feel the hotel will not do this themselves.

◆ Fill the bath with water - not to get in, but to fight the fire with.

◆ Wet towels or sheets and stuff the door cracks to keep out the smoke.

◆ With the waste bin, bail water onto the door to keep it cool.

◆ Feel the walls - if they are hot, bail them too.

◆ If you can block the door with a mattress, do so and block that with a dresser, if one will move - keep them wet - keep everything wet.

◆ Tie a wet towel around your mouth and nose - make a triangle and put the corner in your mouth.

◆ Flail a wet towel around in the room to dissipate the smoke. .

◆ If there is a fire outside the window, pull down the drapes and remove anything combustible from near the window.

◆ If flames are rising up the outside of the building, keep your windows shut.

◆ Bail water around the window.

◆ If the air is clear outside, make a tent over your head with a wet blanket and open the bottom half of the window, enough to get your head out. If the window won't open don't break it as you can no longer keep smoke out.

Elevators

There isn't an elevator made that can be used as a safe exit in the event of a fire. Remember the MGM fire, where one of the ways in which smoke and toxic gases travelled up through the hotel was via the elevator shaft. The problem is most people only know one way out of a hotel - the way they came in and that's usually the elevator. Besides the lift shaft filling with smoke, many other things will go wrong.

Always bear in mind the effect panic will have on normally sane, rational and peaceful people. Everyone tries to get into the elevator in an emergency and fights break out and people are seriously injured. People see elevators as they see lifeboats on a sinking ship, only there are no deckhands at the lifts to ensure an orderly evacuation, even if the elevator was the correct method of evacuation, which it isn't.

Also smoke and heat do strange things to elevator call buttons, controls and complicated, delicate parts. In a hotel in New Orleans guests were called on the phone and notified of a fire on the upper floors. They were in no immediate danger, but were asked to evacuate the hotel as a precaution.

Five of the guests elected to leave via the elevator. In the subsequent investigation it was discovered that the lift only went down two floors and then for some reason started going back up. It did not stop until it reached the floor on which the fire was. The doors came open and then were held open by smoke obscuring the photo-electric light beam. All five guests died of suffocation and firemen discovered that every button had been pushed, probably in panic.

Elevators have killed many people, including firemen. In the mid seventies, several New York firemen used an elevator while responding to a fire on the 20th floor of a building. They entered the elevator, pushed the button for the 18th floor, but the elevator went right on passed the 18th, to the 20th where the doors opened onto an inferno and stayed open long enough to sadly kill all inside. The doors then closed and it returned to the lobby.

Jumping

First let me say something about your ability to control your own destiny when it comes to surviving hotel fires. In the field of Close Protection (Bodyguarding) we have some guidelines as to the location we would wish the rooms to be in for our clients. From a security aspect we never like our clients to have rooms below the third floor, as we described earlier. There are two security risks - first the surveillance risk, particularly on the ground floor and second the risk of someone shooting into the room who can see what is happening inside.

The standard recommendation is, therefore, not to be below the third floor, so as to also be above the height of an accurately thrown object, but equally not to be above the sixth floor. This limit on height is not to do with security, simply that in most parts of the world any higher moves you out of reach of most turntable fire engine ladders.

It is our old enemy panic, which causes people to jump out of hotel windows. If you are on the ground floor you can simply open the window and climb out. From the next floor, you may survive the jump with a sprained or broken ankle, but only on the proviso that you jump out far enough to miss any ledge or window sill on the way down. Many people don't and end up cartwheeling. If they don't land onto their head and kill themselves they end up seriously injured. If you are any higher the chances are you will not survive the fall and had better elect to fight the fire.

Also forget the thought of jumping to what you believe are nearby buildings. Often these seem much closer than they are and what seems a jumpable distance could easily be fifteen feet. As an example of the effect of panic causing people to jump, there was a fire in a hotel in Brazil some years ago where 40 people jumped from windows and 40 people died. Ironically 36 of those jumped after the fire in the building had been put out. Many people survived by staying put whilst those around them jumped to their deaths. So resist the rising panic and think clearly.

Most of the above guidelines were originally produced by a Richard H. Kauffman of the Los Angeles Fire Department, over twenty years ago. His wife had worked in the airline industry and accompanying her on a trip one time, he realised how ill prepared she was in the event of a fire breaking out in the hotel. Kauffman knew that with some 5,000 hotel fires a year the odds are bound to catch up with you. The advice he gave then is no less relevant today and in the majority of the world, particularly the 'emerging' part, fire safety in hotels is no better than it was twenty years ago.

What Richard Kauffman also knew, as a fireman, was that many hotels won't even call the fire department in the event of a fire, until it is too late. Often they despatch one of their people to investigate whether, in fact, there is really a fire and put it out themselves. The last thing most hotels want is a few hundred guests standing around in the rain, in night clothes or less!

In a fire in a hotel in New Orleans, records show that the fire department received only one call and that was from a guest in one of the rooms. The hotel desk had been notified of the fire 20 minutes earlier and had sent a security guard to investigate. His body was later found on the 12th floor about 10 feet from the elevator. The message is if you believe there is a fire get an outside line and call the fire brigade.

There doesn't have to be a major fire for deaths to occur. Kauffman describes very vividly the death by asphyxiation of a man in a hotel through heavy smoke, which had come from some a small fire in a room where there were stored bed rolls.

Corporate Meeting Planners

If you are arranging a meeting or a convention in a hotel, you should pay particular attention to fire safety. As per previous advice, if you have to schedule a meeting, first check the hotel's arrangements for fire detection, alarms, extinguisher provisions, exit routes and employee training. This should be part of a 'risk assessment' procedure for the travel arrangements as a whole.

1. Choose ground level meeting rooms which will be easier to evacuate. Basement, or high floor rooms are not a good choice.

2. Meeting rooms should have adequate exits. Generally, a rule of thumb is that.

50-300 people require 2 exits, 300-1,000 need 3 exits and plus 1,000 need 4 or more exits.

3. Exits should be brightly lit, not blocked by furniture or curtains and be easily opened. They should not be chained or locked.

4. Seating should allow enough aisle space for quick evacuation.

I have seen meeting rooms in many hotels around the world which do not conform to the very basic parameters above, but they were the only show in town. However do the best you can and put the management under some pressure to conform to some basic fire safety requirements.

Some large corporate entities ban their personnel from staying in some hotel chains with inadequate physical and procedural fire safety features.

In summary hotel fires probably constitute one of the greatest risks when travelling overseas, so be prepared both mentally and with a few simple bits of kit, such as a portable smoke alarm. Be selective as to the hotels you use and become familiar with your room and corridor layout to the extent you could find your way out blindfold.

CHAPTER NINE

Security at Airports

I should say first of all, so as to keep matters in perspective, that journeys by air, whether by commercial or private aircraft, do not represent an exceptional danger, even from the hijacker, although it is the likelihood of this we will address in this chapter.

As you are probably aware, there is no common ground throughout the world as to a standard of either security or safety amongst airlines or airports.

Some years ago there was blanket condemnation of both the safety of the Russian airline, Aeroflot and Russian air traffic control, to the extent that the advice was to avoid both. It is the wide divisions in the approach to security taken by many airlines and many airports and it is this disparate approach that increases our risk. As is often the case, we make assumptions that it is only when we are in the Third World that security procedures are lax. The following should dissuade you of this presumption.

Airline Security

With alarming frequency, U.S. Transportation Department investigators, penetrated security at a number of major U.S. airports during months of testing in 1999. They breezed through checkpoints, gates and jet bridges all the way to seats on planes. Given the 'stepped-up' worldwide emphasis on tighter control to deter terrorists, the tests exposed gaping holes in airport security in the U.S.

Investigators reported that 'piggy-backing' (following certified employees through doors and gates) was the most successful method of entry. But, they also found unguarded elevators and once on board aircraft in dozens of cases, no-one was there to challenge them. In still other areas, the investigators deliberately set off 25 emergency exit alarms and in 10 instances, security personnel never responded.

Since the tests, the Federal Aviation Administration (FAA), says it has been running thousands of its own tests and taking enforcement actions. Since the death of 270 people on PanAm flight 103, the FAA, despite the Aviation Security Improvement Act 1990, has made little progress in improving explosives detection through the introduction of new equipment. New devices have been hampered by teething and false alarm problems.

The Federal Aviation Administration - Office of Civil Aviation Security, publish annually a report entitled, *Criminal Acts Against Civil Aviation.* This first appeared in 1986 and compiles incidents which have taken place against civil aviation aircraft and interests worldwide.These are summarised in regional geographic overviews and incidents are also sorted into one of seven categories and compared over a 5 year period.

At airports, your security starts in the car parks, which in certain parts of the world are not the safest of locations.

The seven categories in the *Criminal Acts* are as follows:

1. Attacks At Airports - Incidents include arsons, assaults, attempted bombings, mortar or other projectile attacks, shootings and similar acts directed at airport assets.

Attacks on airports that occur in war zones as part of the fighting between combatants are not included in this category.

2. Bombings, Attempted Bombings and Shooting on Civil Aviation Aircraft - This category records incidents that occur on commercial civil aviation aircraft and which are not part of a highjacking or commandeering. Bombings and attempted bombings include the use of real explosive and incendiary devices, but not hoax or claimed devices.

3. Commandeering - Commandeerings occur when the aircraft is on the ground and the doors are open. There is no distinction made between commandeering aircraft that remain on the ground and those which become airborne. Distinguishing a commandeering from other on-board situations (such as those involving unruly passengers) is determined by one or more of the following: the act involves the claim or use of a weapon; it is committed by a terrorist group; there are deaths or injuries to passengers or crew; or there is premeditation (hoax device, fake weapon, previously prepared note, more than one suspect, etc.). Incidents involving general aviation or charter aircraft are recorded separately and are not included in this category.

4. General Aviation/Charter Aviation Aircraft - Only incidents of significance involving charter or general aviation aircraft are included in this category. These incidents include commandeerings, highjackings and the destruction of aircraft.

5. Hijacking - An incident is defined as a hijacking rather than a commandeering if the aircraft is in an in-flight status, that is once the doors are closed. By this definition, a hijacking can occur either on the ground or in the air. There is no distinction made between hijackings in which a plane does not divert from its flight plan and those which do. Hijackings are distinguished from other in-flight situations by the same criteria used to determine commandeerings. Hijacking incidents involving general aviation or charter aircraft are not included in this category.

6. Off-Airport Facility Attacks - Incidents in this category include attacks against civil aviation assets, such as air navigational aid equipment and airline ticket offices, which are not located within the perimiter of an airport. These targets are attractive because they are unguarded and/or easily accessible.

7. Shootings At In-Flight Aircraft - Incidents include acts in which in-flight aircraft (commercial and general/charter aviation) are fired upon either from the the ground (surface-to-air missiles, anti-aircraft artillery, small arms fire, etc) or the air. The category excludes military planes and some other variables.

The above descriptions were taken from the FAA web site on *Criminal Acts.*

The *International Civil Aviation Organisation (ICAO)* has, for the past 25 years provided the framework for security practices worldwide. Established under the Convention on International Civil Aviation (Chicago Convention) in 1944, the document which created the ICAO gave States the responsibility for safeguarding against acts of unlawful interference. To assist with this the ICAO Council adopted the Standards and Recommended Practices on Security in 1974 and designated them as Annex 17 to the Convention. Whilst incidents have, generally, fallen in relation to both hijackings and assaults on airports, it has not guaranteed safety is neither consistent nor absolute on a worldwide basis.

Often domestic flights are proving 'softer' targets than international ones and we should all raise our alertness a notch when travelling internally in Third World countries, by their national carriers.

Private jets in Third World countries need round-the-clock security.

Tips

◆ If you must drive to the airport, pick a well lit area close to the terminal or shuttle pick up spot. If you feel uneasy about your surroundings, ask the shuttle driver to wait until you safely reach the terminal or your car.

◆ If you check your baggage at kerbside, make sure you see it loaded onto the conveyor belt. Don't assume the suitcase is safe sitting on a cart waiting to go on the belt - it isn't.

◆ Never give you bag or ticket to anyone unless you are at an official security checkpoint or ticket counter. A legitimate airport employee will never ask you to surrender these things anywhere else in the airport.

◆ Laptops disappear with amazing frequency at airports. Never let it out of your sight and don't put it through the X-ray machine - have it inspected. Ensure batteries are charged if you are asked to turn it on.

◆ Don't let anyone cut in front of you, especially if you have put something on the X-ray machine, such as your laptop. He may be trying to reach your goods before you or stall you by setting off a metal detector whilst an accomplice steals your computer.

◆ Don't be 'bumped' or let someone wipe a stain off your clothes - you may be being pick-pocketed.

◆ If you doze off waiting for a flight, loop your arm or leg around any hand baggage.

◆ It is older metal detectors and not X-ray machines which may damage information on hard drives because they create a magnetic pulse. In older X-ray equipment, it is actually the motor that drives the conveyor belt that may not be adequately shielded.

It behoves on companies who send their employees around the world either through their travel agents or their ' in house' resources to research the best and the worst. Much of this is available as 'open' information and published in travel magazines. Passenger screening measures will help to eliminate much of the risk from the hijacker and his weapons, but this is not foolproof, nor does it stop atrocities being committed in the airport itself and this aspect we will look at here.

The vulnerable times during a visit abroad occur whilst travelling to and from the airport, or rail and bus station and particularly during the stay at the hotel. It would be convenient to believe that security procedures at airports around the world are good, consistent and effective. To believe that this is the case means you have not travelled or you do so with your eyes shut. Often what we superficially observe as security at work is no more than bureaucracy at it's international worst. Don't be fooled into thinking that the presence of security personnel equates to effective security procedures.

I can become repetitive about certain concepts to the point of nauseum and no where is this more true than over the psychology of 'denial'. An unassailable belief that "it will always happen to someone else", is the greatest contributor to personal risk. We believe we are safe and we believe institutions are safe, such as Hotels, Embassies and Airports.

As this book was in the process of production the terrorist bombing of the U.S. Embassy in Nairobi, Kenya had killed some 260 people and injured over 500.

The video camera on the roof of the Embassy, monitored by the marine internal guard force, had no facility to record events and so there is no record of people and vehicles prior to or at the time of the bombing. This is a gross act of negligence, but it evidences the attitude that can prevail in even official security circles where the task of protecting people and premises is a full time one. The problem is one of relaxing in the face of the belief that the risk is low therefore a minimalist approach can be taken to security issues. The consequence is, unfortunately, that the premises and people become attractive as a 'soft target' for terrorist attacks.

The U.S Embassy in Lebanon, which formerly sat on the Corniche alongside a busy main road and destroyed by a vehicle bomb was another example. This is in contrast to their existing one, up in the hills and protected with as much consideration as Fort Knox. Again though, at the time of writing, a rocket attack was attempted against this Embassy, but this was a 'stand off' attack as it is 'hard target' and well guarded, both physically and with very efficient local security personnel.

One week after these atrocities in Africa, Northern Ireland suffered one of it's worst bombing incidents when a splinter, Republican terrorist group the 'Real IRA' murdered 28 people and injured 200 in a car bomb in Omagh. Amongst the dead were two Spanish nationals, a twelve year old and a teacher, as well as another twelve Spanish children who were injured. Often visitors abroad find themselves the victims of domestic terrorism and there is little they or anyone can do about it.

It is too easy to say that renowned trouble spots should be avoided, especially when the general belief is that the troubles have ceased, rarely are long term political problems, which have a history of associated violence, ever truly resolved and for those students of current affairs, you will know it is easier to find countries with a history of domestic terrorism than it is to find one's without. That does not mean that we should accept the risks without making an accurate assessment as we outlined in Chapter 3.

Soft Targets

Airports are, like the U.S. Embassies in Kenya and Tanzania, soft targets. When we enter airport buildings our threat goes up. Over the years international airports have seen some of the worst terrorist atrocities against innocent civilians and yet we harbour a belief that security in such environments is good and that security checks on people and luggage going onto planes are equally good. This is a fallacy and you need to travel the world to see the contrast in the provision of security services. I was speaking to a colleague in the security business who has an interest in bomb attenuation equipment. These are products that reduce the effects of bombs, such as 'bomb blankets, curtains, armour for walls and vehicles and who was telling me that there had been three recent incidents in Europe where X-Ray equipment had 'triggered' explosive devices. If you can, try and pick a machine that has few people using it - easier said than done, I know.

Airports have proved to be a prime terrorist target for both attacks, bombings and hijacks. Due to the nature of commercial airlines and airports, the executive is at the mercy of the system, but risks can be lessened if reasonable precautions are taken. The following pre-flight and In-flight guidelines are proven techniques developed from case histories of numerous aviation-related incidents.

Coming into land at a former Soviet bloc, Eastern European airport in a Gulfstream G5 - often security at such locations is poor or non-existent.

We need to keep things in perspective though and the terrorist attacks in the eighties such as those at Leonardo Da Vinci, Rome and Schwechat, Vienna in 1985 by Arab terrorists have resulted in a far tighter level of airport security around the world. There have been no atrocities such as these attacks for many years, but all the tensions still exist in the Middle East and we should still take all precautions.

Broad Principles

◆ Forgetting the extremist actions of terrorists for a minute we need not to lose sight of the fact that international and domestic airports are the haunt of thieves, especially pickpockets.

◆ Generally, you should be aware of the airports which have, acknowledged, high security measures.

◆ Endeavour to book flights with as few stops as necessary - always try to fly non-stop.

◆ It is often difficult, but try and avoid those airlines which are natural targets for terrorist activities as well as those airports which have been subject to attacks. Equally we should avoid those airlines and airports which have a poor security/incident profile.

◆ Carry-on luggage should contain any regularly used prescription medicines, an extra pair of glasses, passport and copies of carefully chosen documents.

◆ Dress inconspicuously to blend in with the international environment.

◆ Do not discuss business or travel plans with fellow passengers.

Prohibited Items

There is a list as long as your arm about what you can and cannot take on an aircraft. Such things as explosives, fireworks, percussion caps, caps for toy guns, All aerosol cans marked as 'flammable', camping gas, butane/propane containers, tear gas, lighter gas and refills for hair curlers, bleach, nitrogen and the list goes on. If you are in any doubt then seek advice. Take nothing which is a weapon, looks like a weapon, or can be used as a weapon. You are advised to take electrical and electronic equipment as hand baggage. If you pack this type of equipment in baggage that is to be checked in then you must declare it. If you don't the baggage may not be loaded onto the aircraft.

At The Airport

◆ The general rule is to plan your arrival at the airport to give you just enough time for all the procedures, in other words you want to limit your time and exposure at the airport. Statistically, the main risk is at the 'check-in' areas. However, the reality of judging the time involved in this process and also the journey to the airport from your hotel, is as scientific as nail filing. You simply cannot judge the precise time required. Journeys necessarily require large margins, particularly if you have to travel through any major city en route to the airport. At the airport there is a complete inconsistency as to the time required to process you through the system. Only recently at Gatwick airport in the U.K I had to wait in a queue for 15 minutes simply to go through passport control and have hand luggage x-rayed. There were some 12 potential locations with 'walk through' x-ray and baggage control, yet and this is in the height of the holiday period, there were only two open.

◆ The second rule should be that if you have confidence in the procedures, through experience and have faith in the time estimate to get you to the airport then you can obey the first rule of security at airports and that is to be there for as short a time as possible. If you have ever flown out of Moscow from Sheremetyeva 2 you will know that when they say leave 2 hours for the process, they are not joking. On many occasions I have got through in less than an hour, but on occasions it has been close to the full two hours. Going in we use the

VIP facilities and are met from the plane, because if you think the exit procedure is a tough one wait till you have to queue with two hundred others to get through immigration.

◆ Phone one hour before you leave home or the hotel to check if the plane is on schedule. You want to know if your flight is delayed so as to decrease your exposure to risk.

◆ Upon arrival at the airport say your goodbyes in the vehicle, if there are any to be said. Unless the people with you can help in any way with speeding up the process, either because of the language or influence, then proceed alone to accomplish the preflight procedures.

◆ Don't get caught by 'baggage handlers'. Manage on your own and be firm. I believe you can even make a scene rather than allow others access to your baggage.

◆ Address baggage with your business address and not your home address. In the U.K baggage handlers have been jailed for being in collusion with burglars and supplying them information.

◆ Whilst you should put the company's address on the tags do not put the company's name. In many Third World, anti-western countries this is a dangerous thing to do.

◆ If you do have 'gold, silver or platinum' airline membership tags, don't not put them on your luggage - they identify you as some-one who may have wealth and status.

◆ Get used to how you will carry your bags if a trolley is not available. Don't look like you are having problems or you will attract the very people you want to avoid. If your luggage is on a trolley keep the sling of your hand baggage or computer case in your hand.

◆ Before your baggage is 'checked' keep your baggage in a tight group on the floor if you have no trolley and keep your hand baggage or computer case in your hand or over your shoulder.

◆ Never leave any baggage unattended- not only from the theft aspect, but because unattended bags, boxes and other items that have no apparent owner are, by default, treated as bombs.

High Tech meets Third World. At many Third World airports, very few security procedures apply.

◆ Losing sight of your luggage may mean that someone can slip narcotics into your baggage for you to carry it for them. In many parts of the world drug smuggling carries with it the death penalty.

◆ Whether it is customs or passport control or security, be as polite as possible. Loose your temper or have a sense of humour failure and you could become a victim very easily. Don't show signs of impatience or frustration and don't criticise 'out loud'.

◆ Do not put your bags onto the x-ray conveyor belt until you are next to go through and keep you eyes on them, particularly computer cases. According to the Computer Security Institute, which works with the FBI in compiling stistics on computer-related crimes, laptop theft has doubled since 1998 and hotels and airports are major danger spots.

◆ Be highly vigilant in crowded, chaotic situations at airports, or bus, metro and train stations.

◆ Be alert to groups of small children, or people crowding around you. If you are bumped into or jostled this could be part of a pick pocketing attack.

◆ Once your baggage check-in has been completed, spend a minimum of time in the public lobby areas - proceed as quickly as possible to the, essentially, 'sterile area' of the departure lounge.

◆ If you have time on your hands then always make use of the VIP lounges, if you qualify. Bear in mind, at this point that there are opposing schools of thought about executive lounges. This advice is because of the benefit of being isolated away from the main public areas which would be the focus of a terrorist attack. The other view is that travellers should keep a low profile and endeavour to mingle with the crowd. The view is that by being seen as someone who uses the executive lounges you are a target for the thief, corporate spy and terrorist. I disagree - the lounge is a safer area and mingling with the crowd does not make you any less than what you are, I'm afraid. There is far more opportunity for the 'sneak thief' to operate in the main public areas than there is in the lounges. Access to the lounges is only possible with the appropriate ticket.

If you cannot get access to a private lounge, look carefully around the airline gate area before selecting your place to sit or stand.

◆ Avoid large expanses of glass.

◆ If it's unavoidable, sit or stand facing away from it.

◆ Sit near or stand with your back to a supporting structural column or wall. By doing this you also limit your field of view of people to 180 degrees.

◆ Do not sit or stand next to :-

Waste paper baskets, unattended luggage, telephone booths, airline ticket processing booths, unidentified enclosures, vendor/cleaner carts, or any other equipment a bomb can be hidden in.

Lockers in which an explosive device may have been left. In reality there are very few airports with free standing lockers in operation, for that very reason.

◆ Avoid being near soldiers, especially U.N or U.S soldiers.

◆ It is good advice to endeavour to be as inconspicuous as possible, even to the extent you buy a local paper. The suggestion is that if you have a favourite magazine to read then do it behind cover of the local paper.

◆ Avoid people who are receiving special attention from the airline, other passengers or the press. Especially avoid large and official looking entourages with dignitaries.

◆ Remain alert in the waiting area.

◆ Don't linger near ticket counters - terrorists target places where the largest number of people may congregate.

◆ Don't become absorbed in a book or business matters - stay alert.

◆ Be alert to an influx of uniformed security, policemen or anxious airline personnel using radios, or if there is a bomb scare, hopefully, not using radios as there is the risk, albeit remote of the radio signal detonating the device.

◆ If you hear something that sounds like a gunshot or an explosion, it might be a gunshot or an explosion - so don't go into denial and think it can't happen. Look for some 'hard cover'.

◆ Be wary of any disturbance, it could be a diversion.

Anticipate problems and your reactions to them. It is only solving half the problem, by maintaining a good level of awareness. If you do not have an 'immediate action' plan in mind, should anything actually happen you will be likely to freeze as your decision making process will simply shut down on you.

Pick out a sheltered area, such as behind a supporting column, vending machine or upholstered furniture.

◆ Be prepared to seek shelter immediately in the event of an incident.

◆ Identify emergency exits in a waiting area. If possible check to see where they lead. Often you can do this through a window as opening the door may trigger an alarm.

◆ If an evacuation is ordered by airport officials, take a position in the centre of the group with as many people around you as possible. Do not take the lead or straggle.

◆ If it is not possible to gain access to a lounge try and identify the departure gate as soon as possible and sit near that. It can be boring, you are away from the main concourse, with no shops, cafes or interest value, but you are away from the main problem area.

◆ Do not become over 'chatty' with anyone, if it exposes your nationality.

◆ In Third World geographies always arrange, in advance, to be met. Public transport should not be an option and taxis your last option. Depending on the standard of your hotel they can send a car for you or ensure a local contact meets you.

Waiting for the plane airside at Almaty airport. On this occasion there were some 7 - 8 vehicles waiting for one private jet. Not many places in the world would allow so many private vehicles airside..

On The Aircraft

◆ However many times you have heard the safety announcement, listen carefully. Procedures on aircraft can change so listen.

◆ We are told to do it and seldom comply and that is to keep our seat belts on unless we have to get up out of the seat. Loosen it but keep it fastened.

◆ Comply with the rule that most airlines have these days which is to switch off all radio equipment (telephones, pagers etc).

◆ When selecting a seat on the aircraft, request a seat next to an 'over the wing' emergency exit. When on the aircraft read the instructions posted on the exit hatch about it's operation. (Personally, I have problem with this as often the leg room in these seats is so generous that unless your seat has an extendable foot rest there is usually no place to put your feet, but that's a personal problem). If this seat is unavailable, select a position near an alternate exit.

◆ Select a window seat if you can - this will put you two or three people away from anyone causing a disturbance in the aisle. Most assaults during a hijacking involve people occupying an aisle seat.

◆ Memorise your passport number so you do not have to reveal your passport when filling out landing cards.

What Not To carry On With You

In the event of a hijacking, the hijackers will usually seize any documents you have on your person or in your hand baggage. Therefore, if possible, don't have any incriminating information included in your possessions in the cabin. You should try not to carry the following for example:-

◆ ID for any military reserve or any police reserve organisation.

◆ Cards showing membership in a political party, action group or any group that can be considered controversial.

◆ Business cards that indicate controversial titles or indicate your position/title. If you are the President of IBM, it would probably pay not to let a hijacker know that fact, so stow your business cards in your checked luggage.

◆ The same applies to business cards with addresses in controversial countries and stationery that has the letterhead or logo or addresses which could be viewed as controversial.

◆ Credit cards issued in the company's name. This is obviously problematic. You would never consign your credit card to checked baggage, but equally there are occasions that you become at personal risk as a consequence of who you work for. The answer is a corporate one, which needs tackling from the company's end. Corporate credit cards should be issued in the name of a group or subsidiary company whose name is anonymous.

◆ Company reports, annual reports that spell out the nature of your company's business. If you work for an armaments company and find yourself in a hijack situation with your P & L accounts on your lap showing how well you did last year in land mine sales - good luck.

◆ Letters that provide sensitive information. Personal data that can be used to pressure you into taking actions or making statements against your will.

◆ Personal financial information - bank or tax statements and any documents that could indicate a degree of wealth that could agitate.

◆ Cheque books or savings passbooks. Both may indicate wealth. Remember wealth is relative.

◆ Obviously expensive jewellery, rings, gold watches, chains etc. I came back from a job in Italy recently and sat next a a very wealthy North American who had been touring Europe with his family. He had sold a business worth millions and was in semi-retirement. As he listed the hotels they had been staying in, it was apparent that they enjoyed only the best, yet he was proud of his attention to detail in the area of personal security as he was wearing a black plastic twelve dollar watch and no other jewellery. He did, however, carry the children's 'spending money' in a black briefcase he had with him and into which he regularly dipped always coming out with cash.

◆ Clothing that sets you apart from the crowd.

◆ Pocket knives or other items that could be viewed as weapons.

◆ Magazines, books, videos that could be offensive to fundamentalist groups. Even leaving countries, such as Algeria, your baggage will be searched by hand, ostensibly to check for devices, whereas in reality they are looking for contentious material such as girlie mags and the like. Don't take them in to countries and don't bring them out.

What To Do If There Is A Hijacking

You must be prepared to look after yourself!

As a general rule, you must become as 'invisible' as possible in order not to be singled out. Some Do's and Don'ts:-

◆ Listen carefully and follow instructions of the hijackers.

◆ Blend in with your fellow passengers.

◆ Do not argue, question, or challenge physically.

◆ The more time that passes the better your chances of release, so, behave rationally to further increase your chance of survival.

◆ Do not volunteer anything and do not volunteer to be a spokesman.

◆ Even if you are accustomed to 'being in charge', do not display authority, disdain or ignorance - be as grey and neutral as possible.

◆ Avoid making eye contact with any of the perpetrators, especially during the first 20-30 minutes of the incident.

Experience has shown that the initial stages of a hijacking, when the perpetrators are particularly nervous and agitated, are the most dangerous.

◆ Plan on a lengthy stay and endeavour to keep track of the passage of time.

◆ Keep your mind active by planning the future and if possible reading.

◆ If the hijackers collect valuables, documents or other personal items, do not attempt to hide or withhold anything. (There is a school of thought, however, that says you should avoid giving up your papers if they single you out by nationality, religion or profession). Carry a family photo, if you at some time have to make an emotional appeal.

◆ Do not ask that certain items - watches, rings and so forth - be retained for sentimental reasons.

◆ Do not ask any special permission to do anything such as smoke, change seats, or go to the toilet, unless absolutely necessary. Consume liquids in moderation with this in mind.

◆ Unless absolutely necessary, do not talk to passengers around you. The hijackers may think that you are plotting something and take action against you.

◆ Also the hijackers may have planted colleagues amongst the passengers.

◆ Remain as calm as you can throughout the incident (you may be frightened, but try to retain your composure) and conserve your strength. While you may feign sleep, you should actually remain awake and alert to everything going on around you. If the incident is prolonged and you need sleep do so, but only briefly.

◆ Accept and consume all food and beverages offered to you by the hijackers. If you are offered alcoholic beverage accept it, but don't consume it.

◆ Do not ask for special foods, drinks or utensils, even if you do not have any, but take what you are given. Be quietly gracious.

◆ Use your time to assess the situation and plan various reactions to the situations which might arise. Note where all the emergency exits are located. Note the movement of the hijackers, crew and other passengers.

◆ Prepare yourself mentally for questioning by the hijackers. Consider whether any of your personal effects could draw attention to you. Formulate reasonable answers to explain your position and effects.

◆ If you are in fact questioned, be as truthful as possible, without revealing information that may cause the hijackers to take action against you. Keep your answers short and limited to non-political topics.

◆ Minimise the importance of your job.

◆ Continue to wear as much clothing as you can tolerate. Clothing will provide some protection if you are shot, or an explosive is detonated near you.

◆ Keep your shoes on. If they decide to shoot people and you elect to make a run for it, you don't want to do it in your socks.

◆ You will probably also wish you had listened to the safety briefing about the location of the emergency exits.

◆ Do not trust anyone else on the aircraft with your thoughts, emotions or plans. The passenger in whom you confide may either be a hidden accomplice of the hijackers or may offer information about you in the hope of ingratiating himself/herself with the hijackers.

◆ Mentally rehearse actions in the event the situation deteriorates to violence and you have to move quickly. Keep the floor area between you and the seat in front of you, clear of clutter, as you may have to crouch down there for protection. Try to have a coat or blanket handy for covering and protecting your head.

◆ At the sound of gunshots or other disturbance, crouch as low as possible and remain in that position until you have no doubt that it is again safe to sit back up or you must take further action for your safety, say in the event of fire.

◆ Whether or nor you try to escape is a decision that must be based on a careful analysis of your situation, the danger you are facing and the possibilities open to you. Evaluate all the factors and reach a reasoned decision. Remember, however, that your decision making faculties will be greatly effected by the pressure and fear of events. If the opportunity is a good one take it. You have nothing to gain by remaining captive unnecessarily if you can get away. Once you have made the decision, do not vacillate - move and move fast. As we discuss later in Chapter 10, if a hostage situation develops, an individuals resolve to act deteriorates over time until any escape, even through an open and unguarded door, becomes psychologically impossible.

◆ Hijackers sometimes release passengers in the course of the hijack. If for any reason they select you do not argue. Leave the aircraft according to the hijackers instructions. You must be prepared to co-operate fully with the authorities, providing them with enough information as you can about the hijackers and the situation aboard.

◆ If the situation continues, try and massage your limbs and move as much as possible without drawing undue attention to yourself.

The Risk

The nineties have seen a shift in geographic emphasis of airline highjackings. We became used to seventies hijackings with a Middle Eastern origin, whereas the nineties has seen a shift of emphasis to the problems of India, Pakistan and latterly Afghanistan.

In March 1991 Pakistani hijackers seized a Singapore Air flight en-route to Singapore with 114 passengers and 9 crew. The seizure ended when Singapore commandos stormed the plane and shot dead all 4 hijackers.

In somewhat the same religious vein 4 Moslem fundamentalists in December 1994 seized an Air France Airbus 300 with 227 passengers and 12 crew. Following the murder of 3 passengers and the release of 63 passengers, paramilitary forces stormed the plane at Marseilles, killing the 4 hijackers and injuring 25 others.

In May 1998, all 29 hostages aboard a Pakistani International Airlines flight, were released following a shootout when Pakistani officials posing as Indians entered the plane.

December 1999 saw 6 hijackers seize an Indian Airlines flight 814, from Nepal to New Delhi. The end of this incident saw India release 3 Kashmiri militants they were holding in jail, sending out a very dangerous message - that terrorism works.

The hijackers objective was to get released the imprisoned leader of the Harkut ul-Mujahadin, (Islamic terrorists operating in Kashmir, a Maulana Masood Azhar. Eventually India's External Affairs Minister flew to Kandahar airport in Afghanistan to deliver the three freed men to the hijackers. This followed a capitulation by the Indian government following one week of terror for the remaining 155 hostages on and the stabbing to death of one of their number.

The Taliban government in Afghanistan gave the hijackers and their freed comrades 10 hours to leave their country. Following the seizure the plane having been refused permission to land in Pakistan, landed first at Amritsar, then Lahore and onto Dubai before being allowed to land at Kandahar. The Afghan authorities' release of the terrorists and the freed prisoners was condemned around the world as was the Indian government's capitulation. A British Foreign Office official said *"the Indian incident has raised the idea of hijacking as a means of getting demands met"*. South Asia has now overtaken the Middle East as the world's terrorism capital, with Indian Airlines, India's state owned domestic carrier, apparently the most hijacked airline in the world, with 11 abductions since 1971.

The Wheel Turns!

The Taliban government paid for their lack of resolve over the Indian incident, when an Afghan airlines Boeing 727 Ariana flight was hijacked by anti-Taliban rebels on an internal flight on Sunday 6th February 2000. In a complete about face the Afghan government refused to either meet any demands, nor negotiate with the hijackers. Having first touched down in Moscow the plane flew on to Stanstead airport in Britain where, through negotiation and toughness all 158 hostages were released unharmed. It subsequently became apparent that the term hostage was a misnomer, as almost to a man all hostages applied for asylum.

General

When booking tickets always have these made in the name of the travel agent and not your company. On occasions you may read advice on travel security which suggests that you do not book tickets in advance, rather get to the airport early and buy them there. This is frankly rubbish. Security depends on known factors, such as knowing that you are most certainly able to depart a country when you wish. These days the chances of turning up at any airport for most flights and being able to guarantee the availability of a seat is remote to say the least. You need to minimise your time at the airport not increase it.

Although these days the rule is not strictly applied, it can be the case with certain airlines that their regulations require that you have personal identification on the outside of your luggage, to help trace lost items. In this case you should use your business address, not your home, but exclude the corporate name.

Try and use your time at an airport to familiarise yourself with the layout. It has paid dividends for me in the past where, through connecting flight delays I have had to race through an airport to a gate and the prior familiarity has helped. In most in-flight magazines you will find good schematics of airport layouts. British Airways has Heathrow and Gatwick and Air France in their magazine has Paris Charles De Gaule and Lufthansa has The German airports. Either keep the magazines and cut these out later or tear them out and build up a file.

Each airport and each country have their own peculiarities when it comes to embarkation procedures and you should try and remember these for future reference. At Charles De Gaule for example, getting through to the specific gate can be a strange experience and when you do you find you are the only one in the departure area as everyone else has descended into the lower departure area where the departure gate is actually located - all very confusing.

Lost luggage

It happens! We may travel in hope, but on occasions hope may not be enough to defeat the machinations of the baggage handling service at some airports. I can think of nowhere where 'hope' needs to come in gallon containers than Heathrow airport, particularly if one is having to transit through and transfer luggage. I learned to my cost some time ago to check my luggage only to Heathrow, collect it and recheck it in for the next flight. The system is overloaded and does not work.There may be other airports in the world as bad, but there can't be many. Cyprus proved another bad spot for me and as I was in transit to Israel the same day the loss of my luggage became problematic.

Try to be the first to the carousel, to avoid theft. Remove any travel tags which identify your origins, but keep them on your possession until you are in the hotel.

There are a few rules to stick to if luggage does go astray.

◆ If the offending piece of luggage doesn't turn up on the carousel, then don't go through customs until you have reported it.

◆ Be able to give an accurate description - size, colour, make, material, distinguishing features etc. To help in this make sure you I.D it inside and out.

◆ Always get the people you are reporting it to to make immediate enquiries whilst you are there and fill out the necessary forms there and then.

◆ Get someone's name, preferably the person you are talking to and a telephone number which will get you straight through to him. Also get the name of the persons opposite number on the next shift.

◆ Give precise details of where you are staying and when you get to the hotel phone back and give your room number.

◆ Make sure the hotel concierge knows you are expecting luggage. I had a situation where the air service people swore a missing suitcase had been delivered and which the hotel refuted. In fact it had been delivered, but the person who had accepted knew nothing about the issue and put it on one side and told no one - a 5 star hotel as well!

◆ The last point is that you must pester people, nicely, but pester. Keep on the phone to them and make them tell you it's whereabouts at all times.

You only have to look in one corner of any airport to see a jumbled pile of suitcases to know someone, somewhere is tearing their hair out. Do not assume that it will reach you without some effort on your part. Repatriation may take one day or four days, so be prepared to re-kit yourself.

If you were going onto a business meeting after booking into the hotel I can only suggest you travel in business attire. If you put it all in the checked luggage you could find yourself at the bankers forum in Hawaiian shirt and shorts.

CHAPTER TEN

Security for the Expatriate

The U.S State Department in late 1998 urged American citizens living abroad *"**to review their security practises, to remain alert to the changing situation and to exercise much greater caution than usual. Large crowds and other situations in which anti-American sentiments may be expressed should be avoided**"*. This was following the bombing of their East African Embassies. Whilst this is a book for the business traveller, it maybe that one day the travelling stops and the expatriate life begins. In that event the nature of ones problems change. Many of the stories we read in the newspapers of kidnappings and attacks on foreigners, more often than not, take place against people who are living in that particular country. The exception is the 'adventure traveller' an ever increasing breed whose travel is spiced up by holidaying in countries whose social stability is tenuous.

The U.S. State Department - Bureau of Diplomatic Affairs, Overseas Advisory Council (OSAC), produced guidelines some years ago which are still relevant and should be the basis of planning one's security initiatives when living abroad. They are available on the internet and I think it is worth quoting the Introduction in full:

"Effective security precautions require a continuous and conscious awareness of the environment, especially when living in a foreign country. Security precautions lessen vulnerability to criminal and terrorist acts and greatly facilitate the assistance the U.S. government can provide. Levels of risk in a foreign country can change rapidly, sometimes overnight and can be triggered by internal and external incidents or circumstances. Continually monitor the political climate and other factors that may impact the level of risk. Security precautions must be constanly reviewed so they may be adapted for effective response to changes in the level of risk".

Whether you are living in a country or intend to be there for a while, register with your embassy or consulate, especially if there is civil unrest. This will include you in the arrangements for evacuation.

The casual businessman if he draws attention to himself may also be at risk. In South Africa on the morning that Nelson Mandella opened his parliamentary session in February 1999 a Canadian diplomat who had arrived in the country to attend the event was mugged in his Cape Town hotel room. One week before that the Korean head of Daewoo South Africa, Yonk Kwoo Kwon, was shot and killed in a car hijack attempt outside his home in Johannesburg.

As an example of how much violence and criminality has taken a grip of South Africa in 1998, 223 police were killed, mostly by attackers who robbed them of their pistols. The expatriate in such environments is increasingly at risk.

Kidnap Potential

The business traveller and tourist has the very real advantage of not staying in one place too long, whereas the expatriate is someone who will eventually become noticed in his community. This book is not the place to analyse the subtle differences between kidnappers for profit, political mileage or hostage taking. In southern Italy it will be purely business, whereas in Russia it could be business or vendetta. The worst countries are as follows (in no particular order of merit) - Columbia, Mexico, Pakistan, Phillipines, Brazil, Venezuela, Italy and Spain (ETA). South Africa is also gaining something of a reputation for itself in recent times.

Latin America is still the leading region for kidnappings with statistics revealing some 6,000 people abducted each year, with Colombia accounting for three quarters of these. Estimates put the ransom figure in Columbia alone to be some $200 million. There are in the region of 2,000 kidnaps in Mexico, but those reported may be the tip of the iceberg and it is believed most go unreported to the police, often because the chances are it will have been the police who carried out the kidnap.

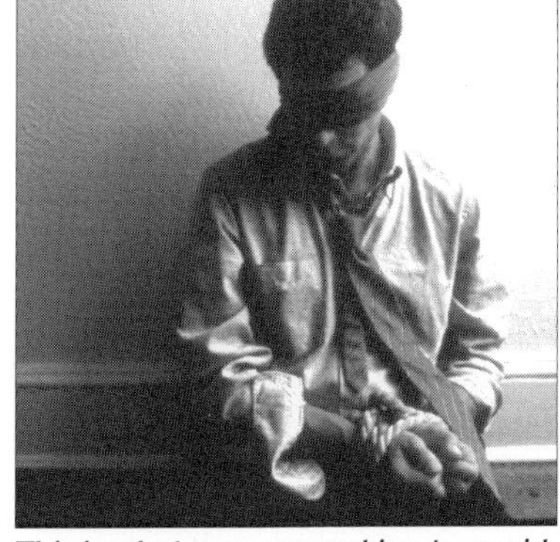

This is what you are working to avoid.

It is sufficient to know that in all cases it is something to avoid. From whatever background or motivation, one thing is essential in a kidnappers or robbers armoury and that is information and theinformation they need is about you.

They need to build up a pattern of your behaviour, addresses, timings, associates, routes, means of transport, security effort, the families procedures, your awareness level and a host of other factors which all contribute to ensuring, as much as possible, that they will succeed with the execution of the plan without danger to themselves. To gather such data takes time and effort and, as a consequence, the businessman who hits town and is away in 48 hours after a succession of meetings gives no potential for a 'would-be' attacker to even begin to build up a pattern and profile about the individual. More often than not the traveller is the victim of the opportunist thief, robber, rapist, or murderer. A kidnapper or an extortionist's attention is turned, therefore, to the expatriate who essentially becomes a victim of his or her environment. A victim in the sense that they fall into patterns of behaviour, believing that even in a known dangerous environment it will not happen to them. Also every expatriate should know that he or she, irrespective of their position in the corporation, represent a potential target. This book is liberally sprinkled with incidents where people of none, or little economic worth have been attacked, kidnapped or killed.

Always remember, it is what you represent and who you represent that makes you a potential target. You represent the West, you represent democracy and you probably represent a Western nation which, in the eyes of many Third World countries, is responsible for all the ills of the world in general and theirs specifically. The U.S. State Department, Bureau of Diplomatic Security sees fit to produce a glossy and expensive booklet entitled 'Terrorist Tactics and Security Practices' to assist people and businesses abroad understand the nature of the risks and how to prepare.

The problems for the ex-pat, as distinct from the occasional business traveller or tourist, is that they establish patterns of movement and behaviour. Kidnapping and assassination attempts take planning, time and detailed execution and are based on having detailed information about the victim. Information is the key to what they do. This is where the intended victim can play the greatest role in his own security programme . Many people believe that theirs is a passive role in the corporate security programme and providing they lock the office, turn on alarms and follow some basic guidelines they are fulfilling their part of the scheme. The expatriate must take much more of an active role than this in his own protection. Techniques of **anti-surveillance, pattern avoidance and information denial**, should all become a seamless part of an executives duties and lifestyle.

A healthy concern for personal safety should not develop into paranoia, rather it should channel into a continuous, sub-conscious state of awareness of one's actions.

The Offenders Need For Information

Hostile actions against an executive ie kidnapping, robbery, ambush or assault are often carried out after careful preparation. Victim selection may hinge on a number of factors, many of which the executive is, unknowingly, in control of. Information is needed to make both the initial victim selection and subsequently to establish daily and weekly patterns of behaviour and analysis made to establish vulnerabilities.

This process will require careful inquiry, analysis of information, observation, reconnaissance, study of timings or routes, mapping and analysis of the residence and place of work. The main emphasis is on surveillance and information gathering and an attack is unlikely unless all of the factors are in their favour. The methods employed will essentially be two --**Information Gathering & Surveillance**

Information gathering may even involve placing someone in the business. The author has many instances of Western companies operating in the former Soviet Union where business's are heavily infiltrated by members of organised crime groups. If they do not directly infiltrate members, they will pressure, threaten, bribe or blackmail otherwise loyal employees to become a regular source of information from the company. Often this information will be of an economic nature so as to assist in theft or fraud, but equally it will include data about the Western management. Be circumspect with members of the press. It has been known for terrorists to pose as journalists, so do not submit to interviews or allow photographs to be taken, particularly in your home or office. Brief your children to be guarded with strangers and under no circumstances must young children be allowed to answer the phone. Servants are another source of intelligence about you, so be guarded in their presence

Surveillance will be used to determine movement, timings, patterns, habits, lifestyle in general and any security procedures in place, e.g. a team of Bodyguards. For example they may establish that you leave your residence every morning at 0730, follow the same route, drive yourself, always drive with your window open and seem totally unaware of what is going on around you. It may be that you habitually go and play squash every Tuesday night and travel home on a deserted country lane. Surveillance will be both static and mobile and may be on foot or vehicle and may involve women and children.

Surveillance can be stationary at the residence, along routes, at work or you could be followed on foot or by vehicle (car and/or bike), or your phones could be monitored as could your mail. Information gathering will also extend to searching and removing both your domestic and business trash. Install shredders at home and the office.

Surveillance is, however, time consuming, expensive and requires manpower and resources. Therefore the more difficult it is for the offenders to get information on a victim the less attractive that victim becomes. This is where you come in. By not falling into regular patterns, timings and habits, you create little opportunity for offenders to set up an attack. The surveillance becomes unproductive and inconclusive. The object for an attacker is to catch a victim completely off guard and take them by surprise.

They know that such a vulnerable victim gives the best chance of a successful attack and, equally, a quick and safe getaway. They will have determined whether the attack should take place whilst the intended victim is in transit, at home, or 'transiting' from his office to the street. Statistics reveal that an executive is more vulnerable to ambushes, kidnappings and assault when he is in transit.

Anti-Surveillance

"Anti-Surveillance is the actions taken by those concerned with the protection of a potential target of terrorism, to detect and in certain circumstances to defeat terrorist surveillance." Whilst this may be directed at a professional protection team it applies equally well to someone living abroad who has to be their own bodyguard. The measures taken are to Locate, Identify, and Report surveillance of all types. Good anti-surveillance drills begin not with techniques but, with an attitude of mind. This attitude firmly states that you are, *'at all times being watched by someone'* and that the perceived level of threat or risk should have no bearing on that simple truth pervading your thinking at all times.

If you do not believe you are being watched, you will have no motivation to act appropriately - BELIEVE.! Anti-Surveillance is broadly what we call 'active' or 'passive'. Active means we carry out certain drills and procedures, both to try and detect any surveillance and also to let the opposition know we have seen them. This is not advised for the expatriate without a security team and we have not included any of the drills in this book.

Passive Anti-Surveillance

This should go on at all times and is simply a continuing awareness and observation to detect patterns or surveillance around you, your family and your business. If you believe you are being watched, this should be reported to the necessary authorities and make any changes to procedure necessary to provide increased protective effort and to make clear to the potential opposition that their surveillance has been detected. **Look For:-**

1. Erratic driving.

2. Early morning appearance - remember - everyone should have a reason for being where they are.

3. The vehicle that does not overtake.
4. Motor cycles.
5. Passengers giving directions.
6. Vehicle occupants with heads bent down - map reading.

Maintain an Observation Log of:

◆ People with descriptions, sex, race, age etc etc and attach a 'nickname' if it helps.

◆ Vehicles - VINs, make, type, colour and bumps and dents.

◆ These must be linked with time, places and circumstances.

Awareness

The basis of spotting people (Anti-Surveillance) who may be watching you is Awareness. Knowing what to look for is irrvelevant if you are not sufficiently Alert to what is going on around you (see Chapter 5). Both an Executive and his family can learn to detect subtle or sudden changes in their immediate environment, in other words they should be able to see the obvious and consistent efforts to survey the family's movement, habits, home or place of work.

One of the most important habits to get into, is to write down descriptions of individuals and vehicles which concern you including some distinguishing features. Notify any suspicions to your regional security manager and, if appropriate, the local police. I say if appropriate, as in many parts of the world it may be the police who are watching you and if you were in Mexico it may be that they intend to kidnap you. So, take advice, particularly from your embassy or consulate as to whether the police should be a port of call in times of difficulty.

Some other general guidelines are as follows:-

1. If you have a choice of company pool vehicles, use them.

2. When walking, walk in company wherever possible and be discouraged from walking anywhere at night.

3. Do not use the same restaurant, club, place of entertainment or other public place regularly.

4. Let the police know of any threats or the possibility of threats which may arise from public or commercial activities. Keep your family in the picture and, wherever possible, your key associates and those trusted close employees.

5. Advise family and business associates not to provide strangers with information concerning executives or family.

6. Avoid giving unnecessary personal details to information collectors in response to their enquiries on behalf of publications, such as business directories, social registers or research projects.

7. Establish simple, effective signal systems which, when activated, will alert business associates, chauffeur, members of the family (and obviously if in attendance the security officer).

8. Refuse to meet with strangers at scheduled or unknown locations.

9. Ensure that an 'Executive Tracking System' is in operation so that family and colleagues are aware at all times where you should be and an approximate ETA, past which point certain actions should taken. This should also equally apply to family members.

10. Know all phone numbers - office, home, police, security company.

11. Establish some simple code words to confirm that everything is alright. Such code words can be used for executive, family and business associates. They will need changing at intervals.

12. Corporate press releases announcing promotions of executives, should not list the executive's home address, nor should they discuss forthcoming travel plans or other activities which will define the presence of an executive at a particular location.

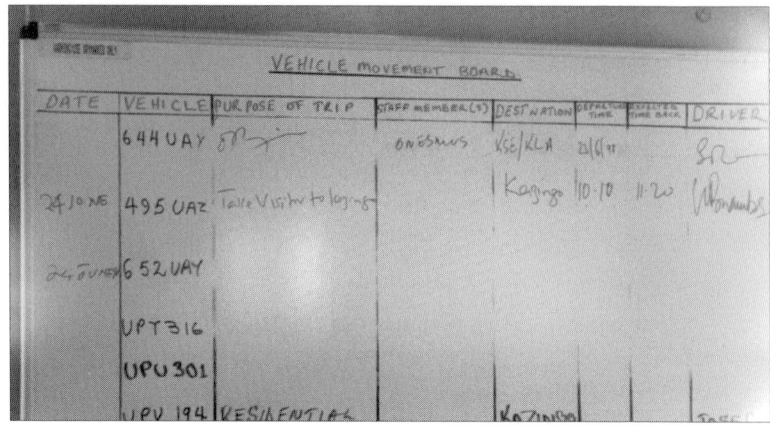

A location status or loc-stat board being poorly utilised in a Ugandan charitable organisation. An excellent concept if it works properly to track executive management and warn others of problems.

13. Press releases should be either without a photograph or else should not show the executive in his office or work location. Use a neutral background for all photographs.

14. Discourage use of name boards on office doors or desks.

15. Encourage a corporate 'clean desk policy' so that no information is available after hours to the not-so-casual observer.

16. Do not have a designated parking space with the company name identified or that of the executive or his position in the company. Park in the general parking area.

17. Senior executives should not work alone.

18. Do not leave travel papers on desks.

19. Do not book restaurants in your own name.

20. Avoid travelling at night.

21. Vary social activities, if at all possible, which may happen routinely week in, week out.

Anti-Kidnap Procedures

If you've got this far in the book you should, by now, be fairly sold on the idea of Awareness being the cornerstone of good personal security. There are endless things you should do and not do, but simply going through the routine won't save you if someone has designs. I'll repeat the key phrase and that is "**being aware is the difference between looking and actually seeing**".

The times you need to be most alert is when you are close to your home and place of work. This is where people will be likely to be watching you so look and note people who seem out of place, who seem to be trying too hard to appear to be 'in place'

Children

Always endeavour to impress on children the need not to give others information. In addition they must also know :

◆ To keep their parents in sight at all times in public places and in shops. If lost they must know to go to a shop assistant and not to a stranger.

◆ Not to go anywhere without permission.

◆ Have a password known only to the family and very close friends.

◆ Not to accept parcels or letters from strangers.

◆ Some local phrases and be learning the language.

◆ To let someone know their location at all times, particularly if they are older and enjoy more freedom.

Parents should ensure:

◆ That children do not get into a car or go into a house without permission.

◆ Do not let them be alone for a minute in a public place.

◆ Ensure they know their address and telephone number.

◆ Do not let them answer the phone, as they can easily be induced to part with sensitive information, particularly about parents whereabouts.

◆ Ensure they know the importance of keeping doors locked and not opening them to strangers.

What Should Your Company be Doing ?

The company should review it's security plans regularly to determine there effectiveness. Company travel arrangements should receive the same level of security as would any sensitive information.

1. Crisis Management Plans

You should know that your company has in place a set of 'Crisis or Emergency Plans', which would cover a number of emergency eventualities, such as 'Kidnap for Ransom'.

If your company's organisation abroad is substantial there may be enough personnel to establish an 'in-country' **Crisis Management Team (CMT)**, which would swing into action in the event of a kidnap, or any other prescribed emergency. If the in-country team amounts to you and a couple of ex-pat colleagues, with local employees then the CMT will be home based.

Be that as it may, there should be a designated team, resourced with equipment, administration and authority to make certain decisions. The CMT members should have received adequate training and possibly role-play scenarios to test their abilities as both individuals and asa team to operate with very high work loads under severe pressure, for long periods. Don't simply rely on a specialist consultancy being able to get someone 'in country' quickly and even if they do, the local situation may be a complete mystery to them. Put as much of it together locally as you can.

2.Risk Assessment

The Risk Assessment for a company operating in a non-compliant or hostile geography must include a security survey of domestic residences, vetting of staff, assessment of common routes, timings, habits and the level of training provided.

This is in addition to the regional, socio/political assessment carried out prior to your company establishing the operation or sending it's people abroad.

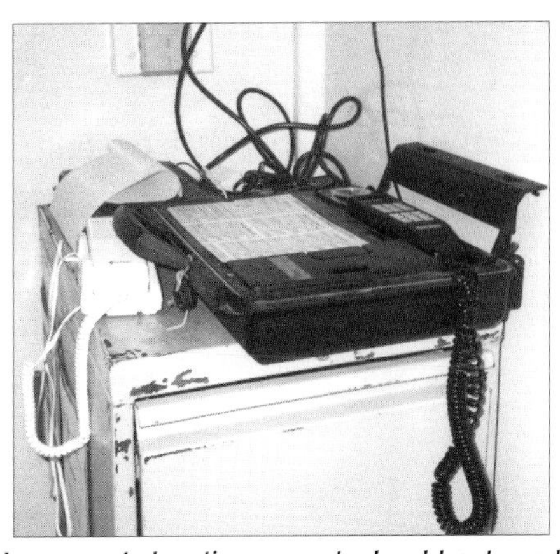

In a remote location, ex-pats should not need to rely on land lines to summon help. A Sat. Com. will be required.

The assessment should also cover the quality of any 'joint venture' partner - e.g. criminal and political links, history, government interference and a history of the company's directors. Whilst not wanting to get into any detail on matters of evacuation, a company must ensure that no plans rely on local police, local militia or military for it to succeed. There must be 'appropriate' vehicles, aircraft, communications, fuel, cash, passports, visas and supplies should the evacuation be overland. A system should be in place which allows future events to be assessed and 'alert states' amended accordingly. The intelligence for this may be gathered back at base, be provided by regular updates from the local consulate or produced by the operation on the ground. It may be an upcoming election, release of unfavourable economic data, or any action or omission by the government which may bring it into conflict internally or externally and lead to social breakdown and possibly chaos and violence.

Litigation

Your company should know that if they have no procedures in place and no people identified who are trained to manage such circumstances as a kidnap, then they could face expensive litigation from their employees should something untoward occur, or from their family should death be the result. It may be that in your particular country your company's operation is just you. If so you need to know that back at base a CMT procedure is clearly mandated and it's organisation and resources are taken seriously by the company and not merely paid lip service.

Special Contingencies

When operating in Third World environments, executives are at risk from a number of potential situations, not simply Kidnap. Often a complete breakdown of the country's stability and social order can occur, or there may be a specific extortion demand for money. The latter may be enforced with the threat of product contamination or a direct physical threat to the executive or his family. The executive may suffer serious injury or illness and in all these cases it may be advisable to 'Evacuate' the person and his family from the country.

Speed of Change

Never forget how one incident in one corner of the world can have a massive impact elsewhere. Nowhere was this better illustrated than with the fall out from the accidental NATO bombing of the Chinese Embassy in Belgrade during the Kosovo crisis, killing four Chinese nationals. The result was a massive wave of anti-American and British sentiment with demonstrations in Beijing, Shanghai and most major Chinese cities by tens of thousands of people. The German consulate was stoned in Guangzhou as were the US and British properties in all major cities. A number of fast-food outlets such as McDonalds and Kentucky Fried Chicken closed and Western films were withdrawn from circulation. The Chinese State had a heavy hand in stoking the fires of resentment through both the press and television, despite their assurances to foreign business of safety. It was reported in the Financial Times that the government controlled media had helped turn the spontaneous anger felt towards the US and NATO into rage. The reporting was partial and highly emotive.

Aid workers in Liberia who were kidnapped in August 1999 described the shock of the attack. They said they were aware of the volatile political situation in Liberia, but admitted they had not been prepared for the experience. *"It was a surprise"*, said one of the captors, Mr David Heed, *"we knew there was tension in the region, but it was definitely a surprise, there was no warning"*. Another hostage Peter Colenso said *"you can make preparations to deal with the situation, but in terms of anticipation, an event like this is very difficult"*.

To ensure people can evacuate swiftly, particularly in times of social disorder or riots, evacuation plans and arrangements need to be in place before the event and the CMT should instigate the various phases of the evacuation as the situation demands.

A corporate body should always take it's lead on evacuation from their embassy. The U.S. particularly has had considerable experience of 'drawdowns' or evacuations and an embassy will establish what are known as 'tripwires' which instigate a predetermined action based on escalating events. There will be issued a Travel Warning which may recommend 'authorised departure' or voluntary evacuation and the embassy itself will reduce non-essential staff.

Whether you and your family are evacuated by your company or your government you should always be prepared:

◆ Assume an evacuation is possible at any time

◆ Determine the 'who and the where' with your family i.e that is who should be contacted and where your family should go in case of an extended evacuation.

◆ Most corporate crisis plans for evacuation will withdraw non-essential staff and family's first and the most important to the business last.

◆ Keep a small bag packed with essentials i.e. clothing changes, dry and non-perishable foods, bottled water and any medications.

◆ You should always maintain in the residence an emergency supply of food, water, fuel and first-aid supplies. It may be you become trapped in the residence for a period and if it is not safe to leave the house you must be self-sufficient. When Western aid workers were eventually rescued from the Liberian capital of Monrovia in April 1996, it was following days of being marooned in their aid compounds. A Peter Chrichton of Action Aid, who was one of seven British aid workers taken from the Oxfam 'safe house' said, *" we have spent a considerable amount of time over the last three days on our stomachs down the back corridors of Oxfam House listening to bullets and grenades slam into the buildings around us".*

◆ In your residence keep all essential papers together and include your emergency cash and credit cards.

◆ If there are children involved discuss what is going to happen with them.

Kidnap & Ransom Insurance

I conducted a very detailed Risk and Crisis Analysis for an organisation operating in Beirut, Lebanon. During a meeting I was presented with an insurance schedule which the senior executive believed to be K & R insurance. On inspection it turned out to be simply 'Key Man' cover - in other words the organisation would be paid a capital sum on the death of the named employees for the amount specified for that person. It was not K & R and would not have been available as a financial resource to assist in securing the release of a kidnap victim. As a matter of interest this organisation had lost senior people to both kidnappers and the assassins bullet during the height of the troubles.

Statistics tell us that about 40% of all hostages are released safely after the ransom is paid. Having the resources to pay kidnappers demands, such as in the form of insurance, should help ensure safety.

By contrast, though, approximately 80% of hostages are killed during rescue attempts as was the case with the tourists in the Yemen. Don't get this out of perspective. Most kidnappings around the world are of local people by local people - landowners, businessmen, politicians etc.

In the main K & R insurance policies are reimbursement ones, that is the insurance company will reimburse the organisation for it's payments and certain expenses incurred to secure the release of the victim. They will usually pay out when the victim is released. The cover will be for the ransom amount (up to a limit), consultancy fees, possibly some other payments i.e. for information and transit cover for loss of the ransom monies during transport. Companies that transact such cover are Chubb, Lloyds of London and AIG, New York, with their 'Worldrisk' policy.

Kidnap & Ransom Consultancies

The K & R policy will also include an amount which allows the organisation to bring in a Kidnap & Ransom consultancy firm. Such firms specialise in providing an experienced management resource to the CMT. K & R consultancies are small in number, but highly experienced in such matters. In addition to the experience of similar incidents, they bring to an organisation a very objective and dispassionate approach to the process of obtaining a release.

It is usually the practice that a K & R insurer will insist on the target company using the services of one of it's 'captive' consultancies to advise on a range of security issues prior to providing the cover. This may include Close Protection (BG) work, Threat Analysis, CMT training. This consultancy would then be well placed, should a kidnap occur, to step into a slot as advisors to the CMT.

At times there is the very evident possibility of 'conflict of interest', with regard to whom the consultancy represents. Whilst it is paid for by the client company, clearly it is there to endeavour to mitigate the insurers potential losses. The two aspects need not, however, prove exclusive and experience has shown that the presence of skilled and experienced consultants benefits all parties concerned, the kidnap victim not being the least of these.

The Kidnap and Ransom Scenario

This usually takes place in the following sequence:-

- Reconnaissance by the kidnap gang.

a. To confirm identities b. establish the place, time and method of kidnap.

- The ambush/attack and abduction.
- Confirmation of the kidnap.
- Identification of the kidnap gang, organisation, or individuals.
- Receipt of the kidnap demand.
- The activation of the Kidnap Team from within the CMT. (nb a CMT may be brought together for emergencies such as product contamination, extortion, bomb threats, or a major disaster such as a factory explosion). CMT members who would be drawn together for a major disaster will not necessarily be the same people who would act in a K & R situation, although some members e.g. finance and legal will overlap.
- Negotiation ◆ Agreement ◆ Payment
- Release ◆ Debrief of the victim and post-incident care

When the sequence is 'bullet pointed' as above it seems a simple and straightforward process, whereas nothing could be further from the truth, but with expert assistance a satisfactory conclusion is, most often, reached. In many parts of the world kidnap for ransom is as much a part of the fabric of the economy as is stock market dealing. It is not the intention to kill the kidnap victim, simply to extort the optimum amount of ransom from the target organisation. By implementing tried and proven negotiating tactics, the victim will be released unharmed. Whilst the experience may be terrifying there is a substantial body of information available from those people who have been through the experience

Hostage Survival

In Chapter 9 we looked at many points to do with our correct behaviour during an airline hijack. Read that section again and link these general points given here. Remember a kidnap or hostage-taking is at it's most dangerous when the captors may be nervous, capable of acting irrationally and easily annoyed. It sounds trite, but be calm if you couldn't escape or fight your way to freedom in the first few seconds of the attack. Don't struggle - violence will be no problem to them. Fighting and struggling are two different things and if the distinction is not clear to you I would suggest you don't know enough about fighting to attempt it. Violence may be used even if hostages are passive, but ineffective resistance could end in death. Also don't make any sudden moves which may be misinterpreted and don't try to be a hero.

◆ If you are taken hostage with others try and remain inconspicuous, avoid direct eye contact and don't give the appearance of observing your captors.

◆ Avoid eye contact and don't appear to be interested in what your captors are doing.

◆ Maintain your sense of dignity, increase your requests for comfort, but in a low key way.

◆ Do what you are told without argument, but try and regain your composure as soon as possible, even if you are terrified.

◆ If questioned keep your answers short. Don't volunteer informationor make unnecessary overtures.

◆ Condition yourself to a lengthy stay, but ensure you have a system to keep track of time. Your captors may try to confuse you by removing your watch and altering meal times, but you can try and keep track of day and night by changes in traffic noise, temperature changes and even bird noises.

◆ Read whatever you can and keep your mind active. You can plan and you can daydream

◆ You should communicate with your captors and let them know you will comply and that you wish to stay alive.

◆ Your best defense will be passive cooperation

◆ Avoid politics or any contentious issue, but listen to their points of view attentively

◆ Avoid and refuse alcohol, but eat and drink when it is offered.

◆ If you find yourself in the middle of a police or military rescue attempt - lie very still on the floor - most hostages are killed in the crossfire when standing or moving.

◆ Keep yourself mentally and physically in good shape. If you can, exercise. Even with limited space this is possible.

◆ Always try and remain positive and avoid a sense of despair. Rely on your inner resources if you can dredge them up.

◆ If you are allowed writing materials all well and good, if not don't let that stop you composing either that novel you always intended to write or try your hand at poetry.

◆ Take detailed note of your captors and your surroundings.

◆ You will be accused of working for your government if the kidnap is political and you must come to terms with being ill-treated.

◆ Try to establish some kind of rapport with your captors. One suggestion is to talk about your family.

◆ If hostages are separated endeavour to establish some systems of communication, but don't jeopardize your safety.

◆ You should make every effort to maintain both your physical and mental health. Work out an exercise programme, however restricted your space and also work out a relaxation programme. Meditation may help.

◆ Eat the food you are given without complaint. It may not look or taste appetizing and a loss of appetite and weight is normal.

◆ Request both medicines and medical treatment. Don't be afraid to ask for anything you want - pens, paper and books for example.

◆ Whilst you may consider escape a possibility you should weigh in the balance the general socio/political climate in the town or region in which you are held captive. If it is strongly anti-Western and you would stand out from the crowd you may not get far.

Hostage Rescue

The attack on the kidnappers in the Yemen and the subsequent deaths of some captives highlights the risks of an armed rescue.

◆ If an armed rescue happens, take cover, lie down and keep still at all costs.

◆ Make no sudden moves which could mistake you as a terrorist.

◆ The point of release whether by assault or consent is a dangerous time with tempers volatile and tensions charged. Give no one an excuse for violence.

◆ Obey the very precise instructions given by the kidnappers or rescuers.

◆ Be prepared for initially rough treatment by the rescuers, including being searched.

Training and Briefings

A corporation has both a moral and legal duty of care to ensure that people it sends abroad are physically and mentally fit to withstand the rigours of the particular country they are posted to. There will always be the chance of 'culture shock' for those people and also their families who are uprooted from the familiarity of home. We are told that the onset of culture shock is likely to be in the second or third month once the novelty of the new environment wears off. Then the reality of the difficulty of living in a difficult environment takes over. Both children and adults can be affectedand can cause sleeplessness, apathy and depression. It can lead to other symptoms such as a reduction in efficiency recurrent minor illnesses and compulsive eating and drinking. It can lead to breakdowns of marriage at it's worst and even the loss of one's job. A company bears a great deal of responsibility in this area in correct selection of personnel, detailed briefings and short term visits initially.

Expatriate experience in Brussels will not equip someone for the rigours of the Philippines or Colombia. A person to be posted should receive training on a wide range of personal safety and security issues, as well as being resourced in the event of an emergency arising, be it immediate evacuation or kidnap for ransom. He might receive a course in 'Evasive Driving' (Anti-Ambush Drills), advanced first aid, cultural awareness and other 'avoidance' skills. The employee briefing should contain - areas to avoid, (clearly marked on a city map), hospitals, police stations, embassies., all relevant phone numbers, suitable restaurants, taxi firms, etc etc.

The following is a list of do's and don't, some of which will have been brought out elsewhere in the book, but are worth repeating:

Don't dress in a way that makes you appear Western e.g. brand's, logos etc.

No signs of wealth - gold, jewellery, watches.

Learn local phrases, if not the language (it still amazes me that companies send their people abroad without any language orientation).

Contact your local Embassy to establish the local do's and don't and the 'where not to go's.

Don't argue politics or express views.

Be friendly to people, without letting them take advantage.

There is a point about such items as sunglasses becoming a barrier to people as are air-conditioned cars, but I would not place too much emphasis on this. Without air-con you will drive with the window open which is not a good thing. If you do talk with people though, remember sunglasses may appear unfriendly.

The more repressive the regime the more care you should take, particularly with regard to your general behaviour. Do not be drawn into political discussions with anyone, however innocent - you could be set up. Also don't be surprised if you are followed. In most repressive regimes around the world the size of their internal security operations would bankrupt most democracies. We have mentioned it elsewhere, but will say it again, do not speak openly on the phone about sensitive business issues - either on a local call or international and your mail may also be intercepted.

When you enter a country which has a history of repression remember they are very sensitive to any form of criticism and ensure you do not have with you any literature such as security department briefings which may show the country in a poor light. The same goes for critical press comments and if you are staying in a hotel expect your luggage to be searched. You should avoid driving yourself, as even the most minor infringement of even the most minor law can be used against you. In this regard endeavour to know the laws, however petty.

As we said earlier, obtain from your embassy a list of places you should not go as a foreigner and never travel alone if at all possible, particularly to remote areas. If you are planning to travel obtain from your Embassy the names of local police chiefs, intelligence officers important political people. Often simply the mention of a name will have a magical effect. People in your organisation should know where you are and when you are expected. Eat and stay at only the Western, chain hotels.

Accept that, on occasions, e.g airports, road checks, government buildings, you will come into contact with police, military and internal security, so keep your temper, keep a smile on your face and never give them the impression that you are frustrated or annoyed about the delay. If they believe you are short of time they will make sure you are.

Bribes, for want of a more acceptable word, make most of the Third World turn. However, never bribe anyone yourself if you can avoid it. If you have the services of a guide or intermediary let him enter into negotiations - often complete strangers will come to your aid to establish the correct deal to be done if they see you are struggling. Always have 'giveaway' goodies such as bars of chocolate, cigarettes, pens, lighters or chewing gum. They can work wonders when used selectively.

Travel by air internally if you can as it is usually marginally safer than going by car. Remember though that thieves and con artists ply their trade at airports.

OFFICE

The office employees and the physical aspects of the office itself can offer good protection for the executive. Good protection means limiting the access of people to the management areas.. Access control should start at the building entrances and at the reception. There should be screening, I.D verification and a temporary badge system in place. No visitors should be left unescorted and staff should come to reception to meet people who have come to see them and not have people simply sent off on their own. They should also be escorted out of the building.

The received wisdom is that executive offices should be in the middle of buildings, but affairs are seldom so perfectly arranged. The object of having the executives in the central core is that people who want to get at them have to pass through additional security controls. An open office environment is also a good arrangement surrounding

Keep an eye out for anyone loitering near your office entrance and don't let people 'piggyback' in with you.

the executive offices, as there is live surveillance when someone walks through the general office as people in these open areas easily spot strangers. Staff need to know that they must either challenge strangers or those people not badged, or if this is thought too dangerous then report them immediately.

Always exclude the executives name from his office door and no name plate on his desk if this is in an open environment and no name, floor or office number from the internal directory. An executive should always vary the times he arrives and leaves the office and also vary his route inside the building, if possible. Sometimes walk up one or two floor before getting the lift, or use other variations to get to his office. Executives should not work alone late at night

All physical, electronic and procedural arrangements are the product of the threat. Where the threat is real, there will need to be panic alarms for both the executive and his personal assistant. There may also need to be a safe room constructed within the office environment as well as at the residence. A well thought out system of CCTV, both at home and the office will be required and if the threat so demands there may need to be a Close Protection team in place. This latter will be, essentially a mobile protective detail, but will give additional support to the more traditional security arrangements within the office environment.

No company names should be painted on the car park. Occasionally, if the building is multi-tenanted this is unavoidable as the landlord may designate specific spaces to his tenants and mark these with the company name. I was working with a company in Europe that was carrying out some factory closures and there was a remote possibility of a backlash from the workers at the head office location. The executives spaces were marked with the company name and we got the people to start using the visitors section until matters had been resolved.

If you are a high profile Western business in certain parts of the world, you don't want your executives' vehicles identified with the company. This is typically how multi-tenanted property identifies car allocation and its not good.. Executive car policy should be secure, anonymous and visible!

The same should apply to company aircraft and vehicles. No logos or names and a severe restriction on revealing corporate travel plans. The arrangement of the executives private office will need consideration, but for more detail see The Modern Bodyguard.

In general terms the following should happen with regard to the running of the office:

Broadly

- Personnel and vehicle access control
- Escort visitors
- Screen mail

Contingency plans for the following:-

- Fire
- Bomb threats

- Explosions
- Hostage taking
- Extortion demands

Any risk assessment needs to determine some or all of the following:

- What is your target potential
- What is the prevailing attitude toward your security
- Is there someone with overall responsibility for the security programme. If it is someone from Personnel & Organisation, who may be more busy with 'relevant' work, as he sees it, then find someone else and ensure they have training in these areas.
- How are your Corporate and local security policies mandated and enforced. Does everyone know what is expected and does everyone participate?
- When was the last 'emergency preparedness' plan developed (fire, power failure, civil unrest, bomb threat, extortion, death, evacuation, K & R, product contamination).
- What kind of physical, electronic, procedural security is in force?
- Do such assets give confidence to local staff?
- Do such security resources, policies and procedures meet the local threat.

Some Suggestions

This is not a list for the professional adviser, rather a list for the 'appointed' individual charged with the security issue.

- Install key card access systems at main entrances and other appropriate doors.
- Issue access control badges, with current photos to all employees, visitors and contractors. Use a different colour badge for each category.

The whole system should be computer software controlled so access cards can be removed instantly and an audit trail of entries produced if needed.

◆ Keep master keys and extra keys locked in a properly designed key cabinet, in a secure room and don't hide the key for the key cabinet in the room.

◆ In high risk geographies develop 'Crisis Communications' among key personnel, families and security officers, involving intercoms, telephones, silent duress alarms, duress codes and other concealed communications.

◆ Have back-up 2 way radios.

◆ Locate executive offices near the inner core of buildings to afford the maximum depth of security and to avoid surveillance from outside.

◆ Arrange offices so unescorted visitors will be noticed. All staff to follow strict access controls - no propped open doors near smoking areas outside or on stairwells and no 'piggybacking".

◆ No nameplates or titles on doors, desks plaques or parking places.

◆ Keep offices neat, tidy and orderly so that strange objects can be easily spotted.

◆ Keep the post room away from executive offices

◆ Keep closets, service openings, telephone and electrical risers locked at all times.

◆ Protect crucial communications and computer equipment with alarms in locked rooms.

◆ Keep publicly accessed restrooms locked at all times and set up a 'key control' system. If a numbered lock only employees should open it and not give the numbers out.

Office Personal Security

Employees should avoid:-

- Stairwells and other isolated areas.
- Working late alone
- Not riding in elevators alone or routinely and not with anyone suspicious.

Your Security Officer should maintain an emergency contact file for immediate access for key personnel containing personal information which can be used in an emergency.

- home address and telephone numbers.
- family members- names, ages, descriptions.
- school schedules, addresses, phone numbers.
- close relatives - names, addresses, telephone numbers.
- medical histories and physician's name, etc.
- any code words or passwords agreed upon.

Safe Room

A safe room in an office or residence may be considered essential in some parts of the world. It should have:

- Steel doors, reinforced walls/ceilings and protected ventilation
- First aid equipment
- Phone and back-up communications
- Fire extinguishers
- Bomb blanket
- Sandbags
- Emergency tool kit
- Torches and spare batteries
- Extra food, drink and clothing

A safe room is not designed to withstand a long siege, rather it buys time until the police or military can get to you. It is essential therefore that they are appraised an attack is in progress.

A newly constructed CEO's office in Beirut. The glass in the windows was bullet-proof, but the frames were softwood! - you need to check all construction work..

The Safe Room being constructed in the office - bullet-proof steel doors and an encased steel lining for the roof space.

Residence Security

When working abroad there is often very little that can be done to improve the physical security of a residence, particularly in rented accommodation. It may not be possible to replace the doors, install alarms and cameras, cut down shrubbery, construct a safe room etc., so security may have to depend more on good procedures than the physical protection.

In broad terms an apartment offers greater protection against intrusion than a single dwelling. Take advice on choosing a 'safe' neighbourhood. In many Third World countries the word 'safe' is relative. The local police and the embassy security personnel will be able to advise on this. The busier the street the easier it will be for surveillance to be carried out and examine the general security precautions in operation in the area such as bars on windows and razor wire on walls.

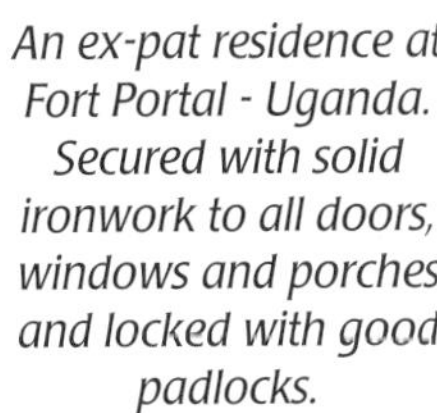

An ex-pat residence at Fort Portal - Uganda. Secured with solid ironwork to all doors, windows and porches and locked with good padlocks.

Generally avoid living on a one-way street or a dead end and property with underground parking and unless it is very tightly monitored and guarded, should be avoided. There should be, however, some means of securing the vehicles overnight such as a lockable garage and avoid parking vehicles on a road. See the property at night so as to determine the adequacy of the street or building lighting, absence of pedestrian traffic and general feel.

Try to live in an apartment building which contains other ex-pats. You may feel you should integrate, but there is safety in numbers of your own nationality or Western inhabitants.

If you choose to live in an apartment building check:

1. Access control of the building, elevators and parking garages (doormen, keyed front door, receptionists etc)

2. Public areas should be well lit after dark (lobby, laundry area, parking lot, etc)

3. Fire exits and doors clearly marked and possibly alarmed to prevent unauthorised entry).

4. Limited access to apartment balconies.

5. Doors to contain 180-degree peephole together with an auxiliary deadbolt or bar.

A private 'ex-pat' residence in Beirut - note the architectural ironwork at all windows - especially important because of the balconies.

A close-up of the ironwork being fitted for the new residence.

The Risk Levels produced by The U.S State Department - Intelligence and Threat Analysis Division are a useful guide to how particular areas can be classified:

CRITICAL: Constant criminal activity is reported and the threat of criminal violence is serious and abiding, with a history of recurrent incidents against expatriate personnel and interests.

HIGH: Frequent criminal activity is reported and the threat of criminal violence is serious, but more sporadic, with incidents against expatriate personnel and interests occasionally reported.

MEDIUM: Some criminal activity is reported and there is potential for serious criminal violence; incidents against expatriate personnel and interests occur, but are infrequent.

LOW: There is little indication of serious criminal activity; incidents against expatriate personnel and interests seldom occur and involve stealth rather than confrontation.

If you have the option to select a property all well and good and if you have a landlord who wants you badly enough he may be willing to substantially upgrade the physical security, even to the extent of installing new doors and frames and improved window security. Over the years I have been involved in the assessment of living accommodation for expats and have, in the main, found most landlords in third world countries very aware of the requirements of Westerners for a secure environment. They know that one of the criteria for selection will be the security and they have usually addressed these issues.

Often though, the standard of construction can leave a lot to be desired and may need further work to bring it up to an acceptable if not quite Western standard. You will often come across very secure apartments, but situated in less than acceptable surroundings. Russia is a classic example.

Despite the installation of IR beams in the garden and motion detectors on the CCTV - it would still be appropriate to cut back the shrubbery and bushes close to the residence.

Most Russian apartments are more secure than fort Knox. They have steel doors, set in steel frames and covered in wood, with enough locks to supply a lock shop. The only way for anyone to get in is to be let in. Leave the apartment, however and your problems start.

The common stairs and corridors are poorly maintained, badly lit, with maybe a non-functional lift. Many robberies and even assassinations are carried out in these locations. Leave the building and matters probably get worse not better.

Domestic Staff

Have all domestic staff thoroughly vetted and ensure complete background checks are done prior to employment. Travel plans, work schedules, business activities, security measures, social habits should not be discussed with, or within hearing range of, domestic staff.

The domestic staff should be instructed:

Not to let strangers into the house for any reason.

Not to mention the executives' work schedules to anyone.

To report any approach by someone seeking information.

In the interests of space I have not included in this book the very detailed information about both residence and office security. For those people who feel they may need such detail can I recommend **The Modern Bodyguard** and also **Streetwise.**

Summary

Be Aware and Alert

Be methodical - forward planning, preparation etc.

Avoid Routine - don't let people be able to set their watch by your routine.

Communications -establish a system of keeping in touch and use the 'buddy system' to force you to do it.

Predictability and Judgment - prepare to be flexible at all times. Keep a 'running assessment' of a situation and remember No Two Are Alike.

I hope you find some information and advice which is of value and may you travel safely.